Joyous
Abundance
Journal

D1533906

JOYOUS
ABUNDANCE
JOURNAL

Petra Weldes

Christian Sørensen

Spiritual Living Press
Golden, Colorado

Spiritual Living Press
573 Park Point Drive
Golden, Colorado 80401-7042

Cover design, book layout & typesetting by
Maria Robinson, Designs On You, LLC. Littleton, Colorado 80121
Set in 11 point Garamond

Printed in USA
Published June 2015
ISBN 978-0917849-39-8

Thank you
Bert, Sherry, Christine, Karen, Susan, and Cheryl
for helping me experience truly joyous abundance in my life.

— *Rev. Petra*

To my son, Trevor Dane,
no greater teacher could a dad ever dream —
bless you on your joyous journey.

— *Rev. Christian*

Joy is the most infallible sign of the presence of God.

— Pierre Teilhard de Chardin

Foreword

One of the greatest things in life is to start the day with the sheer excitement for all the good that Life has in store for you! The *Joyous Abundance Journal* gets you on the right track for each of your next 366 days. Our desire is for you to know a freedom beyond your wildest dream. There is no greater reason for claiming abundance than to experience a richer quality of life through living fulfilled, passionately, and successfully, while enjoying physical, mental, and spiritual health, for as long as you are in this game called Life.

This book helps you to see how Life reflects back to you what you put into It. You'll be inspired to move from being the spectator on the sideline of life into the excitement of consciously manifesting the life you love to live! When you commit to a deeper revelation of Spirit in you, through you, and as you, you'll find an exhilaration that is transforming. You'll come to know that as you change the inner conversations you are having, you'll be changing your future, stepping forth with an unwavering self-confidence in your greater self-expression. Your new focus will be on what's possible because you'll come to know that you are supported beyond your wildest dreams. As you lift your heart and soul to an expanded consciousness, you will come to realize you are so much more and have so much more to share with the world.

Happiness is the natural state that leads you to an extraordinary life. The *Joyous Abundance Journal* is dedicated to empowering you to enjoy life and to fill you with the desire to share your abundant good with others. If you are sharing life with a soul partner, may it be a soul-connecting, juicy, intimate and passionate relationship! Our hope is for you to know how natural it is to have an abundance of laughter, joy, faith, gratitude, and a surplus of cash and resources to be able to come and go where, when, and how you want. Our dream is for you to be able to give to wherever your heart is guided; to support spiritual communities, the arts, and social causes at a level beyond your previous giving.

You are the answer to previous generations' prayers for a world that works for everyone. This journal will help you pay tribute to Life by being a conduit for Life to have Its greatest expression as YOU!

~ Petra Weldes and Christian Sørensen ~

How to Use This Book

Joyous Abundance Journal was written directly to you with the intention to help you engage, practice, respond, and daily explore new ideas that invite you into a fuller experience of yourself and your ability to live joyfully.

As an Individual

As you read each thought for the day, journal, doodle, draw, or comment in whatever way allows you to explore the idea presented. Where are you with it? What do you think about it? How can you engage with it? And most importantly, how can you practice freeing yourself to experience the joyous life that is the Divine Intention wanting to manifest in, through, and as you?

As a Book Club or Small Group

Each month has a theme that is broken into daily topics. Groups may meet weekly or monthly to explore the topics and themes. Meditate on the theme together. Share what you discover in your journal. Discuss deeper practices that will help you and the members of your group. Pray for one another during the meetings, and as prayer partners between meetings.

As a Spiritual Community

Using a journal like this allows your whole community to be on the same page for the whole year. Joyous Abundance can be a wonderful annual theme to focus your year around. The theme for the month can also be utilized by the children and youth. Each week's lesson can be based on the topic within each month's theme. When there are five weeks in a month, this allows for an additional deepening into the overall idea being explored. The individual days provide excellent material, quotes, and ideas for weekly lessons or presentations.

Weekly or monthly study groups can be formed, as mentioned above, in support of engaging with the material and practicing it more deeply. These can take place at your community location, or in members' homes for a more intimate, community-building experience.

January

Visions of Infinite Abundance

January 1–7
How Big Is Your God?

January 8–14
Solid Decisions

January 15–20
MLK (18)
No Is Hard, Sometimes Yes Is Even Harder

January 21–26
Can You Imagine It?

January 27–31
Beloved Community

Don't Just Think It—Ink It

January 1 is a symbolic threshold from the past to the future, from the old to the new. Wouldn't it be nice to have the ability to see what was and apply it to what is forthcoming? January 1 is the first day of the civil year in the Gregorian calendar used by most countries, but definitely not by all cultures. The month is named after the Roman god of doors and gates, beginnings and endings—Janus. He is depicted with a double-faced head, each face looking in an opposite direction, and is remembered at the beginning of important events in a person's life such as marriage or birth. Last night you closed a chapter of your life and today you symbolically start a new one, hopefully taking what you learned to support you on what will come across your path this year.

For last year's words belong to last year's language and next year's words await another voice. And to make an end is to make a beginning.
— T. S. Eliot

Now is the time to reflect upon your life lessons from last year and write down your intentions and visions for this year. Ink it—don't just think it. If you want to be a conduit for the abundant flow of life, you need to put your vision in writing. This will move you beyond the mental sphere of just hoping your good will come. You are here to live as an abundant expression of God, and everything you could ever imagine is yours for the creating. So plan boldly from what you've learned but leave room for the fun surprises of life to lead you even higher in this exciting New Year. Joyous Journey to you!

SPIRITUAL CONTEMPLATION: Write down your insights and life lessons from last year and your intentions and visions for this coming year. Make sure to put this where you'll occasionally see it from time to time during the next twelve months.

AFFIRMATION: This is an abundant New Year that is fabulous to me!

Infinite Abundance

Have you ever tried to count the number of leaves on a tree? Now multiply that by all the trees in your neighborhood—in your state—in the entire U.S.—and all across the globe. Now look into the heavens at night and try to count the stars. Beyond those are billions more in the Milky Way, and beyond that, trillions of galaxies, each with billions of stars.

The universe is abundant, unlimited in every respect; if it were not unlimited it would have depleted itself long, long ago. . . . Instead, what do we find? The fish in the ocean lay so many eggs that if they all hatched, the waters would overflow all the lowlands. The stars in the heavens are beyond counting. The grains of sand on the beaches are innumerable. The leaves on the trees continue to multiply. Nature is lavish, abundant, extravagant.

How many grains of sand are on a beach? How many on all the beaches in the world? How many drops of water in a pond? Now imagine all the drops in the ocean. Everywhere you look, you can SEE the abundance of our Universe. Trust that what you see is a reflection of a powerful Spiritual Truth. The Universe is Infinite Abundance.

— Ernest Holmes

SPIRITUAL CONTEMPLATION: How do you best see abundance in the Universe? Are you looking for it?

AFFIRMATION: I live in an Infinitely Abundant Universe. I see the Abundance of Life and Spirit.

January 3
How Big Is Your God?

All spiritual faiths and traditions agree that for our idea of God to come even close to the reality of the Infinite Presence, we must see It as omniscient, omnipresent, and omnipotent. This means the form from which everything is created is infinite in power and intelligence. It is big enough to hold and manage the creation of a vast and seemingly infinite Universe. It has the intelligence and wisdom to know how to design cells that divide and multiply to become a baby's fingernails and eyelashes. It is present in the smallest quark and photon while showing Its majesty in the beauty of the mountains.

> *The Power that holds a grain of sand in place is the same Power that holds the planets in their places. There is nothing big or little or hard or easy as far as the Power is concerned. It is the same Power working in and upon everything. This is the Power we use.*
>
> — Ernest Holmes

Spirit, the infinite ONE, doesn't differentiate between big and little. It shows up in the smallest to largest of all things. Nothing is too big for Spirit to create. This is the same creative power that moves through you. Nothing is too big for Life so you can focus on a molehill of Abundance, or on a mountain of Abundance. God doesn't know anything about big or little. The Universe has the wisdom, power, and presence to become anything through you.

SPIRITUAL CONTEMPLATION: How big is your God? Is It big enough to handle everything in your life?

AFFIRMATION: Spirit doesn't know big or little, mountain or molehill. I trust in the bigness of my God!

We Are Bigger on the Inside

Science shows us that our bodies are actually more space than anything else. Dive deeply into the center of our own atoms and all we find is empty space, proportionately vaster than that between the planets of our solar system. What is at the Center of all that space?

The ancient mystics taught the practice of the Presence of the ONE in everything. The early Christian theologians knew that "God is a circle whose center is everywhere and whose circumference is nowhere."

Inner space is so much more interesting, because outer space is so empty.

— Theodore Sturgeon

This becomes the intuitive realization of the Omnipresence of the Infinite Reality, right where we are. When you take that centering breath and go within to the sanctuary at the core of your being—there you find infinity—there you find the Presence of the Infinite ONE. We are bigger on the inside than we are on the outside.

SPIRITUAL CONTEMPLATION: Practice taking that centering breath that takes you deep into the heart of your core. Be still. From your center, stretch your inner awareness out as far as you can in every direction. Notice that there are no edges or barriers that cause you to stop. You can go now into Infinity. What do you discover there?

AFFIRMATION: I breathe into my Center, and there I find the vast Infinite Reality of the ONE.

January 5
The Timeline of the Universe

When I took geology in high school, I was fascinated by the idea of geological time. In geological time it takes tens, even hundreds of thousands of years for anything to really change. Annual changes in the earth's crust, for instance, are measured in millimeters, but over the millennia these changes add up to continental drift and even massive slow-motion collisions. The same is true for time as measured by starlight. The distances are so vast that the light from the stars we see has been traveling for hundreds of thousands of light years across space to reach our eyes. This is a completely different time sense than the one that rushes you around from appointment to deadline to a fear that you will never get everything done. This same fear pushes us to try never to make mistakes and to get everything right. When we don't, we wonder if we will ever grow up, or become spiritually mature, or experience true abundance.

We are not limited by actual boundaries, but by false ideas about life and by a failure to recognize that we are dealing with the Infinite.

— Ernest Holmes

Relax. Your life has an even longer time scale than geological time or even time calculated in light years. You are an immortal, deathless being of light, whose timeline for growth and expansion is the eternal, infinite Reality of Life Itself. So remember, you have eternity to get it right, figure it out, and realize your full spiritual reality. Surely along the way you will discover that Abundance is already here.

SPIRITUAL CONTEMPLATION: In the ultimate scheme of the Universe, how critical is this need or problem? In three months, five years, the next lifetime, or over eternity, how important is it really? How does this perspective shift everything?

AFFIRMATION: Abundance, Joy, Health, and Love are my birthright. I have eternity to discover and experience all of Who I Am.

Who Says That's Abundance?

Everywhere you turn, someone is trying to tell you what kind of life you should have to be cool, rich, or desirable. These pile on top of the messages you received as a child from your family, teachers, and friends about what makes you fit in, be successful, or achieve what you are to become in life. But what kind of life do you want to create and experience?

Abundance means so many different things. It means having enough money to have the life that YOU choose. It also means experiencing enough love, friendship, creative expression, spiritual growth, and belonging. Everyone's definition of abundance is different. For one person, abundance may be a big home in the suburbs, while for another it's a cabin in the woods to retreat to on the weekends. For some people abundance may mean the freedom to travel and live in foreign countries, while for others it may mean working to build a fortune at home.

When I think about creating abundance, it's not about creating a life of luxury for everybody on this planet; it's about creating a life of possibility. It is about taking that which was scarce and making it abundant.

— Peter Diamandis

SPIRITUAL CONTEMPLATION: What is your definition of abundance? What does abundance look like to you in your life?

AFFIRMATION: I let go of any outside definition of Abundance. I create and live out my own idea of Abundance.

January 7
Going to the Well

When you imagine going to a well, you think of taking a dipper or a bucket or even a trough to get water for yourself or your animals. The size of the receptacle determines the amount of water, and how much thirst of either people or animals, that you can quench.

Life is no different. An infinite Well of Life, of Abundance, Joy, Love, and Peace is the source of all that nourishes and sustains us. The amount we receive from that infinite Well is based on the size of our minds and hearts and consciousness, for they are the receptacles we take to it. The more open and receptive they are, the more good we can receive—a closed mind and a small heart can draw little. Living waters are available to quench every thirst you have, so bring the largest receptacle that you can imagine and let Life fill you up.

We can make bigger buckets. We cannot make a bigger law. The Law knows nothing about big and little. It knows to do. Since there is such a Law and we are always using It, we are all receiving from Life an objective equivalent of our inward mental attitudes. If we wish more we must increase our expectancy, we must identify ourselves with more.

— Ernest Holmes

SPIRITUAL CONTEMPLATION: If you imagined the current receiving size of your consciousness, what shape and size would it be? In other words, how big is your bucket? Now, can you imagine it being bigger? How big can you really imagine it being?

AFFIRMATION: I go to the well with an open mind and a receiving heart. I draw forth the living waters that nourish and sustain me always.

What Are You Thinking?

If you think you are beaten, you are
If you think you dare not, you don't,
If you like to win, but you think you can't
It is almost certain you won't.

If you think you'll lose, you've lost
For out of the world we find,
Success begins with a fellow's will
It's all in the state of mind.

If you think you are outclassed, you are
You've got to think high to rise,
You've got to be sure of yourself before
You can ever win a prize.

Life's battles don't always go
To the stronger or faster man,
But soon or late the man who wins
Is the man WHO THINKS HE CAN!

— Walter D. Wintle

SPIRITUAL CONTEMPLATION: What is the predominant attitude of your thinking when you imagine the abundant life you want?

AFFIRMATION: I turn away from negative thinking. I know that with Spirit ALL things are possible.

January 9
Yes, You Can!

"I can't" is one of the most limiting things we can say because a Universal Power mirrors back to us whatever we predominantly believe. In psychology it's called "the self-fulfilling prophecy." In sales and success training it's taught as the power of positive thinking. In our spiritual practice we know that whatever we believe to be true, the universe says yes to and creates for us.

You can do what you have to do, and sometimes you can do it even better than you think you can.

— Jimmy Carter

"Yes, I can," on the other hand, is one of the most powerful affirmations we can say because then the Universal Law mirrors back opportunity and possibility. Believe that you can, and you are much more likely to move forward in pursuit of your dreams and the abundant life you desire. You can imagine a greater good in your life. You can allow Spirit to support you. You can set your feet in the direction of your goals. You can learn what you need to learn. Yes, you can do it, and Yes, you can have it.

SPIRITUAL CONTEMPLATION: Where is your belief in "I can't" limiting you or holding you back? How would things change if you believed "Yes, I can"?

AFFIRMATION: Yes I can, because a Power and Presence within me knows what to do and how to do it. Yes, I can!

Solid Decision

Rags-to-riches stories are about individuals who have had enough of their circumstances, went beyond their confines, and made a decision about what to do differently in their life. They didn't just wish upon a star, sit at home, and scratch lottery tickets. They made a solid decision, which is not a wish; rather it's a definite statement as to what you want and then going for it in an acutely focused way. I wish I would stop drinking . . . I wish I was rich . . . I wish I had a better job . . . these are not going to cut it.

> *It is in your moments of decision that your destiny is shaped.*
> — Anthony Robbins

Abundance comes as a result of the decision to experience greater good in your life. Make a commitment to yourself that inspires you to step up your focus of creation. Never allow what has been dealt you to be your final hand. Situations may alter your course but they don't have to deny your abundance. There's always a way to thrive when you have committed to a solid decision.

SPIRITUAL CONTEMPLATION: What would you like to move from your wish list to your fully focused list? What are you willing to do to make this decision a reality?

AFFIRMATION: I am focused on creating my dreams as a reality!

January 11
Farmer in the Dell

Remember the game where all the children skip around in a circle singing "Hi-Ho the Derry-O"? In the center is the kid called the "farmer," who then picks his mate, who picks a child, who picks a dog, who picks a cat, and so on. The group in the center grows until only one kid remains on the outside—and "the cheese stands alone."

Education is what remains after one has forgotten what one has learned in school.

— Albert Einstein

I couldn't wait to outgrow that demoralizing game and the "pick me" mentality. But then came picking teams in gym class, and even more intense, then came dating, which put it on a whole new level of "pick me, pick me."

It can take years before you realize that you don't have to wait to be picked—that you are actually already "it," and you get to do the choosing. You can now move beyond wanting to be acceptable to knowing you are acceptable just as you are. You aren't the cheese standing alone, and you no longer need to grumble about the other kids who are always "it" and get to select the best—because your abundant Good is always available to you too. Do you get it? All you need do is decide to tap into what's in your heart, and it will enter your world. Stop waiting to be picked and know you've already been chosen. The next move is yours. Hi-Ho the Derry-O . . . you'll never stand alone.

SPIRITUAL CONTEMPLATION: Where in your life are you waiting for someone to choose you, or some situation to grace you with its benevolence rather than being the creator of your reality?

AFFIRMATION: My life responds to my choices!

There is no place for hope in prayer; when it comes to prayer you must come from knowingness and certainty. You must trust, declare, proclaim, and affirm. Hope just doesn't have the same kind of oomph or power. In the beginning, it wasn't called the hope of God— it was the word of God. Hope doesn't sound Omnipotent. Heck, it sounds wimpy. Spirit is definite and so your prayerful statements must be as well. Wondering and hoping if good may come of your sweet thoughts have no place in powerful declarations of spiritual truth.

Hope is a subtle illusion. Hope is good; it is better than despair, but it is a subtle illusion and is an unconscious compromise, and has no part in an effective mental treatment.

— Ernest Holmes

In metaphysics there seem to be two very distinct branches of philosophy. One is the mental approach— the other is spiritual. In the mental realm, hope reflects the power of one's mind over conditions. Alternatively, the spiritual approach is a God realization that there is no power over anything because there is no otherness, and therefore hope is a totally irrelevant piece of the non-equation. The Divine Presence opens your consciousness to the flow of abundant good when you open your awareness to God and let It become manifest as you in both word and form.

SPIRITUAL CONTEMPLATION: Where in your life do you need to trade in your hope for a knowing of the spiritual truth of the situation at hand?

AFFIRMATION: I trade in my hope for a Divine Knowing!

Money Doesn't Grow on Trees!

So many beliefs we have about money and abundance are simply weeds that grow a lack and scarcity mentality. Although money may not grow on trees, the Spiritual Truth is that it grows in our consciousness. When our consciousness about abundance and prosperity grows, our money flow increases.

People must realize that no matter how infinite the Infinite may be, it can only become to them what it can become through them. We must look at ourselves with our own eyes. If we could open up, clean house mentally, and get out of ourselves everything that ails us, I don't care what the poverty is or the misery is, everything would be allowed because the Infinite cannot refuse anything.

— Ernest Holmes

Begin to discover and root out all your old beliefs about money—those from your family, from society, and your childhood. In every case these limiting beliefs are not based in Spiritual Truth. Every time you find a lack or limiting thought, immediately replace it with some form of Spiritual Truth: "There is always enough in God." "Spirit is my source and supply." "Money is God in action." Read spiritually based Abundance books and look for Spiritual Truths that you can use to counteract the false beliefs and ideas that are lurking in your subconscious.

SPIRITUAL CONTEMPLATION: What are some of the false beliefs and old ideas you hold about money and abundance? Write them in one column. In the second column write a spiritual truth you can know instead.

AFFIRMATION: I am free from old and limiting beliefs about abundance. I know the Spiritual Truth that God is my Source, and I receive all my abundance easily and with joy!

Have you ever watched a dog chase a cat alongside an invisible electric fence? He runs only so far, then stops rather than crossing that invisible line that would shock him. After having been repeatedly shocked for crossing it, he's learned not to overstep the boundary in order to avoid any further pain. The conditioning element is so strong that even when the electric field has been turned off, the dog won't step over it, no matter how much the cat teases and tantalizes him.

Although the world is full of suffering, it is also full of the overcoming of it.

— Helen Keller

What invisible parameters have you been conditioned to accept? Where do you stop because of painful memories? What if the shocking current has been turned off and it's only hurtful remembrances that are keeping you confined? Let go of being afraid of going too far. Crossing that line becomes imperative if you don't want to live in your preconceived pen. Outside the familiar, you may slip and experience moments of pain after being fenced in for so long because you didn't honor your explorative self. But your natural intuitive self will come alive again with its guidance once you return to listening to it instead of the controlling beliefs that held you back for so long.

SPIRITUAL CONTEMPLATION: What beliefs of containment are keeping you from exploring new possibilities? Your visions of possibility are big because you are big. So step outside of what's got you penned in because the world is waiting for your gifts to be discovered.

AFFIRMATION: My vision is a portal to the other side of the fence!

Gooood Morning

If you've ever felt the presence of God, you no longer feel alone in the world. Having had that experience, you know you are not alone in facing the challenges in your life. This is a sense of freedom you could never know otherwise, because in this knowing, you are not dependent on human intervention to assist you through.

Silence is God's first language; everything else is a poor translation.

— Father Thomas Keating

The Divine hand may look like It's working through someone or some agency, but that is just one of the Infinite channels through which Spirit is showing up in a relevant way in your life. The Presence goes before you to make the crooked ways straight. It also walks beside you, and has your back covered, and paves the way for your experience. This is why a conscious realization of living, moving, and having your being in God blesses you before you even know you have need of it.

So starting off your day in conscious connection with your Source not only can't hurt, it makes the most sense as to how to greet every day of your life going forward. Once the Divine experience is realized, you'll be on the right track for the rest of your day. Your conscious intention establishes what you will manifest. You'll come to know the joyous abundance that appropriately expresses as your life and you'll more easily recognize the activity of the Divine having fun as you.

SPIRITUAL CONTEMPLATION: Take time each morning of this week to consciously connect with Spirit before you get rolling with the day. After reading the daily inspiration, sit with it in the silence for ten minutes connecting you with something greater than the words.

AFFIRMATION: My morning time with God is a priority in my day!

What Are You Putting On?

A visit to the theater is a magical trip as you suspend your responsibilities of daily reality and enter a different paradigm for a journey through someone else's lens of perception. For a few hours another person's reality becomes your story and you are transported to a different dimension for a while. It's as if a space vehicle has lifted the whole audience. The actors and musicians are the crew; the captain is the director, and you all are following by a map drawn by the playwright who's put his story into three-dimensional storytelling.

Out of respect for life, what are you putting on in preparation for a greater reality? What thoughts are you willing to suspend for your emerging story to take you on a new kind of toe-tapping, heart-pounding journey into unknown realms? Are you able to trust God as the director or do you feel you need to be in charge of your whole production? Are you up for an adventure to mysterious parts of your unexplored psyche? What hidden aspects of your personality would you like to delve into? Is it time for a new character to surface in your script?

> *The main factor in any form of creativeness is the life of a human spirit, that of the actor and his part, their joint feelings and subconscious creation.*
>
> — Constantin Stanislavski

SPIRITUAL CONTEMPLATION: Take a trip to the theater and notice the stirring of feelings within: From choosing what to wear, to the anticipation of the drive to the show, what is coming up for you? What are you thinking as you are finding your seat, waiting for the exciting moment the curtain goes up, watching how it ends, and sharing the high points during the conversation home?

AFFIRMATION: I embrace my roles in life!

No Is Hard, But Sometimes Yes Is Harder

Have you ever said yes to someone because you were afraid to say no, and then had to clean up a bigger mess later on? Maybe you allowed an inappropriate behavior of your child slip by while he was young, only to have it magnify and be extremely inappropriate as he got older. Ever take on a project that was way over your head and expertise only to have it blow up somewhere down the line and create a lot more damage than had you said no to it in the first place?

I believe that a life of integrity is the most fundamental source of personal worth.

— Stephen Covey

Everything that comes your way doesn't have to be yours. If selling is not your thing, it's a lot easier to say no to your friend's multilevel marketing business than to have all sorts of hard feelings later on. If you know a relationship isn't for you, whether business or pleasure, rather than dragging it on until an explosive ending gives you an out, say no now. Saying no allows you to say yes to other opportunities in your life. Saying no severs the energetic link to that which, for whatever reason, isn't right. The God consciousness with its Infinite potential is obscured when you hold on to your head tripping instead of speaking your truth. Your time is valuable and sometimes to honor yourself and your projects, you need to say no to some of the requests of the world.

SPIRITUAL CONTEMPLATION: Is there something in your life you need to say no to but you haven't? It's time to speak your truth. It's best and honoring for all concerned.

AFFIRMATION: I speak the truth from my heart!

Letting Life In

I love sitting on my porch where I look into the tops of the trees and down into a creek. I feel like I'm sitting out in the woods, when in fact I am living in a pretty populated, urban-like area. Lingering over morning coffee I can hear the traffic in the background, even an occasional private jet from the local airport. But what I notice is that because I am so open to the stillness of the trees and the peace of the creek, none of these things disturb me.

Let life happen to you. Believe me: life is in the right, always.
— Rainer Maria Rilke

Letting in the parts of life that we love helps move us beyond resisting the things we don't like. Resistance, unfortunately, only causes more of the same thing we are resisting. Resistance is like glue. It makes us more aware of it and actually puts us in a dynamic relationship with the very thing we'd like not to have or experience. So stop paying attention to the traffic, and start paying attention to the trees. It doesn't mean the traffic will disappear— it means you'll stop being caught in tension with it. Miraculously it will fade from your awareness.

SPIRITUAL CONTEMPLATION: What things in my life am I resisting, thereby holding in my awareness. What could I pay attention to instead?

AFFIRMATION: I let go of all resistance to this particular thing. I turn and let the beauty, joy, and abundance of life in. I am at peace.

Making Space for Something New

I love moving, as weird as that may seem because when I pack up to move I release things that I seem to have accumulated. Then I purge again when I unpack. Because we are constantly growing and evolving, things that expressed our lifestyle and inner essence earlier may not anymore.

The sculptor produces the beautiful statue by chipping away such parts of the marble block as are not needed—it is a process of elimination.

— Elbert Hubbard

Sometimes we hang on to things because it's what we have and what we know. The problem is that we hang on long after they stop serving us or being a reflection of who we are. We keep things for sentimental reasons, for nostalgia, or because of who gave them to us. Often we keep things because we don't think that we can have something new or different. Or we keep something because we can't stand the void of an empty space. Yet when we keep something that simply fills up space, or no longer fits us, it means that the space isn't available for something new.

So go ahead, toss it out, whatever you are hanging on to. Then live with the emptiness long enough to let Spirit rush in and fill it in the most miraculous and beautiful ways. This is a powerful way to experience the Abundance of the Universe. Remember that the Universe abhors a vacuum—life will rush in to fill it.

SPIRITUAL CONTEMPLATION: What am I hanging on to? What do I have that I don't even realize I no longer like or doesn't fit me? What am I ready to release?

AFFIRMATION: I release and let go. I make room. I relax into the emptiness. I trust Spirit to bring in something even better and more perfect than was there before.

Attitude of Application

Many of the youth today learn the skills of a martial art, and it's fun to watch the young masters developing their craft. Although they look the part in their freshly pressed uniforms, as they put their routines together, often something is still missing. You'd find out quickly what that is if you were to step up behind them and engage in some playful wrestling. While they may be well schooled in the fine art, they haven't yet moved from practice to real life performance.

Be master of mind rather than mastered by mind.
— Zen Saying

On the path of mastery in the metaphysical realm, there is a plethora of teachers and dojos to learn from. The self-help section overwhelms the shelves in bookstores, and conversations of spiritual insights fill the airwaves. People are talking the talk and more than ever espousing the lessons like candy from a dispenser. Yet the appropriate attitude of application in so many lives has not arrived. Life and its challenges can sneak up from behind and unexpectedly grab you. Will you know how to apply all these lessons to the assailants of constriction, fear, anxiety, broken-heartedness, or medical verdicts? Does the size of the attacker matter and are your moves transferable from theory to application? The only way to find out if you know beyond concept is when life shows you your stuff. Are you ready for your next belt?

SPIRITUAL CONTEMPLATION: Where are you being tested to show your mastery of the forms of this world right now? Where have you not passed in demonstrating your prowess of consciousness over form? Are you ready to walk the talk of lessons learned and put it into action by taking it to the streets of your life?

AFFIRMATION: My attitude is right for applying Spirit in all areas of my life!

Get Affirming

An affirmation is a short positive statement that focuses your mind in the direction of your choice. Keep it short so it's not confusing. If there is a challenging condition in your life, rather than affirming it won't continue, since that would put the energy on the negative, flip it over to the affirmative side and proclaim that spiritual truth for your experience instead. Rather than using generic words or flowery phrases you've heard others use, find the words that conjure up your own feelings and images. No template affirmations for you! Custom all the way.

Why live in a soap opera when you can star in a great love story?
— Alan Cohen

Like an earworm of a song you hear played continuously and find all of a sudden is playing in your head without your intention, affirmations change thought patterns. Repeat your affirmation numerous times throughout the course of your day until you find it running in your awareness like a loop. When it's playing in your subjective you will find it pulling you in its direction and pushing you away from that which doesn't support it. It's a powerful practice to consciously program what you want to attract into your world. When you say, "I am," your whole being perks up to take its orders as to what outcome to produce for you. If you are looking for some change, get affirming.

SPIRITUAL CONTEMPLATION: Is there an area that could use an upgrade in your life? Take that experience and flip it around. Create a positive expression of that change of expression and you have a custom statement for what you want to see. Repeat it a hundred times twice a day for the next week and notice what happens.

AFFIRMATION: I am consciously creating my good!

Go or No Go

Searching for the perfect flight on an online discount travel portal can be an unparalleled convenience or a mind-boggling frustration. It's beautiful when it all comes together—and a complete aggravation when you're left choosing between red-eyes or crack-of-dawn flights with multiple stops including one in the opposite direction of where you are headed. In addition your travel time has been extended to a ridiculous number of hours at an exorbitant price for your inconvenience. You can rant, rave, and complain to non-empathetic

Every head has its own headache.

— Arab Proverb

agents at the airline counter, or whine to your friends. You might consider taking a car, boat, a private jet, or maybe even a camel, but at some point you need to decide if it's a go or no go. Your options may not be optimal, but it's what's being offered at that time and a choice must be made.

If instead you choose to perceive the Divine in this situation you'll find a miracle unfolding before you. The airline may not open a new route at the time you desire, but you might develop an appreciative attitude for not having to walk or take a horse if you attain a God realization around your airline experience. This awareness doesn't have to be sought; it merely has to be recognized where you are. Its Omni-calming Presence is ever available and includes online or at the counter service.

SPIRITUAL CONTEMPLATION: Look for Spirit in your most challenging spots in Life.

AFFIRMATION: Wherever I am, God is!

January 23
What's Motivating You?

One gorgeous weekday afternoon an older man jogged on a track around a football field at a local high school. As he jogged in circles, he noticed that the football team had begun running wind sprints up and down the field. The man decided that he'd continue running as long as the kids did, so he ran and the players ran. And then he ran some more and they ran some more. Despite his significant exhaustion, he decided he'd push himself one more lap, after which he stopped and leaned over in exhaustion, attempting to catch his breath from the hardest, longest workout he'd had in years. As he walked around the field to cool down and the players stumbled off the field from their grueling workout, one teen approached him and said, "Hey mister, I'm sure glad you stopped. The coach told us we had to run wind sprints as long you ran laps. We are all beat!"

Motivation is simple.
You eliminate those
who are not motivated.

— Lou Holtz

Be careful what you set your criteria by. Don't get caught up in an association with that which is not relevant to you. It's easy making comparisons to all sorts of activities going on in the world that aren't pertinent to you. Just because something's caught your attention doesn't mean it's significant to what you are doing. It's fun to find inspiring motivation; just be careful it doesn't take you where you don't want to go.

SPIRITUAL CONTEMPLATION: Have you ever set your standards to something that was not applicable to your situation but somehow you made yourself feel it was? Where did it get you and what did you learn from that experience?

AFFIRMATION: My inner inspiration leads me!

January 24

Can You Imagine It?

My son and I used to love making things out of giant cardboard boxes. A refrigerator box became a pirate ship in the living room, complete with mast, cannon ports, and ship's wheel. A washing machine box became a castle for him to play knight in shining armor. A long thin box became an airplane hanging from his shoulders as he zoomed around the house. It was so much fun to watch his imagination as he saw a real pirate ship, drew up a real drawbridge to the castle, and flew through the air on his powerful wings. What an imagination!

Our brains don't actually know the difference between a real and imagined experience. So as you imagine yourself having more abundance, this is what becomes real to you. Begin to see with the eyes of a child, imagining your apartment as your dream house and your life filled with overflowing blessings. Every time you see what you want in your mind's eye, you are creating it through the Power of the Law. Stop looking at the cardboard boxes of limitation, and start seeing yourself soar! You can experience greater abundance to the degree that you can imagine it.

> *If we keep our thought fixed upon taking the form of some desire in our lives, then it will begin to take this form. If we change the desire then It will change the form. Therefore, there must be a definite purpose in our imagination.*
>
> — Ernest Holmes

SPIRITUAL CONTEMPLATION: What kind of abundance do you want to imagine? Let yourself go—daydream about the life you want to experience. Write down some descriptive words and phrases, not about the form, but about the experience. Let it become real to you in your imagination.

AFFIRMATION: I imagine greater Abundance in my life, today!

Visions of Infinite Abundance | Can You Imagine It?

January 25
The Lessons of Earth School

Earth School is always in session. Every day we have the opportunity to invite growth and to let a little more of our greatness out! Every event, activity, and interaction is an opportunity for mindfulness and spiritual practice. The question is only "Are we paying attention?"

As individualized expressions of the One Universal Mind, the one thing that stands out is that we are not "robots or automatons" like Holmes describes in *The Science of Mind*. We have free will and can choose. We can choose to live a life in alignment with Spiritual Truth, or not. This is Spirit's great gift of Love to us—that we are left alone to discover the truth of our own being. How do we do this? By learning from our choices.

In school, you're taught a lesson and then given a test. In life, you're given a test that teaches you a lesson.

— Tom Bodett

SPIRITUAL CONTEMPLATION: What subjects are you currently taking in Earth School? To which lessons do you need to pay more close attention?

AFFIRMATION: I pay attention to the lessons my choices teach me.

Unpackaging Your Perceptions

Let go of the illusion of attempting to get somewhere and relax in the timeless here and now so you might observe with ease and grace all that transitions through your awareness. Create space in your awareness so you can allow happenings and understandings to present themselves without your packaging them in preconceived notions inside your head. In doing so, you will bring a mindfulness to the experience that is not entangled in the particulars of the moment and autonomous of the happening.

> *Things are as they are. Looking out into the universe at night, we make no comparisons between right and wrong stars, nor between well and badly arranged constellations.*
>
> — Alan Watts

When you can let go of the need to identify and label, you will find liberation and can go large or small, unfocused or specific, depending on the appropriate call of the moment. You can enter specific stories or conflicts without needing what you want for your happiness to happen. You are no longer dependent on outcome, which frees you to see a larger truth than what your mind has conjured up. You are witnessing your consciousness, actions, and growth in relation to what is playing out in your world. You are freed from the pain or pleasure by just noticing it and making room for whatever you find going on in a wakeful awareness, so you can move on.

SPIRITUAL CONTEMPLATION: Find some time to just sit and notice all thoughts and circumstances that come to your awareness without judgment. Instead of pushing anything away, resist not and let it have space so what's next may now float into your wakeful, witnessing self.

AFFIRMATION: I see without judgment!

January 27
The Paradox of Gratitude

Yes, you can literally "thank you" your way into something more and better than you have right now. No matter how stuck or uncomfortable your life may be, looking for something to be grateful for sends a whole new message to the Universe. The Law of Attraction is forever operating, and it attracts to you the very thing you are focused on. So if you are constantly focused on what's not working, how much you don't have, or whatever is wrong—guess what? The Law is simply going to continue to mirror that back to you.

If the only prayer you ever say in your entire life is thank you, it will be enough.

— Meister Eckhart

Now you don't have to lie and be grateful for the things you don't like. That's just silly and you won't believe it anyway. No, what you have to do is simply find positive things to be grateful for, even if they have nothing to do with what's causing your unhappiness. Be grateful for what is working in your life or what small things you do have or the good that you are receiving. This then becomes the predominant thought that the Law of Attraction will use to re-create your life.

The paradox of gratitude is that by being grateful for what is now, you can literally "thank you" your way into new.

SPIRITUAL CONTEMPLATION: What are you grateful for?

AFFIRMATION: Thank you for all the good, all the love, all the joy in my life. I am grateful for the abundance I have.

Beauty Is in the Eye of the Beholder

One morning in Costa Rica, I awoke to find the volcano perfectly etched against the dawn light. As I watched over my morning coffee, the mountain grew a cap: a perfectly circular cloud called a lenticular cloud. As the sun rose and the cloud grew, the mist of the rain forest began to rise. Over time the volcano was shrouded in clouds once again. That was a breathtaking morning, and I was so grateful to have been awake to see it. Beholding the symmetry of the mountain in the pearly light over the lush canopy, while hearing the birds calling back and forth to each other, was an opportunity to behold the Presence of Life Itself.

This is the same wonder I experience when I gaze into the face of my son, enjoy a moment of peace in my home, or experience the power of prayer. Everywhere we turn, there is an opportunity to behold the Presence of the Divine. It's easy to see in the drama of nature or in a foreign land. Yet it also is present right in our own backyards and in the familiar faces and places of our ordinary lives. Your only job is to be present to it, so you can behold it.

> *People often say that "beauty is in the eye of the beholder," and I say that the most liberating thing about beauty is realizing that you are the beholder. This empowers us to find beauty in places where others have not dared to look, including inside ourselves.*
>
> — Salma Hayek

SPIRITUAL CONTEMPLATION: Where in your life, person, place, or experience, can you behold beauty rather than the something else you may be focusing on?

AFFIRMATION: I cast my gaze upon what is beautiful right here and right now. I behold the Present of the ONE in my life today.

Receiving the Gift

A spiritual community I had started in the Northwest decided to remodel a space to create our own sanctuary. Our community came together in a barn raising–like experience and put in hundreds of hours over the next two months to create our new home. It then became clear that we needed a podium for our new sanctuary; and since podiums are a tool of a minister's trade I was delegated to find one I liked. Whew, now that was a challenge. Not wanting a large, imposing thing to stand behind, or a Plexiglas see-through stand that felt like a business meeting, I searched and looked in every catalogue I could find.

Human life runs its course in the metamorphosis between receiving and giving.

— Johann Wolfgang von Goethe

Then one day an eighty-year-old gentleman from our community offered to build me a podium. He'd just retired and taken up woodworking and wanted to give me a gift. In the past I would have said no. Not feeling worthy, not wanting to put him out, afraid that I wouldn't like it, or wondering if I could make sure he did it right, somehow I would have managed to reject the gift. This time I simply said yes. To my surprise he measured my height and carefully quizzed me about my furniture style. Two months later he brought me the most simple, light, and beautiful podium I had ever seen . . . all because I was willing to accept his gift.

SPIRITUAL CONTEMPLATION: How are you with receiving gifts? Do you reject them? Try to control them? When have you allowed someone to gift you in a way that truly filled your heart and life with abundance?

AFFIRMATION: I accept my good through the gifts that others give me. I release any need to hide, deny, or control how my good comes to me.

Season for Peace and Nonviolence

The sixty-four days between the dates of the assassination of Mahatma Gandhi on January 30 and Dr. Martin Luther King Jr. on April 4 are a time to consciously practice sixty-four ways to implement nonviolence. Throughout this season for peace you can read inspiring quotes for reflection and contemplation. You may also choose to espouse and affirm peace, or allow your daily spiritual practices to revolve around peaceful actions. You are a spiritual leader and how you respond to the confrontational dynamics of life will demonstrate to all that you're deeply grounded in peace.

Must the citizen ever for a moment, or in the least degree, resign his conscience? . . . I think that we should be men first, and subjects afterward. It is not desirable to cultivate a respect for the law, so much as for the right.

— Henry David Thoreau

Peace is not a passive choice—it is a courageous one. King, Gandhi, and His Holiness the Dalai Lama are examples of bold individuals who didn't lie down for peace but instead took a stand that didn't include guns in order to have their principles prevail. Mahatma Gandhi's Satyagraha, which is loosely translated as *soul force*—an insistence on truth or truth force—is a particular practice within nonviolent civil resistance. His approach influenced Nelson Mandela's struggle in South Africa as well as the campaigns of Martin Luther King Jr. and James Bevel during the civil rights movement in the United States.

SPIRITUAL CONTEMPLATION: Where in your life are you tired of the oppression going on? Are you willing to change that without a violent approach?

AFFIRMATION: I am moved by the soul force and am insistent on truth being expressed!

January 31
Beloved Community

You can do spiritual work alone in a cave or in your home, but in a community with others it's give and take, sharing and receiving. When the artistic director of our community recently made her transition, the choir showered her husband with continual love until he surfaced stronger again. Learning with others brings a diversity of perspectives around abstract concepts.

I have to tell you, I'm proudest of my life off the court. There will always be great basketball players who bounce that little round ball, but my proudest moments are affecting people's lives, effecting change, being a role model in the community.

— Magic Johnson

Welcoming a child into the world with a spiritual family committing to life-long support is comforting. Celebrating the times of joy and supporting during times of pain are gifts of community. To grow with individuals of like mind in affinity groups of a larger family is empowering. To have a shoulder to cry on with someone who understands your spiritual beliefs is calming. When you have friends to sing, dance, and feast with, you are never alone.

Buddhists call their community a *sangha,* meaning a fellowship or group you share and spiritually grow with. In order to help build the sangha, you must continue to develop your inner qualities so you can contribute to the group. The beauty of community is that other members may awaken you to areas from your inner work that can still use some attention. Be grateful for your spiritual family and trust the process.

SPIRITUAL CONTEMPLATION: What keeps me from engaging more in spiritual community?

AFFIRMATION: My spiritual community is a blessing in my life!

February

Abundant Love

February 1–7
Worthy of Love

February 8–14
Your Valentine

February 15–21
Spiritual Partnership

February 22–29
Letting Go of Good to Make Room for Great

Young, Precious Expressions of God

Born of the womb that birthed the heavens, your child is much more than you see. But are your plans for your child more important than the child? Do you keep your children so busy that they have no time to daydream or be themselves? By attempting to keep your children constantly engaged and gratified, you become their hostage and not their parent. Know, instead, that you can show them a quiet, joyful way of being.

Children must be taught how to think, not what to think.

— Margaret Mead

Children learn to love themselves from how you treat them, so be mindful and present in their presence. Treat them with respect. Love and guide them without manipulation and they will learn to trust themselves. Overly protective parenting will teach children to fear disappointment. Allow them to make their own decisions and they will learn to trust themselves. If they fail, it's all right because they will survive just as we all have. Better, they will become stronger because of that failing. Express your love and confidence in their ability to deal with what's at hand and stay away from the shame and blame game. Always have room in your soul to hear the voice of that young precious expression of God in front of you. The gift of the heavens will far exceed your dreams.

SPIRITUAL CONTEMPLATION: In what ways do you impose your will upon a child, denying his or her soul's personality the ability to develop? How can you be with a child in a quieter way, like a walk or meditation?

AFFIRMATION: I honor the unique expression of my child!

American folklore claims that a furry rodent, like a groundhog or hedgehog, makes an appearance in the middle of winter on Candlemas Day, and thereby predicts the next six weeks of weather. In Europe it's a wolverine, badger, or scared bear that comes out of its den and does the prognosticating. Screwy as it sounds, this divination of weather is actually an ancient tradition dating back to the pagan festival of Imbolc, which was an astronomical midpoint between winter solstice and the spring equinox and was associated with the goddess Brighid. She represented the light half of the year and served as the power bringing people from the darkness into the spring.

> *The eternal hourglass of existence is turned upside down again and again, and you with it, speck of dust!*
> — Friedrich Nietzsche

It is said if the groundhog emerges from his burrow and doesn't see his shadow, good weather will soon arrive. But another six weeks of winter weather are in store if he does. However a lot depends on what direction the little guy is facing and whether or not the sun's shining. He can't see his shadow if he's facing the sun, which is a good metaphor for us all: shadows disappear when we face the light. So on this Groundhog Day come out of a hole you may have found yourself in, face the light, and watch the shadows disappear from your world. It's all contingent on your viewpoint: it's either six more weeks of winter or only six more weeks until spring.

SPIRITUAL CONTEMPLATION: Where are some shadows looming large in your life? Instead of perpetuating the reoccurrence of them for another six weeks, try turning your perspective to a different direction—face the light and watch the shadows fall behind you.

AFFIRMATION: I feel the warmth of the light upon my face!

February 3
A Little Childish . . .

Every one of us has an inner child who continues to play out the feelings, emotions, and behaviors of our childhood. She constantly tries to get from others what she didn't get from her parents. Unfortunately she attracts people just like those from her past and tries to manage her adult life with the same strategies or emotions that she's had since childhood. Yet decisions made from a child's point of view with a child's emotions are unlikely to operate successfully in an adult world. This inner child is not the child who will lead us into the Kingdom of Heaven. She is more likely to lead us into continually re-creating our childhood relationships and issues.

> *It sounds corny, but I've promised my inner child that never again will I ever abandon myself for anything or anyone else.*
>
> — Wynonna Judd

We can help prevent our inner child from running (ruining) our life by giving her what she needs. This means we become the parent to ourselves. We give to her the love, approval, recognition, care, and support that we didn't get as a child. In this way we show ourselves that we are, in fact, lovable, worthy, capable, and that we belong. This opens the door to our Higher Self, our spiritual essence. We begin to realize that the Divine Presence, in us, as us, is giving to us the very thing we are giving to our inner child. All the love, approval, acceptance, recognition and support are always, already there.

SPIRITUAL CONTEMPLATION: How is your inner child running your life? What does she need from you? What do you need from yourself, as the Divine Presence in you? Spend some time giving it to yourself.

AFFIRMATION: I love myself. I accept and approve of my Self— my inner child and all the ways I do my best. I recognize my unique beauty and I care about the things that are important to me!

A Lot Childlike . . .

What is this childlike quality to which the Kingdom of Heaven belongs? Without romanticizing or overindulging our children, can we discover what the Master Teacher is referring to? We know children can be cruel on the playground, wholly absorbed in themselves, and developmentally unable to make good decisions. Yet we also know that an infant or toddler can capture and maintain the attention of a whole room full of adults. While we may seek to correct the six- or eight-year-old, we do nothing but encourage the toddler who is just learning to walk. Even in our teenagers, under the hair and attitude, there is a precious possibility that is still unfolding.

> *Jesus said, "Let the little children come to me, and do not hinder them, for the kingdom of heaven belongs to such as these."*
> — Matthew 19:14

Our children love their parents long past the point when some parents deserve it. There is an innocent expectation, a profound faith in a child's reliance on those around him to provide for his needs, to nurture and love him. In the absence of serious neglect or abuse, our children continually express wonder and awe toward life, love toward others, and an openhearted engagement with life.

SPIRITUAL CONTEMPLATION: What childlike qualities cause me to feel I am living in the Kingdom of Heaven? What experience/ skepticism/worldly wisdom prevent my living FROM those qualities, thereby keeping me out of the Kingdom of Heaven?

AFFIRMATION: I live my life with an open heart, with awe and wonder at the beauty and mystery of all Life, including the people in my world. I release old stories or hurts that stand between me and my experience of the Kingdom of Heaven.

February 5
Magical Flavors

Preparing a meal for those you hold dear is an abundant expression of love if you enjoy cooking. Creating magical flavors from mere words on a page and a dash of your imagination is a gift. As you prepare the table, light the candles, and choose the perfect drink, you wait with excitement to see how it will be received. And yes, you want it received with joy, but remember that the joy you just experienced in creating this feast is your gift no matter how it is received. Because you put the spice of your heart and soul into your creation, in a way there's a part of you that is taken into their being as the food is eaten. You cannot separate yourself from your creation.

Cooking is like painting or writing a song. Just as there are only so many notes or colors, there are only so many flavors—it's how you combine them that sets you apart.

— Wolfgang Puck

That part of you that is love and caring enriches their body, mind, and soul.

SPIRITUAL CONTEMPLATION: Prepare a meal for a loved one and notice all the love and good thoughts you add to the mix.

AFFIRMATION: I add love to all my creations!

February 6

I Love Myself, Just the Way I Am!

The self-help movement has done so much to support improvement in every area of our lives. We can improve our relationships, communication, businesses, and financial strategies. We are also admonished to improve our health, fitness, and overall well-being. These are all worthwhile endeavors. Then we are told we should improve our teeth, our hair, our clothes and our car. We are bombarded with ways to improve every facet of ourselves, even when those parts of us are just fine.

> *Love yourself first and everything else falls into line. You really have to love yourself to get anything done in this world.*
>
> — Lucille Ball

This is where self-help can escalate into self-judgment and even self-hatred. Constantly focusing on improving ourselves can easily imply that there is something basically wrong or flawed with who we are and how we show up in the world. It's extremely important for us to first become comfortable in our own skin—to be okay with ourselves, warts and all! Yes, we want to grow and improve so that we can become more of who we are and express more of the joyous God-self that is the truth of our being. Then we can focus on improving the things that really make a difference or help us to contribute more to life, to our families, to the things that matter to us.

SPIRITUAL CONTEMPLATION: Which parts of your life are you improving because you think there's something wrong with you? Which parts of your life are you improving so that you can expand and grow?

AFFIRMATION: I love myself, just the way I am. I focus on improving only those things that allow me to grow and expand.

Worthy of Love

There was a time when I wondered whether anyone would ever love me—really love me, the way I wanted to be loved. But because I knew all my faults and flaws, I didn't feel worthy. So I focused on all the ways I could love and take care of others so that they would love me in return. How silly. No matter how much I gave, what I got back never seemed like enough.

You yourself, as much as anybody in the entire universe, deserve your love and affection.

— Buddha

It was many years before I realized that it wasn't because I wasn't being loved. It was because no matter how much someone loved me, I didn't believe it, so I couldn't let it in. No matter how much I did or worked or gave, it never seemed to turn into what I "thought" I deserved back. The reality was, I was letting in just exactly what I thought I deserved.

Learning that Spirit is Love, and that Love is the impulsion of Life itself, and that Love is always available, I began to practice being the love I wanted. Not doing to get, simply being love. I also decided that no one could love me until I loved myself. Saying "I Love You" to myself was hugely difficult at the start. As it became easier, and I really began focusing on my own unique and precious being, I noticed that people seemed to love me more. What really happened is that I let in the Love that was always there, because I finally felt I truly deserved it. Wow, did the Love in my life increase tenfold! And I was able to give so much more real love, without trying to get something back!

SPIRITUAL CONTEMPLATION: What are you doing to get love? Begin to tell yourself "I love you" with the same openhearted feeling that you say to your child or loved one.

AFFIRMATION: I love me. I stop trying to get love. I freely give love. We are all worthy of Love!

There is a story of a poisonous tree proposing the question of what to do about it. You could stay away from it and lose the experience of that part of your yard. You could attempt to prune it to control it. You could build a fence around it to keep everything at a safe distance from it. You could cut it down and totally eliminate it. Or you could appreciate it, allowing it to reveal its secrets—perhaps discovering its many medicinal blessings and cures while enjoying the gifts of its shade on a hot summer day.

No snowflake ever falls in the wrong place.
— Zen Proverb

When there is a toxic situation in your life, stop ingesting the poison, but don't just eliminate it without having it reveal its gifts. You didn't come across this circumstance (or tree) for no good reason. You are never in the wrong place at the wrong time. If something has brought you to your knees, pray to understand what the message is, because if you don't, you will continue to suffer, never knowing the remedy that the tree, the situation is offering. Rather than clear-cutting the forest and leaving a desolate and barren landscape, recognize the value of adversity. Be patient in your discovery and revelations as life reveals its secrets.

SPIRITUAL CONTEMPLATION: What situation in your life would you prefer to have just disappear, rather than love it enough to have it reveal its gifts to you?

AFFIRMATION: I am patient in my understanding of life's revealing!

Is There Such a Thing as Unconditional Love?

Agape, a lovely Greek term used to describe the love that the Divine has for Its Creation, is often translated as spiritual or unconditional love. Loving everyone unconditionally is a wonderful ideal. The only problem is whether we actually know what unconditional love really means. Too many of us had families in which only conditional love was present. How can we love unconditionally if we don't have an experience of it in our own life?

Ask and it will be given to you; seek and you will find; knock and the door will be opened to you.

— Matthew 7:7

Spirit, the Divine Presence of Love, is truly the only unconditional Presence; everything in creation is a condition and therefore relative to everything else. Yet we all have an inner sense and desire to experience unconditional love. So there must be something within us that recognizes it and longs for it. This is an expression of our yearning for the Divine Presence. The longing for a love so palpable and complete that we never question its presence is what drives us to seek God. The wonderful promise from all the saints and mystics of the ages is that when we seek, that which we are looking for immediately reveals Itself to us.

SPIRITUAL CONTEMPLATION: Become aware of your yearning for Unconditional Love as a yearning for the Divine Presence. Be present to the revelation of this Presence as the answer to the very thing you are seeking. When and where do you experience it the most?

AFFIRMATION: The Love I am seeking is seeking me. As I turn to the Divine Presence, It immediately shines Its Love through me.

What Is Unconditional Love?

Sometimes I'm gone all day and sometimes I travel for days at a time, yet when I come home my cat is there. She never scolds me or shuns me. She is always happy to have me brush her, pet her, and sit with her. Our dogs unfailingly meet us at the door with wagging tail and bright eyes. They haven't counted the hours we were away or resented the time we were busy. Every time they greet us, it's with an open heart and a readiness to be fully present.

In this way our pets teach us about unconditional love. It doesn't keep score, assign blame, harbor resentment, or need for someone to be different. Good day or bad, centered or not, our pets are there to be with us, sharing the gift of their presence and love. Now this doesn't mean that they don't want things from us—food, walking, brushing, and attention. Nor does it mean that they don't misbehave, act out, or pick up on our emotional state. What it does mean is that regardless of that, they continually come back to being a joyful loving presence.

> *Unconditional love really exists in each of us. It is part of our deep inner being. It is not so much an active emotion as a state of being. It's not "I love you" for this or that reason, not "I love you if you love me." It's love for no reason, love without an object.*
>
> — Ram Dass

SPIRITUAL CONTEMPLATION: What do you think unconditional love is? Who teaches you about unconditional love the most?

AFFIRMATION: I am a joyful and loving presence. I am open-hearted, without blame, resentment, or keeping score.

Falling in Love!

There's nothing more lovely than the first blush of love. The glow we feel and the beauty we see make everything in our life feel like more than it was before. We want to be with our beloved, we love everything about them, and we agree with everything they say! What is this feeling but a profound sense of connection and oneness? We feel safe enough to open our hearts and connected enough to go beyond our usual limitations. It's delicious, and we long for it to last a lifetime.

Love is the self-givingness of Spirit into creation.

— Ernest Holmes

This love is a human expression of the profound Love that is the Divine Presence. Every time we allow ourselves to fall deeply in love, whether romantically, or with a friend or a child, we are falling in love with the Divine. This sense of connection and oneness is the truth of our soul's being. Spirit has given Itself, all It is and all It has, into us. We are ONE with Spirit. We are reminded that we can see with the eyes of Love, sing with the heart of Love, and glow with the Presence of Love every moment of every day. Spirit, as Love, is always already there.

SPIRITUAL CONTEMPLATION: Imagine snuggling up in front of the fire with the Beloved. Imagine that Spirit's Love is so present that you are always connected as one. Imagine falling in love with the Divine.

AFFIRMATION: I am falling in love with the Divine. I feel connected and one with all Life. Everything is precious and beautiful.

More Than Enough Love

Have you ever tried to give all your love away? Imagine it right now. Give your love, like a beam of light from your heart, to every person you can think of. As much as you can give, does it get used up? Imagine feeling love and being loving toward others. How about if you are loving to the clerk in the store and the person on the freeway and the woman in the elevator and the clerk behind the desk. Is it used up now?

Love is the best medicine, and there is more than enough to go around once you open your heart.
— Julie Marie

There is always enough love because our love flows from an infinite wellspring, an eternal presence of Love. We can never run out. There is no shortage of Love, ever, for us to bring into the world. The only time we feel like there isn't enough is when we are concerned that there isn't enough coming back to us. Yet the people who love us draw from that same infinite wellspring, so how can they run out? They may run out of patience, or understanding, or maturity, or their ability to cope, but they can't run out of love.

See yourself as the giver and receiver of Love from this infinite well. Notice that some conduits are bigger than others, some may have a kink in the hose, but there is more than enough love to fill up and flow through every pipe!

SPIRITUAL CONTEMPLATION: What causes you to feel or believe that there isn't enough love—in you or in someone else? Turn your attention to the Wellspring of Love and feel Its unending Presence.

AFFIRMATION: There is more than enough love in Spirit as me to share and express. Love is overflowing in my life.

February 13
Love Is Always the Answer

When I find myself judgmental or angry with people, I can obsess about them for days. It's as if I've rented out a room in my mind into which they've moved. They are there every time I sneak a peek through the door and I can have endless conversations with them in my mind. This will go on for a ridiculously long time until I find a new place to stand and a new way to see the situation.

Inner peace can be reached only when we practice forgiveness. Forgiveness is letting go of the past, and is therefore the means for correcting our misperceptions.

— Gerald Jampolsky

"If love is always the answer," I ask myself, "what does Love look like in this situation?" It doesn't mean accepting negative behavior or wanting to have these people as my best friends. It does mean that I look at them with softer eyes. I seek to behave toward them in a kind, compassionate, loving manner without giving up being firm and clear and having boundaries. Finding a place to stand in Love means that I stand on Spiritual truth and see from that perspective. I move from my little human ego to my eternal universal Spirit. I see with the Loving Presence of Spirit. In that moment, compassion, understanding, and forgiveness replace judgment and anger. Even if the other person doesn't change, I'm no longer hooked, and everything instantly changes between us. Love is abundantly present; we just have to choose that as our place to stand.

SPIRITUAL CONTEMPLATION: Whom have you allowed to rent a room in your mind? Imagine bringing Love to the situation. How does this change things?

AFFIRMATION: Love is always the answer. I choose to be Love and bring Love to each situation and circumstance.

A popular hagiographical account of Saint Valentine is that he was imprisoned for performing weddings for soldiers (who were forbidden to marry) and helping early Christians who were persecuted by the Roman Empire. According to legend, during his imprisonment he healed the daughter of his jailer. An enhancement to this story states that before his execution he wrote a letter to her and signed a farewell, "Your Valentine."

Love touches the heart and soul. That is its playground. When you are in the presence of a lover, there is an inner aliveness that heals all that aches. Concerns vanish and life is a bit brighter.

For it was not into my ear you whispered, but into my heart. It was not my lips you kissed, but my soul.
— Judy Garland

For that instant in time, you walk in heaven and you are not troubled by the future. The only moment that fills your awareness is the now moment. In the presence of love you feel the courage and support to make all visions possible. Taking the noble stance for what you believe, is the right thing to do; it seems logical to follow your heart irrespective of how things fall. Chivalry is not dead to the heart that is in love.

SPIRITUAL CONTEMPLATION: Write a hagiographical account of how you would like your contribution to the world remembered.

AFFIRMATION: I am an expression of love!

Splitting Your Focus

A martial arts student approached his teacher with a question. "I'd like to improve my knowledge of the martial arts. In addition to learning from you, I'd like to study with another teacher in order to learn another style. What do you think of this idea?" "The hunter who chases two rabbits," answered the master, "catches neither one."

And if a house be divided against itself, that house cannot stand.

— Mark 3:25

Where in your life do you find yourself divided? What are you straddling and not fully committing to? There are all sorts of clichés written about the lack of commitment: Either get on the boat or stay on the dock; you'll fall in the water if you keep straddling the decision. You have to go deep if you want to find the gems in life. You can't run around digging a dozen shallow holes if you want a deep well to bring forth the spring water. Fish or cut bait.

SPIRITUAL CONTEMPLATION: Where and how are you splitting your energies in life? What's keeping you from being able to commit and go deeper in the experience?

AFFIRMATION: I focus with ease and go deep into all my experience!

Being a Doormat

Unconditional love is a powerful acceptance of others' beingness and the unique way they show up in the world. We see through the behaviors that are merely the expression of past experience and false beliefs to the essential reality of another. Unconditional love does not need people to be different from what they are, but this doesn't mean that we have to accept every-thing they do or say. Being a doormat and enduring behavior that is not acceptable is not unconditionally lov-ing either another or oneself.

You teach people how to treat you.
— Dr. Phil

Learning to separate the behavior from the person frees us from needing people to be different. This means we don't blame, or point fingers, or try to fix them. It also means we take ownership of our reactions, trigger points, and old patterns. We share our feelings, needs, and requests in a loving manner. Others are free to try to understand and respond in a way that is supportive. They are also free not to. Allowing them the freedom to respond or not, also allows us that same freedom. This is all about compatible behavior, mutual values and needs, and learn-ing to get along. It is possible to love someone unconditionally with-out wanting to hang out with him or be in his life.

SPIRITUAL CONTEMPLATION: Do I confuse tolerance of unaccept-able behavior with unconditional love? Can I feel unconditional love while still asking for what I need and want?

AFFIRMATION: I ask for my needs to be met without making someone else wrong. I no longer accept unacceptable behavior in my life!

February 17
Understanding

Have you recently sat with the one you love, held her hand, looked her in the eyes and asked her, "Do I understand you enough? Is there anything you'd like me to understand more? Is there a way you would like me to love you better?" You must sincerely and continuously delve into the soul of your beloved, for people grow and evolve and the person you loved yesterday is not quite the same today. There have been challenges and blessings on their path that added to their complexity. Just sharing space and successfully maintaining the routine aren't what build intimacy. How do you know how their dreams have morphed, what wounds have been opened or hurts inflicted, if you don't check in with them? What are their desires of this day rather than of days past? Are you loving someone from the past who lives in the same body?

When we talk about understanding, surely it takes place only when the mind listens completely—the mind being your heart, your nerves, your ears—when you give your whole attention to it.

— Jiddu Krishnamurti

True love requires understanding. If you are not willing to sit with the mystery to explore the realms beyond the surface, you'll never discover the unspoken realms from the soul of your loved one. It takes time to communicate and understand. It can be uncomfortable and exciting, revealing and impactful. But how can you fully love if you don't know the truth, and how can you be loved if you aren't truly known? With understanding, true love will surely grow.

SPIRITUAL CONTEMPLATION: Create a safe environment where you won't be interrupted and your heart will hear without judgment or defense, and take the hand of your loved one and ask if there is anything you need to know to love her better.

AFFIRMATION: I allow myself to be vulnerable to love in a deeper way!

Snuggling Up Together!

Let yourself love. There is something so wonderful about having a romantic relationship, if that's what you want. Of course, it's not necessary for a fulfilling life, but if you enjoy being in a relationship, you have to open yourself up and allow love to flow. This means allowing your heart to be open. It means letting go of protections and barriers that have kept you safe. Yes, we've all been hurt, betrayed, and disappointed by people. But you are spiritually maturing now! Your new consciousness will attract someone from a new level of maturity and openness if you will allow it.

> *To open your heart to some-one means exposing the scars of the past.*
> — Unknown Author

Allow yourself to be vulnerable and trusting. Strive for deep and radical honesty that is caring of how things are said. See yourself and your beloved as capable of growing into a mature and healthy relationship. Allow yourself to really enjoy all the benefits of being together—snuggling, talking, walking, caring, vacationing. Let go of any need for it to be perfect—just treasure every moment for what it is.

SPIRITUAL CONTEMPLATION: Begin by imagining the kind of door you have protecting your heart. Simply become quiet and allow it to reveal itself to you. Notice its texture and size. Begin to imagine it becoming clear and then permeable. You are in charge of what comes in and out of it, so it can be anything you want to imagine.

AFFIRMATION: I fling open the door to my heart. I no longer need to protect myself. Spirit's Love is all the protection I need. I allow Love to flow freely in and out.

February 19
It Takes Two and the Space Between

A healthy relationship requires both people to be fully invested in it while not becoming absorbed by it. For if we become completely absorbed by each other, we may begin to think that it's our partner's job to make us feel fulfilled. We may also start to resent the time he wants us to spend with him if we're not taking time for ourselves. Ultimately this sucks the relationship dry because nothing new enters into it.

Give your hearts, but not into each other's keeping. For only the hand of Life can contain your hearts. And stand together, yet not too near together: For the pillars of the temple stand apart, And the oak tree and the cypress grow not in each other's shadow.
— Kahlil Gibran
on Marriage

But when we are each active in creating fulfillment in our own life, the more we have to bring to our relationship. We bring the things we are learning, our need for support, and times for celebration into the space between us. This way our joyous love is nurtured and enlivened by each of our lives. We each bring ourselves to the relationship rather than trying to find ourselves in it.

SPIRITUAL CONTEMPLATION: What new things am I bringing to my relationships? Notice where you are absorbed in a relationship and where you are lifted by one.

AFFIRMATION: My relationships are nurtured by my spiritual deepening, personal growth, and creative fulfillment. I have so much to offer to my relationships and I rejoice in what they bring to me.

Karma or Dharma?

Karma relationships are those that we call into our life in order to learn and grow and work out our issues. These are the ones in which we attract someone who is really the opposite of us in some significant way. Initially we love it—eventually it really irritates us. All the arguing, and need for them to be different is simply our unwillingness to learn what they are there to teach us. We will be in these relationships over and over again as long as we are unwilling to move into new ways of being. I think of it as our being invited to move toward the middle, toward each other in a way that allows both sides to actually be available to us. When I can speak AND

Don't you dare, for one more second, surround yourself with people who are not aware of the greatness that you are.

— Jo Blackwell-Preston

be quiet, for instance, then both are readily available to me to choose from.

As we mature and grow into our greater self, and when we have released many of our old patterns and unhealed past, we become ready for Dharma relationships. In Dharma relationships we do not face toward each other, but rather we grow and learn side by side. We are mutually supportive of each of us living our purpose. The relationship itself may become a vehicle through which we express and live our purpose. These relationships are truly building Heaven on Earth.

SPIRITUAL CONTEMPLATION: Which of my relationships are, or have been, Karma relationships? Which ones are Dharma relationships? Am I ready to move from Karma to Dharma relationships?

AFFIRMATION: I release any unwillingness to learn what you have to teach me. I move toward that which you are inviting me to grow into. I am free to live my purpose!

February 21
Spiritual Partnership

Love really is everything it's cracked up to be. You just have to remember it's not always spiritual peaks: sometimes it means having to clean up the messes. Growing together, developing a more passionate bond of friendship, and continuously falling in love again and again with the same person—this is what defines the truth of love. It's important for you to connect and talk with your loved one, letting them know you hear them, see them, and appreciate them in the midst of your daily routines.

We come to love not by finding a perfect person, but by learning to see an imperfect person perfectly.

— Sam Keen

When you two have a tussle, attempt to remember that what is coming up for you is something that has been denied within yourself. Look within, not without, for the change of heart. If you are unable to find resolve within, it's futile to pursue the change somewhere else. Mother Teresa said, "If you judge people, you have no time to love them." Stop pouting, forgive your loved one and yourself, and get on with loving. Get back to supporting each other's dreams and bring the spice back into your life.

SPIRITUAL CONTEMPLATION: Where have your concepts of love gotten in your way of experiencing love? How can looking within yourself lead you to be a greater lover of life?

AFFIRMATION: I love to love with my partner!

Love Is a Mathematical Equation

A version of "love your neighbor as yourself" can be found in every faith tradition around the globe. It is a powerful spiritual practice of love, yet too often we have taken it to mean "love your neighbor more than yourself" or "before yourself." This teaching has been turned into a practice of sacrificing our sense of self and living as a martyr, with an underlying lack of self-love or even self-loathing.

> *Love your neighbor*
> *as yourself.*
> — Matthew 19:19

Yet the statement is actually a mathematical equation of equality. Anytime a statement uses the word "as," it equates the two things, which is exactly what we learned in eighth grade algebra: an equation always maintains the equality of the two components. Therefore you can't love your neighbor without also loving yourself.

Love your neighbor as yourself is both a description of how life works as well as a prescription of how we can actually experience more love. Everything I do to you, ultimately I do to me, because we are one! Everything I do to me, I do to you, because ultimately we are one.

SPIRITUAL CONTEMPLATION: Spend time contemplating the equality of the two sides of this statement. Which side do you need to spend some love on to bring the equation back into balance?

AFFIRMATION: I love my neighbor as myself. I love myself as my neighbor.

February 23
Barns

Driving through any rural American landscape you can still find barns with a beauty that comes from having weathered decades of seasons. They're part of our cultural landscape and heritage and remind us of a time of self-sufficiency, family enterprise, and resiliency. But as family farms disappear and new owners sell off the barn wood for decorative furniture, new buildings made of steel take their place.

No memory is ever alone; it's at the end of a trail of memories, a dozen trails that each have their own associations.

— Louis L'Amour

The landscape of your world will also evolve over a lifetime, with only memories to linger to tell of a time that has passed. What you do with them is your choice. Will they drift into the unkempt realms of decay through forgetfulness or will they be restored through your attention? Will they be abandoned and replaced by the modernization of what seems like better experiences? Or is there a way to preserve your history, have it beautified, and make you more intriguing while you continue to progress into the evolving new era?

SPIRITUAL CONTEMPLATION: Is there a valuable piece of you no longer honored that you are leaving behind? What can you do to have it be part of your landscape rather than letting it fade away?

AFFIRMATION: I honor my path to where I am now!

The Trance of Error

Error is a tricky little bugger because it doesn't arrive with a bell ringing around its neck. There is no "Ta-Da, here I am! Watch out for me, because I'm about to create some doubt in your life." Alert spiritual practitioners, however, will always catch error appearing as a person, place, thing, or condition because they know that error is never actually any of those things.

When you embrace the reality that God is Infinite and is all there is, you know that there's no ultimate reality to disease, lack, or whatever error is showing up.

> *Each of us literally chooses, by his way of attending to things, what sort of universe he shall appear to himself to inhabit.*
>
> — William James

You choose which reality you want to live in. If you believe that God is the substance of all, then you must agree that error is an illusion. No doubt every day you face strong materialistic beliefs defended by the world of form. But when you are one with the spiritual consciousness of God, the hypnotic nature of error is irrelevant. Never believe the suggestion of an illusion that has lodged itself in your human consciousness. Instead, go straight to God consciousness and wake up there knowing you are in full integrity with your truth.

SPIRITUAL CONTEMPLATION: What trances of limitation are you caught in? How has erroneous thinking left you believing the challenge in your life is a person, place, thing, or condition?

AFFIRMATION: I awaken from the trance of error into the consciousness of Oneness!

Bad Boys and Sassy Girls

You've got your warm, fuzzy spiritual teachers who are kind and caring, and will love you along the path. And then you've got your bad boys and sassy girls who are annoying, mischievous, and even offensive as they disturb and frighten you into your spiritual realization. They don't give you syrupy platitudes or sugarcoat their expressions. They'll scare you to death because the old must die for the new to be born, and sometimes a startling shock is the only thing that can shatter the egoic defense.

A student wanting to impress his Zen Master said, "Everything is empty. I am nothing; there is nothing to be done." Suddenly the Master hit him on the head with his stick. Angry and about to hit the Master back he asked, "Why did you hit me?" The Master answered, "If everything is empty, nothing . . . so where is your anger coming from?" The student was perplexed and had no answer. The Master laughed and went away.

— Zen Story

Waking up is not always a comfortable experience. Sometimes the truth hurts and the consequences can be startling. Sacred cows can't be slaughtered by niceties, and your very belief system must be challenged. The teacher who wants your praise more than your grief is not the one who is going to push you over the edge. The greater emergence of spirit in your life cannot fit into old familiar patterns of behavior, and sometimes it just might take a bad boy or sassy girl to knock you into Infinity.

SPIRITUAL CONTEMPLATION: When have you had a rough teacher shock you into greater awareness? Could you have ever gotten that understanding through sweetness?

AFFIRMATION: I trust the perfect teachers of my spiritual path!

It's All How You Look at It

A story is told of a snail that was mugged by a turtle on the streets of New York while he visited the great city. In the courtroom, the judge asked the snail to describe what happened. The snail's response was brief: "I don't know, Your Honor. It all just happened so fast." Life all depends on one's perspective. One person's battles may be another person's ease. Individuals creating a financial flow of seven or eight figures a year may have difficulty grasping the perspective of the layaway plan others use in department stores. Everyone has their own expansive and constrictive perspectives. Your growth comes when you know where yours are, not judging others for the levels in their life.

> *We don't see things as they are, we see them as we are.*
> — Anais Nin

Everyone believes their own perspective is the right and sometimes only one, but why would they be called perspectives if there weren't more than one? Believing what you see is the absolute truth can lead to trouble if not all-out war in the world. As the Course in Miracles asks, "Do you prefer that you be right or happy?" Love is your willingness to feel differently instead of having to say to another, "You are wrong."

SPIRITUAL CONTEMPLATION: Where in your life are you holding too rigidly to a perspective? Where would it be beneficial for you to shift how you perceive? Ask yourself in that particular situation, do you prefer to be right or happy?

AFFIRMATION: My perspective is forever expanding!

Seeing with the Eyes of Love

I struggled with my relationship with my father for years. He drank and smoked and cursed life until the day he died; he always needed to be right and have the last word. He was also generous and smart and funny and could tell a story like no one else. Growing up in his presence was not easy but neither was it without some amazingly wonderful times and experiences.

Love is when you look into someone's eyes and suddenly you go all the way inside their soul and you both know it.

— Unknown

But when I started my spiritual journey, I needed distance from my whole growing up, so I didn't speak to him very often. Instead I kept trying to see him as a child of God and trying to love him from afar.

Then one day I realized that my father acted and loved in the only way he knew how. I began to understand his struggle as an immigrant to the U.S. and his deep desire to care for his family. I discovered a place of compassion within me that allowed me to see his pain, fear, and deep disconnection—and I found those same places within myself. We weren't so different.

In that moment when I began to see him with the eyes of Love, I could see the truth of who he was. Did this miraculously change him? No. But it changed me. I no longer needed him to be anyone different. Over time our relationship strengthened and softened. I became grateful for all he'd contributed to my life and the ways he'd tried to love me. When I sat by his deathbed, I knew he was returning to the heart of Love. I'm so grateful that I didn't miss out on the Love he came here to be.

SPIRITUAL CONTEMPLATION: Who would benefit from your seeing them through the eyes of Love? Can you see that they were, or are, doing the best they can?

AFFIRMATION: I see everyone from my past with the Loving eyes of Spirit. I know each person is a unique and precious expression of the One Presence.

Letting Go of Good to Welcome In Great!

A friend once said to me, "Don't let your good stand in the way of your great!" What a powerful truth! Often I cling to something I know and settle for that which I have because there's a little belief back there that says if I let go of this person or relationship that is okay, or even not so great, whatever is on the other side will be worse. Why is that? Why wouldn't it be better? Why do we think that we won't have something as good as what we have now?

We cannot let our angels go. We do not see that they only go out, that archangels may come in.

— Ralph Waldo Emerson

We live in an abundant, loving, and powerful Universe. As we grow and mature, spiritually deepen and heal, we attract a new life out of our new consciousness. What we attracted before was from the consciousness of what we could accept before. But now as we grow in Spiritual Truth, we expand our consciousness, which will also expand the person, relationship, and love we attract. Clinging to or settling for less simply keeps us from experiencing and expressing the greater Love that we now know we are. Trust that a greater love, more joy, and a fuller, richer life really are waiting on the other side of letting go.

SPIRITUAL CONTEMPLATION: Who or what are you clinging to or settling for? What good is standing in the way of your great, in relationships or in life?

AFFIRMATION: I accept my greater good as Spirit flowing into my life. I let go of anything unlike the Love that is Spirit's presence in my life.

February 29
Leap Year Bonus!

If the Divine deposited 86,400 blessed gifts into your life, but at the end of the day none would carry over and all would be deleted, how would you choose to use them? In each of those moments, your life can be either turned around or thrown away. Are you going to withdraw every second from your deposit? What are you going to do with this moment in time?

The present moment is filled with joy and happiness. If you are attentive, you will see it.

— Thich Nhat Hanh

There is no going back in the stream of time. We lose what we fail to use. Too many of us take these seconds for granted by not valuing the gift they are. Ask someone who narrowly avoided a car accident, or an athlete who won silver in a race at the Olympics the value of a second. Do you want to tell someone that you love them? Do so now while you have a chance. Is there someone who needs your forgiveness . . . how about giving it this day? This Leap Year Day is a present, an extra gift with many possibilities where the magic and wonder of life can emerge. It's a gift of 86,400 blessed moments from the Divine. Why wouldn't you use every single one of them for your greater good rather than have them vanish at the end of the day unused?

SPIRITUAL CONTEMPLATION: The gift of this extra day of the year is very special. You are given an additional day of life every four years. What extraordinary occurrences are you going to direct with these 86,400 Divine moments?

AFFIRMATION: I live every second as a gift from God!

March

Deciding to Be Abundant

March 1–7

The Discipline of Deciding

March 8–14

Come to the Garden

March 15–25

Is There a Ceiling to Your Abundance?

March 26–31

Eostre

March 1
Hold Please

Some businesses seem to think it's acceptable for us to guess our way though a voicemail labyrinth, only to get lost and have to call back and start the whole process over again. They might save money by denying us human contact, but we lose. We waste valuable time spending all those hours on hold. But don't be a victim and give your power away to frustration. Find another provider instead of the corporation that strung you up in their bureaucratic business-centric web.

The masses never revolt of their own accord, and they never revolt merely because they are oppressed. Indeed, so long as they are not permitted to have standards of comparison, they never even become aware that they are oppressed.

— George Orwell

Spiritual principle doesn't know large or small, so if you allow yourself to be mistreated by a computer system why do you think your responsiveness would be stronger in other matters of your world? How in the world can you power up your faith to reclaim your authority for your body if it's not well, or your life if it's out of order? All of life is a reflection of your consciousness, whether it's mechanical or human. The question is how you handle what's showing up for you. Does your response come from a victim mentality or from your unshakeable power? We are always at choice—we are never not at choice.

SPIRITUAL CONTEMPLATION: Where in your world are you tired of "the system" abusing you because that's just the way it is? What alternatives do you have to being taken advantage of?

AFFIRMATION: I reclaim my power of choice in all areas of my life!

Forgot to Pray

Imagine that upon leaving this world you are brought to a Divine storehouse whose halls are lined with endless doors decorated with nameplates. You come to one that has your name emblazoned across it as if you were a rock star, and although your host encourages you not to look inside, you are insistent. So the door is unlocked, and you are greeted by ceiling-high shelves of unopened, dust-covered, and dated boxes.

Excitedly you tear the lid off one dated from just last week to discover it's a blessing that you never claimed. From the previous year is that huge break at work that you never asked for. From your youth is the blessing of the ideal person just waiting to share the

Start living now. Stop saving the good china for that special occasion. Every day you are alive is a special occasion. Every minute, every breath, is a gift from God.

— Mary Manin Morrissey

gifts she has to deliver to your life, but you never asked her out. From childhood is the dream you never dared to dream because it seemed too big and held too much potential for disappointment. Here they sit unopened, box after box from your lifetime filled with blessings you never prayed for, for fear they were too good to be true for you. All this abundance belongs to you but was never delivered, because you failed to ask.

SPIRITUAL CONTEMPLATION: When in your life have you not embraced the blessings that were being offered to you—good ideas, prospering good fortune, or the ideal individual who would have enriched your journey? Accept God's blessing now—don't hesitate to open your gift of good that is already waiting for you.

AFFIRMATION: I always remember to embrace my gifts of God!

March 3
How Long Do You Have To Hang On

You know no one is perfect, but for some reason you don't feel that applies to you. Your standard is higher than human perfection and you berate and beat yourself for anything less. Try making it okay that you are still evolving and getting better, and know that Life doesn't hold anything against you. You've been forgiven for any trespasses you may have made, no matter what! So find peace that although you may not be as spiritual as you would like, you are getting there.

After all these years, I am still involved in the process of self-discovery. It's better to explore life and make mistakes than to play it safe. Mistakes are part of the dues one pays for a full life.

— Sophia Loren

If your child were to slip into a ravine and yell out for your help, would you check to see if her room had been cleaned and the bed made before you responded ? No, you'd run to save your child's life without any judgment just as Life doesn't focus on your past gaffes before it responds. There is no desire to make your journey through this world an unhappy one. There is no kind of God who keeps track of all the mistakes you've made and bases Its responsiveness on your behavior. There is no God outside of you sitting in judgment. Get rid of that nagging feeling that God is not happy with you and get on with creating your abundant good.

SPIRITUAL CONTEMPLATION: Where in your life are you beating yourself up for some past behavior? Life is not holding you hostage anymore, so how about letting it go now?

AFFIRMATION: I now forgive myself for any past mistakes!

Decide to Be Happy!

Raymond Charles Barker wrote a great book called *The Power of Decision* in which he states that we are all as happy as we decide to be. So how do we decide to be happy, healthy, wealthy, and fulfilled in our life? How do we decide to contribute and make a lasting impact on our family and the world?

We decide—by deciding! When something happens that could fluster, upset, or destabilize us, we decide to be happy instead. No complaining, whining, moping, or groaning. Of course this doesn't mean when a serious conversation needs to be had, that we don't

Decision is a sharp knife that cuts clean and straight; indecision, a dull one that hacks and tears and leaves ragged edges behind it.
— Gordon Graham

have it. Or when something important needs to be looked at we ignore it. But it does mean that we don't let negative things dictate our overarching attitude.

Mother Teresa was asked how she remained peaceful and joyful in the midst of abject poverty and disease and the constant demands on her time. She shared her secret: every time she got into the elevator or walked up and down the stairs, she would smile. This decision— to smile, to be happy—lifted her whole being and reminded her that she always walked with support and love, no matter what she was facing.

SPIRITUAL CONTEMPLATION: Decide to be happy, right now in the midst of whatever is going on. Don't whine, complain, judge, or feel like a victim. What does it feel like to simply decide to be happy?

AFFIRMATION: Today I decide to be happy. Spirit, as my source, is more than enough to meet every need.

March 5
Intention or Magical Thinking?

An intention is like buying the ticket for the cruise. We've set our mind on something, and we allow that to move us toward it. Without a clear intention, we don't know where we are going or what we want. I think of a powerful intention as an actual movement in consciousness that activates the Universal Laws in service to our intention.

Each decision we make, each action we take, is born out of an intention.

— Sharon Salzberg

It's not enough just to think about something, however. You actually have to act on it for things to happen. Simply saying "Oh, I meant to do that" or "I think about being abundant" isn't enough. Our intention must lodge so deeply in our consciousness that we begin to act and move from it. Otherwise we are simply indulging in magical thinking: "If I think about abundance, somehow God will reward me with abundance." Actually God is already all the abundance there is, right here and right now. Intending to behave, speak, and see abundance is a deliberate way of being and seeing that is not fooled by conditions, circumstances, false beliefs, or old feelings. The power of intention is that it moves and changes us. If it doesn't, it's merely magical thinking.

SPIRITUAL CONTEMPLATION: How am I allowing my intentions to move me? How am I seeing, speaking, and behaving differently because of an intention I have set?

AFFIRMATION: I set powerful intentions for my Abundance. I speak and act in alignment with my intentions.

The Discipline of Deciding Means Declaring Only Abundance!

Discipline, deciding, and declaring—three really strong words that invite us to take charge of our own life so that the Universe has a clear and open channel into which to pour Its Love and Abundance!

Discipline means that we train our mind, like a puppy, to go only when and where we tell it, and not to make messes in our beautiful abundant home (life). Discipline doesn't have to be mean or harsh. It's constant, consistent, and loving redirection, just like you would give to that cute little bundle of fur.

Talent without discipline is like an octopus on roller skates. There's plenty of movement, but you never know if it's going to be forward, backwards, or sideways.

— H. Jackson Brown Jr.

Deciding is exercising our power of choice. Yes, Life and Love are moving through us, but Spirit can become for us only what we choose. Deciding means that we are willing to say "I choose this!" I choose Abundance rather than lack. I choose Joy rather than unhappiness. This means we are deciding the kind of life we want to have.

Declaration is effortless when we have the discipline to decide. Because we consistently choose our greater good, we speak about that, rather than continuing to affirm its opposite. Declaring our good also means that we are actively engaged in focusing on it.

SPIRITUAL CONTEMPLATION: Am I disciplining my mind to pay attention to what I choose? Am I choosing my life, or waiting for Spirit to somehow lay it on me? What am I declaring in the casual conversations in my mind and with my friends?

AFFIRMATION: I am disciplined in deciding for my good and declaring for my abundance!

Seeing with Abundant Eyes

Everyone shows up differently—in the ways they love and speak, and the things they value. Deep spiritual living allows us to see and celebrate all people's precious uniqueness without requiring them to be like us. We may decide their way doesn't suit us, so we choose not to hang out together or work together. Look carefully at that person who irritates you, pushes your buttons, or simply seems to be running through life on a very different track from you. Remember, everyone is here to give and receive love. Seek to discover their way and you will see them blossom before your very eyes.

Abundance is not something we acquire. It is something we tune into.

— Wayne Dyer

This is just as true with the things we decide are important to us or create an abundant life. Every one of us does this differently. Decide what you think is an abundant life. It may be traveling around the world for years and living with the local people on money you earn washing dishes. It may be creating jobs for thousands by developing a new business or patenting a new invention. It may be spending hours with your paints or with your children. There is no "right" way to be abundant—there's only your way.

SPIRITUAL CONTEMPLATION: What makes you feel really luxurious and abundant? What allows you to feel like you are really living your dream and making your contribution?

AFFIRMATION: I am deciding to be abundant my way. I seek only those things that add value and meaning to my life. I am not fooled by other people's ideas of how my life should look.

A Feather a Day!

One year I took a three-month sabbatical in Europe and spent most of the time on my own, exploring the countryside, small towns, and delicious cafes. It was a time to rediscover myself and the joy I have in my own company, although I also made amazing connections with people, saw incredible art, and walked through the pages of history. Every day felt like magic and I lived in gratitude for the blessing of this experience.

My sabbatical stretched me in many different ways, like having to come to grips with my fear of traveling alone. But I met each hurdle with a profound belief that Spirit would lend me the wings to fly and that I would soar through this experience with great joy! Every day I trusted that magic would happen and that I would be completely supported in every way.

> *By intuition we already know that we are One with the Infinite. We must come to recognize the Universal Spirit, with which we commune and in which we live and move and have our being, as a constant source of inspiration and of guidance.*
>
> — Ernest Holmes

When I returned to the U.S. after this wondrous journey I brought with me almost sixty feathers I'd collected along the way. Almost every day I'd find one somewhere. It didn't matter if I was walking through a town or through the woods, feathers were everywhere, and every one I picked up reminded me that Spirit was present, supporting me every step of the way.

SPIRITUAL CONTEMPLATION: How do you know Spirit is supporting you? Are you noticing or seeing Spirit's signs? What signs does Spirit leave in your path so that you will know that Spirit is present?

AFFIRMATION: I see Spirit's support everywhere I look. Spirit's signs of love and abundance are present every day!

Thoughts Are Things

Our thoughts form the mold of our life and the beliefs in our subjective mind. Those things we hold to be true are exactly what the Law of Attraction operates upon. So if we want to attract something different, we have to create a different belief. This creates a "new thought" which becomes the magnet for our new experience.

Resolve a thing into a thought, change the thought, and that automatically changes the thing.

— Thomas Troward

We can change what we hold to be true about abundance by collecting evidence in support of it. Begin looking for all the ways nature is abundant. Look for all the ways abundance shows up in your life. Focus on abundance everywhere you can find it, see it, and talk about it. You begin to see that abundance is your birthright and believe that it is possible for you to experience. Stop telling any story to the contrary because that provides your mind with conflicting and competing evidence, and your magnet then tries to attract opposite things at the same time.

SPIRITUAL CONTEMPLATION: Imagine that your thoughts about abundance clump together to form an actual magnet for your good. Let's say the spiritual truths you believe create the positive pole and your past experience or old beliefs create the negative pole. Which side of your magnet is doing the most attracting? How is that playing out in your life?

AFFIRMATION: I think and affirm great abundance for myself, and for all people everywhere. I am a powerful spiritual magnet attracting great good into life!

Its Time Has Come Through You

When an idea whose time has come must birth, it will always find its way to enter into human consciousness. In that moment, the idea enters into the field of possibilities from the infinite, undifferentiated Allness through the person who receives the inspiration. The concept of a personal computer, for example, occurred to an individual who then made it available to everyone else in the world. As far-out as the concept of wireless communication may have once seemed, at the moment it entered into the human consciousness through a visionary, it became available to us all.

> *Wisdom begins in wonder.*
> — Socrates

A business person, knowing full well that what is stirring in his consciousness has an uncanny ability to be popping into awareness in many locations, may rush his product to market for fear someone else may beat him there. Artists, however, know that if they don't share what they can see and hear, it may never be known because they may have been graced as the sole proprietor of this vision. You are an integral vortex for the abundant potential of the infinite to make its way into form. Once you have caught the vision of something greater, it has entered into the human consciousness through you. So now what are you going to do with it?

SPIRITUAL CONTEMPLATION: What has made itself known within your consciousness and is waiting for you to do something with it?

AFFIRMATION: I am the birthplace of a new Divine idea!

March 11
Our Subjective Reality

There is one Life, Power, and Presence in the Universe—we call it God, Spirit, Consciousness. Great thinkers have called it a Universal Mind, the Divine Intelligence behind all of creation. Psychology has revealed that we not only have a conscious mind with which we think and choose, we also have a subconscious, or subjective, mind that stores everything our conscious mind has experienced. Here is where all our beliefs, habits, and patterns of thinking are laid down as neural pathways in our brain. Once these grooves are established, our mind tends to think along those same lines, over and over again, thereby forming the mold that the Universal Law uses to create our world of experience.

Man's outward life is a result of the subjective state of his thought. The thinker is conscious mind, but when he thinks he lets fall the forms of his thought into Subjective Mind, which is the Universal Medium of all thought and action and, as a result of this, the Creative Medium at once sets to work to produce the thing outlined.

— Ernest Holmes

Affirmations, new ways of thinking, reading, and learning spiritual truths—these are all designed to provide your conscious mind with new ideas that must be given as much or more attention as the old ones so that new pathways can be carved into the brain. "Synapses that fire together, wire together." Consciously firing new synapses with affirmations and spiritual truths literally rewires our brain, which then creates an entirely new subjective reality. This is what creates the new mold for our life of increasing abundance.

SPIRITUAL CONTEMPLATION: Notice how much mental energy and time you give an affirmation or new idea compared to the habitual thoughts that run around like monkeys in your mind.

AFFIRMATION: I am in charge of my mind. I choose to focus on abundance thinking, spiritual truths, and powerful affirmations. I spend more mental energy on this than anything else.

What Do You Want?

I bought and remodeled a condo when I became an empty nester. It was both exciting and a bit overwhelming. Originally I thought I wanted a condo in a certain part of town. Then I wanted a little house by the lake. After that I realized what I needed to do was give myself permission and time to explore—what did I really want? Finally I realized that I needed trees and a certain environment—everything else I could work with.

> *It comes down to a simple question: what do you want out of life, and what are you willing to do to get it?*
> — Unknown

I then found the perfect condo, but it needed a huge facelift and I ended up having to remodel it from top to bottom. Weeks of stores and tiles and paint colors also left me wondering how it would all go together. I'm not a designer! Again I realized that I needed to give myself time and permission to explore. I began to notice the kinds of colors and styles that repeatedly caught my eye, and as I collected samples I saw that a pattern was emerging. I could really see which things I liked and which ones I chose only because I wondered if they might in some way be "better." Finally I decided to focus just on the things I liked, and after three months of remodeling, I moved into a gorgeous, contemporary condo that looked different from anything I originally would have said I wanted, but is exactly and perfectly ME.

SPIRITUAL CONTEMPLATION: What exploration do you need to do to discover what you like and want? When are you overly influenced by what others might think or what you think you should want?

AFFIRMATION: I take the time to explore and discover what I like and want. This makes my life feel so much more abundant because it suits me.

Come to the Garden

Planting a spring vegetable garden demonstrates a belief in the good that tomorrow holds. With the perfect balance of water and the appropriate amount of sunlight, nature will bring you the nectar of the gods. But this delectable harvest of fresh vegetables also depends upon a rich soil teeming with life-giving nutrients.

God Almighty first planted a garden. And indeed, it is the purest of human pleasures.

— Francis Bacon

The best time to plant a tree was twenty years ago. The second best time is now.

— Chinese Proverb

Likewise is the garden of life. The creative process of seed, soil, and plant is a great metaphor for the thought seeds you plant into the creative law that says yes to what you believe, and these thoughts manifest as the form in your life. Selecting the seeds—your thoughts—is a conscious decision of what you'd like in your world. The soil—the Law—says yes to what you plant; it doesn't say, "I don't like those choices, choose again." Then the law of growth takes over as you continue to add affirmative support, trusting in the natural unfoldment of what you have planted.

SPIRITUAL CONTEMPLATION: What thought seeds are you planting in consciousness? What weeds would you like to uproot from your world? How can you better enhance your thoughts around what you've planted?

AFFIRMATION: My thought seeds bear wonderful fruit!

Spirit Is Sufficient!

We contemplate the Abundance of the Universe and focus on Spirit as the Source of our prosperity. The Divine Reality is the well-spring of our good—we are drawing from an infinite, unlimited supply. This means that Spirit, as Source, has more than enough for all our individual and collective needs and is sufficient to all our needs.

Let's take this one step further, however. "God is my sufficiency" is true in EVERY area of our life. It's not just that Spirit is the Source of our abundance—it also means that relying on Spirit is enough. Spirit, by Its Presence in us, as us, fulfills every need—for love, friendship, health, and creativity as well as abundance —not by drawing those things to us, but by already being those things for us, right here and right now.

> *God is my sufficiency.*
> — Joel Goldsmith

So the act of relying on Spirit is what allows Spirit's abundance to be revealed as already present. The act of turning to God, the Spiritual Truth, fulfills the need, even before we ask.

SPIRITUAL CONTEMPLATION: "God (or whatever term speaks to you) is my sufficiency."

AFFIRMATION: God is my sufficiency!

Decide to Be Grateful

Never underestimate the power of appreciation. Appreciation moves us from a fear-and-lack mentality to one of having and enjoying. It's a powerful discipline to decide to appreciate what you have rather than focus on what you don't have. Remember that whatever you focus on grows!

Gratitude unlocks the fullness of life. It turns what we have into enough, and more. It turns denial into acceptance, chaos to order, confusion to clarity. It can turn a meal into a feast, a house into a home, a stranger into a friend.

— Melody Beattie

Appreciate your bills—you received good value for them whether they're for your home air-conditioning or gas to get where you want to go. Appreciate your income regardless of how much it is—it's one of the many channels through which your good is flowing to you. Appreciate all the unexpected income, gifts, sales, discounts, and free things that you enjoy. These are more of the channels through which Spirit supports you. Appreciation reminds us that it's all good and it's all God!

SPIRITUAL CONTEMPLATION: What parts of your abundance and finances do you have trouble appreciating? Begin to find a way to appreciate these very areas.

AFFIRMATION: I appreciate every check I write and every deposit I make. Every one of them represents abundance moving in my life.

What's Holding You Back?

There was a time in my life when it seemed like everything was just too much trouble. It was too much trouble to pack a picnic and go to the lake . . . too much trouble to do the research on where to take a vacation . . . too much trouble to learn about marketing and budgeting to build the business. Every time I tried to go or do or create—it didn't happen because it was simply too much effort or seemed like a bother.

I had to learn not to wait until I felt like doing it. I also had to learn not to wait on other people. If it's important to me, something I enjoy or want to do, I am responsible for moving forward on it. I am responsible for deciding to do it and then following through on it. I know that when we move on

Doing what's expected of you can make you good, but it's the time you spend going above and beyond what's required that makes you great!
— Josh S. Hinds

our decisions and intentions, the whole of the Universe is there to support us.

SPIRITUAL CONTEMPLATION: What keeps you from taking that trip, or a day at the park, or starting that creative project? What keeps you from moving forward on creating or enjoying your abundance?

AFFIRMATION: I willingly move on and apply myself to those things that I want to enjoy, create, or share! I no longer wait for anything or anyone.

Deciding to Be Abundant | Is There a Ceiling to Your Abundance?

March 17
Being a Detective for Good!

My son loves shows like *CSI* and *Law & Order*. He loves the investigation and the sleuthing that bring some surprising evidence to light. It's always something that wasn't expected and he loves the surprise, but also the rightness of how things work out.

Wouldn't it be amazing to move in our life with the same investigative intention, looking for the surprising evidence of how things really do work out? Yet how many times do we actually collect evidence, both current and past, of things that haven't worked out? Our minds are trained to look for and find the thing we are most focused on. If we are focused on lack and fear, our minds will show us all the ways that these are playing out. But if we focus on our good, the things we are grateful for, and what really is working, then our minds have to go out and collect that kind of evidence instead. Like a great detective, our minds will filter out all those things that distract from the hunt, and focus on those things that take us to the truth.

> *The plain, practical, everyday problem of moneymaking is a definite part of living and the answer to it is summed up in these words: Prosperity awaits man's recognition and acceptance of it. Or it can be stated another way: Your financial success already exists, but it is waiting for you to see it and accept it as your own.*
>
> — Ernest Holmes

SPIRITUAL CONTEMPLATION: Become a detective in your life, sleuthing out the evidence of abundance in your life and seeking clues for all the ways you are supported.

AFFIRMATION: I actively look for clues that I am supported and abundant. I am delighted at how much good I discover.

The Power of Four Letter Words

Every significant decision we make is either motivated by love or by fear. Fear causes us to make contracting and limited decisions that have predictable outcomes and are designed to keep us safe in a controlled environment. Generally speaking, these decisions come from limited and false beliefs we hold about ourselves and about life.

Love leads us to make expansive and empowered decisions. Love is the very self-givingness of Life to Life. It is an outward flow and the more it is shared, the more it grows. We can always tell when our decisions are based on our spiritual knowing because the end result expands and grows us.

There are two basic motivating forces: fear and love. When we are afraid, we pull back from life. When we are in love, we open to all that life has to offer with passion, excitement, and acceptance. . . . Evolution and all hopes for a better world rest in the fearlessness and open-hearted vision of people who embrace life.

— John Lennon

SPIRITUAL CONTEMPLATION: Think about how you use and share your wealth. Think about how you talk about and work with your finances and investments. Are you motivated by love or fear?

AFFIRMATION: I allow love to motivate my decisions about my wealth and finances. This expands my good in more ways than I can count.

March 19
The Poisonous Arrow

A man was once struck with a poisonous arrow, and in order to save his friend's life, his mate removed the arrow before the poison spread through his body. Imagine, however, if the man didn't want the arrow removed until he knew who shot it at him and why, their age, their clan, and the kind of poison they used. If he were to wait for all these inquiries to be answered, he'd die.

Whether the world is finite or infinite, limited or unlimited, the problem of your liberation remains the same.

— Buddha

Life is precious and brief, and sometimes we get so caught up in our metaphysical demands that we forget to take care of the matter at hand. You don't have to have all your questions answered before taking the necessary action in your life. Getting lost in the speculative while life passes you by is a waste of the gift of living. If you are being poisoned, get the poisonous expression out of your life. Then you can do all the contemplating you'd like until you figure out enough lessons. But if you are dead because of your inaction, contemplation isn't going to serve you very well in this world.

SPIRITUAL CONTEMPLATION: What poisonous situations are you presently involved in that you haven't removed yourself from? What's the purpose of remaining attached to the poisonous pump? Remove the toxicity from your lifeline now.

AFFIRMATION: I remove all points of poison from my life!

Is There a Ceiling to Your Abundance?

I love having my house cleaned. My favorite day of the week is coming home to refreshing sheets and shiny floors. I've worked full-time my whole life and raised a child, so having someone else clean my house was a huge boon to my sanity and time management. The only problem was that my mother had opinions about it. Subtly, but clearly, she let me understand that she thought I should be taking care of all that myself; after all, she did, and she had certainly taught me how.

> *It is certain that you cannot believe in abundance while identifying yourself with lack. Forget the lack and think only of abundance.*
>
> — Ernest Holmes

As I began working with my abundance consciousness and looking for my lack-and-limiting thoughts, I noticed how uncomfortable my mother's judgment made me. And I realized that for years, I'd used *her* level of abundance and prosperity as the ceiling for my own because I didn't want her criticism. That way if I never had more than she did, we'd always be on equal footing, and she wouldn't have something else to judge about me. WOW—what an eye-opening revelation that was!

I worked diligently on releasing any concern about her, or anyone's, judgment or opinion of my prosperous and abundant life. Now when someone says to me, "You take more vacations than anyone I know," I joyfully reply, "Yes, and isn't it great!" I celebrated the day my mother told me, as she turned seventy, that she had finally hired someone to clean her house!

SPIRITUAL CONTEMPLATION: Explore what ceiling you might have put on your abundance. Is it an old belief about wealthy people or spiritual people? Is it a subtle message from your family or friends?

AFFIRMATION: Spirit's abundance flows effortlessly through all of life. I release any concern about someone else's judgment or opinion. I accept my abundance.

Vernal Equinox

The vernal equinox is that time in the Earth's annual cycle around the sun when night and day are of equal length. It's a time of balance when one side is the dark half of the year and the other is the light. It's been marked since the most ancient of days, as when the Sphinx aligns directly with the rising sun, while in Cambodia the temple of Angkor Wat has been designed so there's a three-day lead-up to the spring equinox when its highest tower is crowned by the rising sun.

Spring is nature's way of saying, "Let's party!"
— Robin Williams

Seeds planted in the fall burst forth from the earth, and birth triumphs over death. It's a time when the powers we've been developing through the winter can be put into creating . . . the time of the alchemical process . . . and the time to initiate a new order within your life. Access the vibrant energy of nature for healing and accelerate your growth by opening yourself for the newness of this amazing season of spring.

SPIRITUAL CONTEMPLATION: Can you feel a tipping point in your life toward a new transforming energy, changing an otherwise heavy vibration to that of a lighter one?

AFFIRMATION: I love the Spring!

How masterful are you at stalling? Can you come up with all sorts of excuses, both lame and creative, for not completing what's before you? Good intentions may fill your mind and a plan and time to finish the task are at hand, but somehow you drag your feet and find other things to do instead: wash the dishes, fold the laundry, run an errand. In the meantime, you are perfecting the art of the stall on the project you really do need to conclude.

One of these days I'm going to get help for my procrastination problem.
— Unknown

There is an empowering quote that says, "I can of mine own self do nothing, the Father that dwells within me does the work"; however I don't think Spirit is going to write your business proposal without your hand, heart, and brain involved. That project waiting for your attention needs your time to find

If it weren't for the last minute, I wouldn't get anything done.
— Unknown

completion. There aren't two, you and the Father—that would be two-ness not One-ness. There is the one life force, the Divine essence, waiting to be called into action through you, as you. When you put no other power before God, your stall tactics have no ability to deny the power of the presence seeking to fulfill your vision.

SPIRITUAL CONTEMPLATION: What are some of your favorite stall tactics? What projects that you'd love to see completed are on stall mode right now? Go complete them and find how much freer you feel.

AFFIRMATION: I complete those things that are near and dear to my heart!

Healing Body, Mind, and Computer

Nothing is more frustrating than finding your computer inoperable when you finally find the time to work on a project you've postponed until the last minute. Somewhere in the cloud or the server, the gremlins are having fun at your expense and all the glitches have united their forces to frustrate you. Maybe it's just that Mercury went retrograde and the heavens have conspired against you. But whatever the reason, your computer isn't working and you're infuriated or at least annoyed, neither of which helps you find a solution.

Never trust a computer you can't throw out a window.

— Steve Wozniak

Well, this then becomes your spiritual practice: recognize that computer repair is not God's domain. Divine intervention for your laptop is always possible, but usually guidance from another person and tapping the correct combination of keys seem to be the channel that Spirit works through. Grace can enter into the resolution only when you stop cussing at your screen. So relax and await the realization of Grace to emerge in what you are looking at. Grace is not a power but a presence, and in the presence there is no need to battle any annoyance. Be still and allow Grace to be Grace. Grace will function as guidance, wisdom, harmony, wholeness, and inspiration while revealing all that is necessary with whatever is before you.

SPIRITUAL CONTEMPLATION: Where do you give your power away to inanimate objects? How can they become your spiritual practice?

AFFIRMATION: I now sense Grace in all areas of my life!

Cyclopes Aren't Good for Business

I was driving down the road when from the backseat my son said out of the blue, "Cyclopes aren't good for business." Initially I spent my time wondering where that non sequitur came from, then I realized that he is absolutely right. Having a single focus, attempting to resolve all issues the same way, and seeing everything through a single portal of perception —these don't bring the diversity necessary for dealing with the dynamics of business or life. Difficulties usually can't be solved all the same way and all at the same time. Line them up, face them, and take one on at a time. You probably already know what's wrong and more than likely it's something you don't want to deal with since it's a problem.

It ain't what you don't know
that gets you into trouble.
It's what you know for sure
that just ain't so.
— Mark Twain

Don't trick yourself into a false perception of the difficulty, however. An impartial attitude may not always transform the situation, but it will transform you. It will take your single-sightedness off the effects of the situation and reveal the cause. Look at the facts, not just what others tell you. Be willing to engage other people to help create as many answers and resolutions as possible and then implement the best one. Assess what unfolds. You'll come to see that stepping back and opening both eyes wide with a positive attitude is the best way to move forward through the issues at hand.

SPIRITUAL CONTEMPLATION: What issues can't you see your way through? Step back to gain a broader vision of the scene, line up the challenges, and pick one to bring your higher positive attitude to address.

AFFIRMATION: My perspective expands at points of contention!

Deciding to Be Abundant | Is There a Ceiling to Your Abundance?

March 25
Authentic Expression

No one likes to feel used or manipulated. It ruins the bond of trust. You connect more by being honest and transparent than calculating and shrewd. When you come from your heart, there is no patronizing or public condemnation, no sarcastic jabs or put-downs. Care enough about people to put them first and really hear what is coming from their heart. Authenticity has gentleness and clarity.

Soul is about authenticity. Soul is about finding the things in your life that are real and pure.

— John Legend

It doesn't matter how polished your communication skills are; what makes the difference is how authentic you are. People want to know and feel the real you. You don't need to be a slick communicator in order to move people—what's most effective is your authentic expression. It's said that Richard Branson froze the first time he was asked to give a speech, but despite being scared to death, he was still an effective communicator. Connecting with people is the key to effective communication, and that is done by coming from your heart.

SPIRITUAL CONTEMPLATION: Where do you find yourself being a little too caustic and abrasive in your communication with others? How could you back off a bit and become gentler in your authentic expression while still communicating your perspective?

AFFIRMATION: I come from my heart in communicating with others!

Be Part of Nature

When you're rushing around in a hurry, stop and contemplate: nature doesn't hurry, and yet everything is accomplished season after season. The grass that is supposed to grow, grows and water doesn't try to flow, it just does. The action is quite effortless when in alignment with the expression of life. This doesn't mean there aren't obstacles to move through or around, but there's a spontaneous ease of appropriate action, something we'd be pretty smart for taking into consideration in our life.

> *Nature does not hurry, yet everything is accomplished.*
> — Lao Tzu

When the logical, calculating mind is in high gear it can impede the effortless flow of nature's wisdom. So when life throws you some curveballs and challenges, relax rather than tensing up. When you notice yourself stuck and straining in effort, pause. Go outside, breathe in some fresh air and realize you are not your mind—you are who uses your mind. Nature is not in any kind of hurry, so why are you? Relax. The grass grows, the water flows, and so do you.

SPIRITUAL CONTEMPLATION: Where in your life do you feel stuck and there appears to be an urgency to get through the challenge? Visualize water coming to a blockage on its path and see the water building up behind the blockage until it effortlessly moves around and over it, continuing on its perfectly timed journey. Now take that urgent challenge and visualize it in that flow, effortlessly moving beyond whatever is in your path in perfect timing.

AFFIRMATION: I move with the perfect flow and timing of life!

Eostre

Eostre, the Saxon goddess for whom Easter is named, later became Ostara who was known as a fertility goddess with a passion for new life. It is said that her presence was felt in the flowering of plants and birth of babies. Her magical companion, the rabbit, a well-recognized rapid reproducer of life, joined her in bringing new life to dying plants while offering eggs, which are obvious symbols of fertility. All the symbols used in spring festivals in the past express gratitude for the gift of life and abundance.

> *The symbolic language of the crucifixion is the death of the old paradigm; resurrection is a leap into a whole new way of thinking.*
>
> — Deepak Chopra

Earlier celebrations were about happiness and life, so how did what we recognize as Easter today change to the consecration of suffering and death? Early observances were about the birth day and preparing for life, not about execution and the alleged afterlife. These festivals don't require a belief in an event that may or may not have happened, but something that is happening in your life now. Let the holiday lift you in the joyous awakening of new life and its triumphant return over slumbering nature.

SPIRITUAL CONTEMPLATION: What's been slumbering that you feel awakening in your soul? What is it that wants to hatch into a new expression this spring as part of your life expression? Give it some space and a celebration because you've been chosen this spring to midwife it into expression.

AFFIRMATION: I align with the awakening life of nature in me!

Breaking the Karmic Chain

People often put such an energetic *Whoa!* about the probability of breaking free of karma. They believe that when you get on the karmic wheel you're there for a long time. Yet the chain is being broken all the time. Some people who were on their last borrowed dollar have turned their life around and are now sitting on top of the world. And what about those people with a terminal illness and only a few months to live who years later are still around telling how they beat their life sentence?

> *Karma, when properly understood, is just the mechanics through which consciousness manifests.*
>
> — Deepak Chopra

In the spiritual consciousness there is no law of dis-ease and no bondage to cause and its effect. Any time you touch the spiritual consciousness and achieve any sense of freedom, the power of grace enters into the equation. Spiritual realization is what sets you free. It doesn't matter what the mistake has been, it can all end in a moment when grace touches down. But then, as the saying goes, "Go and sin no more." If you return to the same old behavior and consciousness that brought the error to you to begin with, you are back on that karmic wheel. But if in the freeing moment of higher realization you decide to no longer perpetuate what was, then what can be will show up for you.

SPIRITUAL CONTEMPLATION: What karmic chain would you like to break free from? If you knew that all you had to do was discontinue the behavior and thinking that got you in a present predicament, would you really let go of them?

AFFIRMATION: I am now free from my karmic discomforts!

Possible or Impossible, You Decide!

"I can't," "I don't know," and "I haven't" are all ways in which we reaffirm our lack and limitation. We have something within, however—the Presence of Spirit as us—that does know, that can, and absolutely has everything needed for an abundant life. We shift our focus from the impossible to the possible by realizing that all we have to do is create the space in our consciousness for a larger idea. The "how" is up to an incredibly powerful and intelligent universal law. We don't actually have to know how, because It does.

Decide what you want.
Believe you can have it.
Believe you deserve it
and believe it's possible
for you.

— Jack Canfield

So the question is, what we are going to decide. Do we decide that this spiritual stuff really works, and that we're going to step out as if that were actually true? Or do we continue to look for evidence that it hasn't been true in the past, and therefore it can't be true for our future? It's all in what we decide to focus on and speak into reality. To God, everything is possible. We have to decide if that's true for us, too!

SPIRITUAL CONTEMPLATION: How often do I decide to limit myself in ways that keep me from living the abundant life that is my birthright?

AFFIRMATION: All things are possible for me, because all things are possible for God as me!

Who You Are Is Enough

Have you ever pondered the deep philosophical question as to why Cinderella's shoe didn't disappear when everything else went *poof* at midnight, including her other shoe? Imagine if she had gone to the party as who she really was; she would never have had to leave in such a panic if she hadn't been in a disguise to begin with. Life is inviting you to show up as who you are, not who you are pretending to be.

Cinderella was being her true self until she lost her confidence and ran. It's after you have touched your dream

He loves me because I'm me.
— Cinderella

that a part of you can be scared and a piece of you is left in it. It's just not very often the dream comes knocking on doors in your neighborhood tracking down the owner of that piece. It might have played out well for Cinderella, but it would serve you better to stop waiting for the lost piece of your dream to find you. Stop using the excuse that you've got nothing to wear and you're too busy. Put on what you've got and get going to the party. Life has invited you to come as you are. So stop wishing on a star for some fairy godmother to come along to spruce you up, because who you are is enough to make your dreams come true.

SPIRITUAL CONTEMPLATION: What excuses do you tell yourself for not going for your dream? What pieces of you have you left behind in your dream that you are hoping will come find you? What can you do to retrieve that last piece of you?

AFFIRMATION: Who I am is enough for my dream to come true!

March 31
Mental Bombs

What mental bombs do you launch into your world? What less-than-kind energetic expression are you responsible for detonating? Where and with whom do you have an inner battle going on? Do you feel there is a mental or emotional war raging inside of you? Some peace advocates are among some of the angriest people you'll meet, but if you want peace, you must be peace. Just because you hold it together on the outside and don't go off on someone doesn't mean you are an expression of peace. You might have the world fooled, but check your blood pressure and see how attuned your body is to your vibrations of consciousness. Then realize the world you walk in is also picking up on and reflecting your vibrational contributions.

> *To work for peace is to uproot war from ourselves and from the hearts of men and women. To prepare for war, to give millions of men and women the opportunity to practice killing day and night in their hearts, is to plant millions of seeds of violence, anger, frustration, and fear that will be passed on for generations to come.*
>
> — Thich Nhat Hanh

Compassion arises from within our heart. Compassion is what will transform the world. Our expressions of caring will still the wars of this world—shipping all the arsenal of this planet to outer space will not. Weapons will just be created again if there is hatred in our hearts. What we focus on is what will materialize in our world, which is why it's important to have our kids rehearse in their minds and hearts those things that will bless this world and not destroy it or them. What visions would you wish your children to review and practice in their soul?

SPIRITUAL CONTEMPLATION: Where are you hurling bombs upon the world? What can you do to stop contributing to the warring energy and replace it with a compassion for the situation at hand?

AFFIRMATION: I bring compassion to my war-torn thoughts!

April

Our Purpose Is an Abundant Life

April 1–7
Living a Mighty Purpose

April 8–14
Making a Living or Making a Life?

April 15–23
Passover (22/23)
Heaven with Eyes Wide Open

April 24–30
I Rest in God

Scary Stuff April Fools

Imagine if news reporting was just one big hoax? People easily believed Orson Welles's *War of the Worlds* broadcast in 1938. What would happen today if it were reported that the planet is getting healthier; war as an option is outdated; global abundance and health are breaking out all over; and nontoxic, renewable free energy is now available to everyone on the planet? Do you think people would believe these as easily as the negative reports of doom and gloom in the world? Having these headlines bombard the collective consciousness might actually create some competition and bring about good fortune for all people.

Perhaps known as the original media hoax, the BBC "reported" on April 1, 1957, that Switzerland was experiencing a bumper spaghetti harvest. Viewers called in wanting to know how they could get their own spaghetti plant. According to the online Museum of Hoaxes the BBC responded, "Place a sprig of spaghetti in a tin of tomato sauce and hope for the best."

— The Swiss Spaghetti Harvest

In his song "Imagine" John Lennon hoped that the world could become one. Maybe if global unity and peace were heralded in horror and fear-based headlines, they might sell. Maybe people would believe that unity and peace were actually happening and peace would break out all over. So let the headlines read today —"FLASH: Random Acts of Kindness Breaking Out Globally, Warring Is Over, Soldiers Laying Down Their Guns and Refusing to Fight, The Climate Is Perfect, Government Really Is for the People by the People, Cure for Cancer Found." . . . Now that's scary stuff!

SPIRITUAL CONTEMPLATION: What are some of your dream headlines?

AFFIRMATION: I am a deliverer of the Divine Dream!

What Is Our Purpose?

I do not want it written on my tombstone, "She certainly worked hard!" Nor do I want "She answered all her e-mail." We are not here on this planet just to work hard or to clear our inbox. While our work may be important to us, we are actually here to express service to Life. We are the place where the Universal Presence pierces the space/time veil so that It may enjoy and express and experience Itself as an individualized self, in addition to the purely undivided, oneness Self of its Universal state. This makes us a microcosm of the Macrocosm or the incarnation, the Divine sons and daughters of a Universal Reality.

> *I am come that they might have life, and that they might have it more abundantly.*
> — John 10:10

Our purpose to express and experience Life as us means that we are not here to suffer, toil, or await a future reward in Heaven. Since we are the ONE manifesting as us, EVERYTHING is already available to us. We simply get to pick and choose which portions of that EVERYTHING we want to experience. Therefore, we are to have an abundant life, a life that has everything it needs to fully express itself. This is our nature, our birthright, and the very promise made so that we may be to the ONE all that we can fully be.

SPIRITUAL CONTEMPLATION: Simply be with the idea that your primary purpose is to BE the ONE as you; that your sense of separation is not bad, it's just not the truth of who you are. How are you living out your purpose?

AFFIRMATION: I am a place where Spirit is made manifest. My life is for the sheer joy of living!

April 3
A Mighty Purpose!

The problem with happiness is that it is fleeting and ephemeral. It seems that the more we chase it, the less of it we experience. When I stopped chasing happiness—after failed marriages and a broken career—and turned my attention to my purpose in life, I began to ask questions: "What am I here for? What is my contribution? What is my reason for being?" As I discovered my purpose—with my home and family and through my work—I noticed that I worried less and less about being happy. The more I gave of myself through my gifts and talents through my purpose, the more satisfied I became with my life and myself. Somewhere along the way I discovered a deep, ongoing joy that had nothing to do with whether an event turned out or someone liked me or I had a good time at a party. I realized that this joy was so constant, that I was easily happy most of the time. Happiness had come in on the wings of my purpose in life.

This is the true joy in life, the being used for a purpose recognized by yourself as a mighty one; the being thoroughly worn out before you are thrown on the scrap heap; the being a force of nature instead of a feverish selfish little clod of ailments and grievances complaining that the world will not devote itself to making you happy.

— George Bernard Shaw

SPIRITUAL CONTEMPLATION: Are you chasing happiness? Are you living your purpose? Spend time thinking about what you are doing that causes you to feel satisfied, like making a real contribution. Follow that, and happiness will steal in while you aren't looking!

AFFIRMATION: My happiness cup overflows when I contribute my gift to the world or my family, my art or my career. I recognize my mighty purpose and move steadily toward it. This brings true joy to my life.

Who Do You Think You Are?

Sometimes we think that if we could just figure out the purpose God has for us, we will be rewarded with wealth and fulfillment. We want a sign, preferably a neon arrow, to show us which way to go. But this way of approaching purpose assumes a duality between God and us. From this point of view, God is out there directing and judging us. Then we experience life as a series of lessons and rewards based on whether we think we are, or are not, in line with "God's Plan for us."

God is to us, as we think God is. Because God is the impulse of our very life and is already fulfilling Itself

God has said, "I am to My servant as he thinks I am."
— Prophet Muhammad, Hadith Qudsi

simply by being us, and has given us the Universal Laws that are the keys to the Kingdom, our purpose is to be and express, become and experience LIFE in the unique and precious way that is the way God shows up AS US. Our purpose is to BE GOD AS ME, as the best ME I can be. This means that we seek our innermost talents and strengths, our deepest, truest desires to express and serve, knowing that they come directly from the impulse of God. God is a Unity with us. God is as close as our heartbeat, as near as our breath, and as present as our hands and voice, as we move out into the world. Every act in alignment with God AS US fulfills our purpose, and we find ourselves wealthy heirs to the Kingdom of Heaven every day.

SPIRITUAL CONTEMPLATION: I am not my job, career, or any role I play. These may be ways in which I express and experience my purpose. I am an incarnation of the Divine Reality; God's only plan for me is one of Freedom. The freedom to be ME!

AFFIRMATION: I am free to be me. My purpose is to be the best ME I can be. This is fulfilling God's purpose to be Itself in, through, and AS ME!

April 5
Integrity

Integrity isn't so much about what you say; it's more about who you are and what you do. It's what steers you through life. It establishes your priorities and behavior so when you are morally challenged you know how to respond. It doesn't matter how spiritual you are; from time to time you will cross a contradictory emotional battle within your soul as to how to be with the question at hand. You have found your edge and soul-stretching moment. You are often confronted with contradictory circumstances between what you want to do and what you know is correct to do. Your integrity brings clarity to these moments.

Real integrity is doing the right thing, knowing that nobody's going to know whether you did it or not.

— Oprah Winfrey

Integrity will not allow your actions to defy your heart. When you're coming from a place of deep integrity, your conduct will be congruent with your heart's desires. Your head won't be tripping out on your past choices but instead will be free to live with a great sense of inner peace. Your integrity allows you to decide who you will be regardless of the dynamics of your world. Your values are what keep you from living as a split personality between who you want to be and who you are in the world by freeing you to be a whole person aligned in spirit, soul, and action, no matter what comes your way.

SPIRITUAL CONTEMPLATION: Are you the same person no matter whom you are with or what the circumstance?

AFFIRMATION: I am living my life from integrity!

Enjoying the Purpose of Life!

Native American traditions teach that wealth is a state of mind no matter what your material status. It's primarily a state of fulfillment, having enough to be and do what makes our heart sing. Our engagement in life, in our own life, creates the feeling of wealth. When you enjoy what you have and what you are doing, you are rich beyond measure.

How often are we engaged in things because we think we should be, or need to, at work or in our families? We compromise our integrity, our health, or our true desire, because we think that's what it takes to succeed, get to the top, or have the wealthy lifestyle we are sold on TV. But this kind of stress burns people out, causes damage to our health, and cynicism or resignation in our hearts. With that going on, it just doesn't matter how much stuff we own or how many titles and promotions we get.

> *Abundance does not come from working "hard." It comes from learning to enjoy the effort of our tasks.*
> — Otter on a Rock

This idea is captured beautifully in the age-old adage—"It's not about the destination, it's about the journey"—and how you are living/walking it. All you have in life is how you spend your time. Does the way you spend your time make you feel like you are fulfilled and wealthy—or stressed and depleted?

SPIRITUAL CONTEMPLATION: When you no longer enjoy the tasks before you, should you press on? Do you secretly believe that all your suffering will deserve a reward?

AFFIRMATION: I live my life to the fullest. I enjoy the journey of my life. I enjoy everything I have and do.

April 7
Temperance

If you ever flood the engine in your car, the last thing you should do is keep pumping the gas pedal and flood it even more. If you've got an itch, a little scratching is divine but to keep digging at it is not. If you find something frustrating and you keep ruminating on it, it will only drive you crazy. Sometimes backing off and giving space to what should work is effective, but overdoing isn't. A bit of temperance can make a big difference—moderation is a significant key to success and an abundant life.

Joy, temperance, and repose, slam the door on the doctor's nose.

— Henry Wadsworth Longfellow

As uninspiring as it sounds, temperance helps you find harmony between your desires and wants, and creates a balance in your emotional and mental fields. When you can moderate your indulgences you will find equilibrium in your life. Temperance will assist you in trusting your inner guidance and finding the right blend of certainty in your life.

SPIRITUAL CONTEMPLATION: Where are you stepping on the gas and flooding your world with insane behaviors that don't serve you well? Where would backing off with a little more temperance help balance your world and bring more insight in those spaces?

AFFIRMATION: I live with the perfect blend of ideas and action in my life!

Are You a Blessing?

Every time we interact with others, whether at work or at home, we have the choice about our contribution to the interaction. We can choose to be critical or judgmental, closed or reactionary, indifferent or apathetic. Every time we look out at the world we can curse those who aren't doing it right, be fearful of people and events, or throw up our hands in "ain't it awful" thinking. The problem, of course, is that life mirrors back to us what we put out. So imagine all these things now coming back to us, impacting the quality of our life and our abundance.

When you focus on being a blessing, God makes sure that you are always blessed in abundance.

— Joel Osteen

What if, instead, we decide to enter every interaction as a benevolent presence? Benevolence is defined as the "desire to do good to others; goodwill; charitableness." Therefore, being a benevolent presence means we have a charitable inclination toward others and seek to have goodwill in our interactions. This changes our impact completely. Even though we might have to tell a difficult truth or draw a boundary with someone, we do so without anger, hostility, or the need to make someone else wrong. We might not agree at all with something that is going on in the world, but when we do something about it, we do so with the desire to be a blessing, not to curse those involved. The energetics is completely different and blesses all those involved.

SPIRITUAL CONTEMPLATION: How can you be more of a benevolent presence at home? In your workplace? When discussing current events? In participating in transformation and change?

AFFIRMATION: I am a benevolent presence wherever I go. I am a blessing to others and I am blessed in return!

April 9
Mi Casa Es Su Casa

Guests who can take care of themselves while they stay with you are so much easier to have around, aren't they? There is joy in the hospitality, and the burden of having to be responsible for their good time is lifted. Make yourself at home, mi casa es su casa, my house is your house, and we can share in creating the magic of being together.

He who brings a tale takes two away.

— Irish Proverb

There is equality in the home and not a burden on the host to produce the pleasure for the guest. It's not a hotel with room service—it's a home where we are alike.

As you walk this earth as its guest, take care of it as your own. It's as if the earth is saying, "My good is your good to enjoy not destroy. Respect it, honor it, and share it." You wouldn't take from a friend's house what is not yours, nor is it appropriate to exploit what the host shares with you. You want to leave a friend's place with a mutual sense of shared blessings. When your journey through this world is complete, will you leave the place blessed and enhanced by your time? Did you contribute to the conversation of the culture, will the youth who follow you carry the grace from your consciousness, and are your parting gifts of beauty lingering like trees for generations long after your presence has left?

SPIRITUAL CONTEMPLATION: What kind of guest are you? Are you needy or are you a gracious contributor?

AFFIRMATION: I am a blessing wherever I go!

Making a Living or Making a Life?

Making a living may be simply paying the bills and getting by. Or making a living may be going for the big bucks, the successful career, and the name in your field. Making a living may mean you aspire to live in a big house and drive the best car, or it may mean you are free to travel and indulge in your hobbies. Making a living may be all you've ever asked for from your work or career.

Making a life, however, is about the sum total of the life you are living. Not just success and work and money, but also relationships, health, creativity, and self-expression. Making a life is living

Having a purpose is the difference between making a living and making a life.
— Tom Thiss

the life you choose and creating the life of your dreams—not purely in form (although it may include form) but more in experience and the quality of every day. In addition, making a life is giving your gift and your contribution to the world. It means you know what fulfills you and what you have to give.

Making a living can become depressing. Making a life is always about expressing Spirit in, through, and as you.

SPIRITUAL CONTEMPLATION: What's the difference between making a living and making a life? How does knowing your purpose make the difference? Which one are you doing?

AFFIRMATION: I am making a life through my choices and activities. I express my purpose and my being through all the ways I contribute to the world.

April 11
Celebrating with Others!

"Why does she always get picked?" This thought ran my life for a number of years. I was envious because I wanted to be chosen, so I trash-talked about her to anyone who would listen. "Well, you know those rich people aren't really happy" also ran my life for many years. It helped me feel spiritually superior, while I felt inferior in terms of my abundance and wealth. I also realized that when good things happened for me, I was reluctant to share them because all my friends responded in the way I used to respond, with envy or negative talk.

Instead, I have an abundance mentality: When people are genuinely happy at the successes of others, the pie gets larger.

— Stephen Covey

Then I began to live "we are all one in God" so that the way I treat another is the way I treat myself. First I began to give myself what I thought others should be giving me. Then I began to see that people are people—and there are happy rich people as well as poor people, and unhappy poor people as well as rich ones.

I discovered a whole new way to grow my abundance experience —to truly and really celebrate every time someone received good— whether a promotion, money, an unexpected windfall, or just generally more abundance. Genuinely celebrating others' good actually raised my own ability to accept that this good is possible. Then I realized that if it could happen for another, surely it could happen for me.

SPIRITUAL CONTEMPLATION: How do I respond when someone else receives a great good? What needs to shift for me to learn to genuinely celebrate others' good?

AFFIRMATION: I celebrate the good that others in my life are receiving! I genuinely enjoy the good that is showing up in everyone's life!

A young archer once approached a master teacher and expertly shot an arrow into the center of the bull's-eye a great distance off. Swiftly, he followed with another and split the first arrow in two. "Beat that," the arrogant youngster boasted. Gesturing for the young archer to follow him, the wise one headed up the mountain to a cliff overlooking a deep canyon that was spanned by a weathered gray log. With great composure, the master walked to the center of the log, and in one smooth stroke, pulled an arrow from his quiver and let it fly straight into the trunk of a tree a great distance away. He casually backed off the log and turned to the youth. "Your turn," he said, without an ounce of ego. The young archer stared into the sprawling cavern below and started to shake uncontrollably. No way was he going to be able to put a foot on that log, let alone take a shot at anything from the middle of it. "You have great control over your bow," the great teacher said, nodding to the student, "but little over the mind that lets loose the arrow."

Man stands in his own shadow and wonders why it's dark.
— Zen

There is a big difference between learning the principles of truth and applying them in a precarious life situation. Master teachers will help guide you into arenas where you must learn to calm your mind in order to call upon your learned skills.

SPIRITUAL CONTEMPLATION: What life situations look very difficult for you to cross? What skills do you have that you know work in calmer situations? Are you ready to calm your mind and step into the middle and take the shot?

AFFIRMATION: I find the calm within as I successfully cross the biggest chasms in my life!

April 13
Is It Really Enough?

The primary synonyms for enough are "sufficiency" and "plenty." Yet often we want more than enough. We tend to feel that "enough" is barely what is necessary. Yet sufficiency really does mean that all our needs are met and plenty implies that it is not meager, but bountiful. I often equate our insatiable desire for "more" with the fact that so many of us overstuff ourselves at Thanksgiving or at a restaurant with today's ridiculously large portions. It's as if we think that if we aren't stuffed, then it's not quite good enough. Yet enough, really is enough. Actually, at a good meal, we can equate enough with being satisfied.

For me, the opposite of scarcity is not abundance. It's enough. I'm enough. My kids are enough.

— Brene Brown

So really the question isn't whether it's enough, but whether we are satisfied. Are we satisfied with the way our needs are being met and the life we have, or are we infected with the disease called "more"? Now clearly we need more if we actually don't have enough money to pay our bills and save for the future, or enough food for ourselves and our children. That's clearly "not enough" and we are not required to settle for anything less.

Why do we think that "enough" isn't adequate or satisfying? Spirit is satisfied expressing through a joyous, happy, and growing life. When we are joyous, happy, and growing, our life is enough and we are satisfied and fulfilled. That really is enough!

SPIRITUAL CONTEMPLATION: How do you relate to the words "enough" and "more" and "satisfied"? What can be learned from this about how you approach your abundance and your life?

AFFIRMATION: Spirit is enough for everything I need. I have enough. I am enough! I am fulfilled and satisfied with my life.

The Joy of Circulation

I was invited to be interim minister of a spiritual community that had been reduced to twenty people and was over $50,000 in debt. In six months we had grown and were completely out of debt. What was our strategy? We started tithing. Immediately on Monday morning we gave away 10 percent of every Sunday's offering. Every week! Within a year I had helped them hire a full-time minister. She served for almost three years, but when she left, the community again numbered twenty people and was $30,000 in debt. Once again I was asked to be the interim minister, and once again we started tithing, every week. We were out of debt in four months.

> *The kabbalists of Tzfat connect the primal urgings toward abundance with the date of tithing fruit because they saw that God's shefa, abundance, would keep flowing only if a portion of it were returned to God, the Owner of all land and all abundance.*
>
> — Rabbi Arthur O. Waskow

Tithing is the training wheels we put on to grow our abundance. Tithing teaches us to use the Law of Circulation. It reminds us that all of life is in the form of cycles and circulation— whether it's the weather, water, ecosystems, or the seasons. Everything moves in circles, even our breath. God is forever showering us with Life, with abundance. We have to move with the circulation to keep it flowing and growing. "Give and it shall be given to you, pressed down, shaken together, and running over!"

SPIRITUAL CONTEMPLATION: Where in your life do you effortlessly participate in the flow of circulation? In what areas do you cling or hoard?

AFFIRMATION: Everything is sourced from the One and belongs to the whole. I am a good steward of the abundance in my possession. I neither hoard nor cling. I allow it to freely circulate!

April 15
Tax Time

Taxes—you can let them depress you as you fill in every calculation with agony—or you can get to work with excited expectation in the discovery of what you created in the previous year. Allow tax time to be an insightful and fun way to observe where you sent your dollars, which are, after all, a reflection of your current energy exchange.

I don't blame or complain about things, like the economy, the government, taxes, employees, gas prices, or any of the external things that I don't have control over. The only thing I have control over is my response to these things.

— Jack Canfield

As the saying goes, render unto Caesar what is Caesar's—do your taxes and get back to your life's work. You are here to be a creative expression of Spirit. Unless your call at this time is to be a changer of policies and expenditure plans, do not make trouble out of life's situations. Deal with what is, without creating any additional emotional issues. Let any tension, stress, or thoughts of scarcity fade into the nothingness from which they came. Know that your reality is based upon the abundance of the universe. Any behavior patterns of lack that distort the plentiful circulation of God as your life, need no longer affect your inspired awareness. Knowing that God is your source, find joy in contributing to the common well-being of the nation, which continues to create a safe world in which you prosper. Recognize the abundant flow of good as your life now, and you'll find yourself in paradise with a sustained consciousness of God's grace as your sufficiency.

SPIRITUAL CONTEMPLATION: Take a look at your energy around paying taxes. What can shift in you to make it a more positive experience?

AFFIRMATION: I am grateful to live in an abundant world and share from my bounty!

To Open the Door to Abundance, Begin with What Is

Craving things, needing stuff, and wanting the latest gadget are not true expressions of abundance. Focusing on what we don't have makes us work even harder on our abundance. We succumb to false stimulation and desires that are heightened by advertisers playing on our egoic need to compare and our belief that our good comes from buying or owning.

When we understand the way all things actually exist, rather than how we would wish them to, then the riches of all the ten directions and the three times, as vast as space, become ours; and anything else pales in comparison.

— Martin Kovan on Buddhism and Abundance

We are meant to live an abundant life that is rich in meaning, purpose, contribution, and joy. This will most certainly include "things" that are means to the end of helping us express and experience our purpose. Other things are ends in themselves, such as the belief that "when I have that boat, then I'll be happy!" or "when I get that job, or promotion, or check or . . . (fill-in-the-blank), then I'll be happy."

Begin with who you are, why you are here, and what you have to share. Claim that everything you need to express your purpose and share your gifts is already manifesting itself for you, easily and effortlessly. Notice how your abundant life grows and expands in ways that are truly amazing!

SPIRITUAL CONTEMPLATION: Are there things you want out of an ego need or sense of lack or less than? Begin to focus on things that are required for you to express and experience your joy.

AFFIRMATION: I release any sense of comparison or "less-than" thinking. My life fully supports my true purpose.

Heaven with Eyes Wide Open

As you develop your meditation skills through regular practice, you get to the point when some steps to a clearer connection are no longer necessary to reach those higher states of awareness. Whereas once you had to close your eyes to shut out distractions, you can now keep your eyes wide open to tap into the awareness beyond form and see as Spirit sees.

My soul can find no stairway to Heaven unless it be through Earth's loveliness.

— Michelangelo

Since form follows consciousness and heaven is a state of consciousness, it seems logical that heaven can find its way into your awareness demonstrating as your life now. You don't have to wait for some far-off distant time or place to be in heaven. Why would you need to close your eyes to enter heaven if you realize you're already in the midst of it? You can choose to be in heaven, or you can choose to point out all the ways you are not. Either way, the choice is yours.

SPIRITUAL CONTEMPLATION: Look at all the conversations you have that take you out of the experience of heaven on earth. Where can you shift your perspective to see you are in heaven now?

AFFIRMATION: I am in Heaven now!

Increase and Multiplication

Today, I accept God's gift of abundance.
Today everything that I AM and have, that is Good,
is increased.
I identify everything I do with success.
I think affirmatively.
And with all my prayers, I accept abundance.
Whatever I need, whenever I need it,
wherever I need it, for as long as I need it,
will always be at hand.
I no longer see negation
or delay
or stagnation
in my undertakings.
Rather, I claim that the action of the Living Spirit
prospers everything I do,
increases every Good I possess
and brings success to me and everyone I meet.
Everything I think about and do
is animated by the Divine Presence,
sustained by the Infinite Power,
and multiplied by the Divine Goodness.

— Emmet Fox

SPIRITUAL CONTEMPLATION: Take time to notice what you tend to focus on—what's not working, or what is? What's stuck, or what's moving? What areas of your life are you most obsessed with? Are you affirming increase and success in those areas?

AFFIRMATION: I claim that the action of the Living Spirit prospers everything I do, increases every Good I possess, and brings success to me and everyone I meet.

Guiding Gifts of Grace

When we first begin to study metaphysical teachings, we often attempt to have God intervene on our behalf. Isn't that what we were taught prayer was for? To get God to heal the body or a relationship, or produce the cash to buy that new house or car, or bring peace to the planet. But eventually you'll come to understand prayer is not about the individual attempting to enlighten God, but rather making yourself available to the abundant power of the Divine. Prayer in its highest mystical form is connecting with the Divine realization and being the place of the Divine's emergence of the truth—opening yourself to the guiding gifts of grace and losing your desire to inform the Infinite of your desires.

There is something in every one of you that waits and listens for the sound of the genuine in yourself. It is the only true guide you will ever have. And if you cannot hear it, you will all of your life spend your days on the ends of strings that somebody else pulls.

— Howard Thurman

The concept of God "saving you" belongs in a bygone era because there is nothing to be saved from. If you want to be freed from the pains of this world, you must enter the spiritual realm where you will live from the awareness that it is all God and the issues at hand carry absolutely no weight or power in that realm. There is no disease, lack, or pain in the kingdom of Divine Awareness. This recognition will dissolve all false appearances that might show themselves as real in your human walk through this plane of existence.

SPIRITUAL CONTEMPLATION: Where are you giving your power away to the forms of your material world? How can you perceive them as a non-power in the spiritual light?

AFFIRMATION: I see as Spirit sees!

It's a Different Proximity

We are now a planet that has been made intimate by our environmental concerns and water, food, and fuel shortages. It's an altogether different proximity than we have ever experienced before: weapons of mass destruction pointed in all directions, climate changes messing with our planet, financial markets tied together, and technology keeping a virtual eye on everything. Whether you like it or not, we are an interwoven global family being pulled more tightly together. What you do impacts the whole. It's not very probable that this one human family is reverting back to our days of isolation from one another.

We will be known forever by the tracks we leave.
— Native American Proverb

We need to promote development that does not destroy our environment.
— Wangari Maathai

Treat the earth well.
It was not given to you by your parents,
*   it was loaned to you by your children.*
We do not inherit the Earth from our Ancestors,
*   we borrow it from our Children.*

— Ancient Native American Proverb

SPIRITUAL CONTEMPLATION: What is your contribution to taking care of our planet?

AFFIRMATION: My contribution makes an impact because of our connectedness.

Ignoring the Alarm

Climate change is our youth's civil rights movement of this era. Whether you believe the weather is doing something drastically different or not, there is no denying the uprising of the collective voice that is saying enough is enough to the abuse of this planet. We can no longer take, take, take, and trash, trash, trash without destroying the balance of our delicate ecosystem. Ignoring the alarm is no longer an acceptable choice. The snooze button has been hit about as many times as possible.

Climate change is a terrible problem, and it absolutely needs to be solved. It deserves to be a huge priority.

— Bill Gates

Rather than submitting to climate despair or taking the gamble of doing nothing, we the people must take the lead in showing and discovering new ways of being on this planet. Alternatives and resolutions are already available but a new meme must be embraced for behavior to change. It's obvious that the billions of individuals who share this planet are depleting the common resources at an unsustainable rate— we are at a point where a leap must be made to a new way of being together. The human species has always made that evolutionary leap when it had to, and there is no doubt it will again. But the time is now, and the now generation is leading the way. Lend them your ears, your heart, and your cooperation—for this earth belongs to them and future generations.

SPIRITUAL CONTEMPLATION: Take some time exploring what you can do to make less of an impact on the planet. Investigate alternative ways of behavior that are more environmentally friendly, and have some fun and radical conversations with your friends about that.

AFFIRMATION: I hear the climate alarm and awaken to ways of being more harmonious on earth!

Celebrating Earth Day

Earth Day is a time to pause and remember the blessing this planet brings to us. It's a day of collaborative demonstrations around the planet to help raise awareness of the dynamics that are shifting the balance of our home. This beautiful blue marble that supports our existence as it floats in an expansive universe is more than just something we can take from, however, and we are now becoming aware of a possible Armageddon scenario. Although many refuse to accept this, others are able to read the planetary facts and use the information to help usher our global family into its next evolutionary expression.

> *Walk as if you are kissing the Earth with your feet.*
> — Thich Nhat Hanh

We will figure out how to feed eight billion-plus people on a daily basis, and provide them with power and daily essentials without destroying the planet. We will come to an understanding of how to return more to the environment than what we take. Humans have always taken that leap to the next rung of the evolving spiral and we will do so this time, as well.

There is no going back to how it was in the good old days. But there are bright days ahead. So during this Earth Day celebration, learn what's happening on the planet; you might find it scary, but don't forget to explore the volumes of answers that are emerging to support all of us now on this beautiful Earth.

SPIRITUAL CONTEMPLATION: What can you do now that can make a difference in living in balance on the planet? What are some of the answers emerging from today's philanthropists, innovators, and technology that can be a planetary changer? Share your research with some of your friends and watch what happens to the conversation.

AFFIRMATION: I trust the future for the next generation is in good hands today!

April 23
We Don't Truly Own Anything!

I love the song "Colors of the Wind" from the movie Pocahontas. It's a lovely description of the Native American understanding that we can't really own anything. The trees and the land, the water and the sun, these all flow from the Great Spirit and belong to all of us. I have a friend who says the same thing about her money and prosperity. She is constantly reminding people that it all comes from the One Source and doesn't belong to us. We surely can't take it with us, so it's ours to enjoy and share only in this lifetime.

To live a pure unselfish life, one must count nothing as one's own in the midst of abundance.

— Buddha

Everything in the physical world is only on loan to us for the time that we inhabit these bodies and walk around on this planet. When we truly realize this, we stop clinging, hoarding, or worrying about money. It would be like worrying about our next breath. It's there for the taking, right when we need it. But we don't keep it. We actually have to exhale before we can inhale again.

SPIRITUAL CONTEMPLATION: Imagine that everything you have and own is on loan to you for your sojourn here and that you are the steward of it while it is in your possession.

AFFIRMATION: Everything I have is on loan. It is mine to enjoy but not to keep. I effortlessly share my abundance with others.

I Rest in God

One of the big challenges on the path to spirituality is confronting an early religious upbringing that speaks of a god outside you who is waiting to do something for you only if you do the right thing. This serves only to anchor a belief in a mythological god. It's hard to forsake the old ways of thinking that you are separate and apart from God. You'll come to know your true nature, however, when you understand the Infinite includes you. Because you are one with the All-Knowing, your needs can be met before you even know of them if you can get your little-mindedness out of the way. You'll be able to rest with no concern for tomorrow in the knowledge that God is the very essence of your consciousness. There is not God and you—there is only Spirit appearing as you.

> *We carry inside us the wonders we seek outside us.*
> — Rumi

SPIRITUAL CONTEMPLATION: What earlier religious beliefs do you hold that puts God outside of you?

AFFIRMATION: I rest in knowing all my needs are provided for now!

A Different Kind of Prayer

Prayer and spiritual contemplation are not only for times of need. When your cup overflows and life is pouring its magnificence into your life, that is also a time to pray. Keeping your mind fixed on the Joy and Abundance you are experiencing is a powerful form of praying without ceasing! This is the prayer of Gratitude.

You pray in your distress and in your need; would that you might pray also in the fullness of your joy and in your days of abundance.

— Kahlil Gibran

SPIRITUAL CONTEMPLATION: In your quiet time contemplate your abundance and joy. Take time to enumerate it all and then revel in how Spirit is showing up in your life. Today, pray without ceasing a prayer of gratitude.

AFFIRMATION: I am grateful for the joy and abundance in my life. I am grateful for love and friendships. I am grateful for fulfilling work and a satisfying contribution to humanity.

Masterful at Excuses

Have you become so masterful at excuses that you actually believe them? Do you tell yourself that it's the other person's fault? Does the voice inside your head ask, How could they have done this to me? Is your excuse loop telling you it's the government's fault, and do you try to place blame by asking why your body is failing you? Whatever your excuses, are they so good that you're convinced they are the truth? When you battle something, it lives on in your energy. Metaphysicians, however, disengage their attachment to duality and become a transparency for the Divine to flow through.

> *Ninety-nine percent of the failures come from people who have the habit of making excuses.*
> — George Washington Carver

The consciousness that is without excuses is a Divine Consciousness and a spiritual power that can move mountains to bring heaven to earth. Spirit is Infinite and doesn't know large or small because It is all. It doesn't matter whether It's addressing a common cold or the fourth stage of cancer, Spirit can transform it all back into wholeness. The abundance of God is not concerned, whether it's your personal bills or the national debt. God doesn't know size—It responds only to totality of consciousness.

SPIRITUAL CONTEMPLATION: What are your favorite excuses? What "truth" do you believe in that doesn't support your life? What kind of shift must you make in consciousness in order to be a clear place for the abundant good to flow in a greater way in your life?

AFFIRMATION: I drop my excuses and embrace my greater good now!

It's Not as Bad as You Think!

Bad things happen to even the best and most spiritual of people. While 90 percent of what we used to worry about are things that we now realize were never really an issue, 10 percent are. The key to meeting any condition that is less than we want or hope for is in our response to it. We can become victims of a circumstance by looking at all the negative things, by worrying about how everything will work out, or by continually rehearsing the litany of issues that we are facing. Unfortunately, this just keeps our eyes, mind, and heart focused on the problem.

When you are down to nothing, God's up to something.

— Author Unknown

The key is to meet these circumstances with the deep knowing that there is a Power and Presence for Life and for Good in the Universe that we can turn to and draw from. We can affirm for ourselves that we have the strength to walk through it, the wisdom to handle it, and the guidance to know how to proceed. We can feel the love of the Presence as well as of family and friends as we work our way through the challenge. Keeping our eyes, mind, and heart focused on these things supports us in rising above a victim mentality and keeps us focused on that which we are committed to manifest and experience.

SPIRITUAL CONTEMPLATION: What am I obsessing about that keeps me in the hole? How could I think about this from an unlimited, spiritually grounded perspective? What if Love and Wisdom really were present in me as I walk through all of this? How would I feel in moving through it?

AFFIRMATION: It is not as bad as I think it is. I turn my eyes, heart, and mind to the Wisdom and Intelligence of the Universe. I turn my energy to knowing the Presence walks with, through, and as me.

From the Inside Out

Have you ever been in a house where someone with a cold was coughing and sniffling, and you used all your energy to surround yourself with thoughts of immunity so you wouldn't catch it? You created something like an energetic bubble around yourself so nothing could get in and get you. An alternative approach might be to imagine that there's nothing to protect yourself from. And rather than surrounding yourself in the light of protection, you simply tap into the energy flowing out from the center of your being from an unending source within. There is nothing to fight or rebel against—perceive, instead, an outflow

To keep the body in good health is a duty . . . otherwise we shall not be able to keep our mind strong and clear.
— Buddha

that doesn't allow anything in. You can take it one step further and see that what's flowing through you is not only moving through you but is actually filling the whole house. Then see it fill the whole neighborhood or community. If you're really into it, see how far this abundant energy can reach. Life flows from the inside out, and its stream clears away all the garbage with its flow. Allowing the stream of life to move through you so nothing adverse can come upstream is a great purifying and cleansing approach. No battles necessary—just allow the Life.

SPIRITUAL CONTEMPLATION: Practice the exercise above and see how far you can allow your energy to flow from the inside out. Then sit and notice how good it feels to be purged by that flow.

AFFIRMATION: I am an expression of the Life Force!

April 29
Pulling Back

Can you be aware of inner feelings and outer activities without being them? Are you able to notice that you are independent of these expressions—that you are not them? Can you move your consciousness around and place your attention on the inner and outer goings-on while at the same time realizing you are not those things? The question is, who is the "who" that is aware of them? Where do you think your exploration of consciousness might take you if you investigated the awareness that observes your world, rather than investigating the events themselves?

The moment you start watching the thinker, a higher level of consciousness becomes activated. You then begin to realize that there is a vast realm of intelligence beyond thought, that thought is only a tiny aspect of that intelligence.

— Eckhart Tolle

When it looks at particulars, your myopic vision brings your attention in on the mind's chatter. You are so much more than that! When you're in a meeting, have some fun and try pulling your awareness up to a higher perspective of what is happening around you. Take your awareness to the ceiling and notice the whole room, the people's intensity and the engagement in their positions. You will then have just freed yourself from the draw of that realm and the activity of the room by moving your awareness. You are the witness of your life—you can enter in and out of any charged situation at any time. It's an extraordinary realization, and sadly so many have forgotten this ability. Remember: you are the observer and not the experience.

SPIRITUAL CONTEMPLATION: What experiences in your life do you believe you are? Take an experience as your laboratory and try pulling away to a higher perspective. Then go up another rung and notice the activity from an even more elevated perspective until you're aware that you are the observer and not what is happening.

AFFIRMATION: I am the observer of my life!

Getting Past the News

It can be challenging and disheartening, listening to the news. It seems as though something awful is always happening somewhere. We can long for the seemingly easier, better days of the past. Or worry constantly about an inevitably dimming future. We can feel overwhelmed about what any one of us can do.

Yet we know that the news doesn't show us reality, neither human nor Divine. There are always new ideas being brought forward. There is always great good being done in the world. The evolutionary process is always taking place—Life seeking to be and express more of Itself through creation. This very impulse is the light behind new inventions, different models of business and government, and the restoration of wholeness in places that have been devastated by pollution or war. Each place where this impulse is brought forward, it is done through people around the globe just like you.

> *New arts, new sciences, new philosophies, better government, and a higher civilization wait on our thoughts. The infinite energy of Life, and the possibility of our future evolution, work through our imagination and will. The time is ready, the place is where we are now, and it is done unto all as they really believe and act.*
>
> — Ernest Holmes

SPIRITUAL CONTEMPLATION: Do you allow the news to devastate or depress you? How could you see the world from a spiritual point of view, while acting boldly toward the future that you desire for all of us?

AFFIRMATION: I look for positive and good news around the world. I lend my consciousness wherever there is good work and restoration taking place. I support our evolution into who we are collectively meant to be!

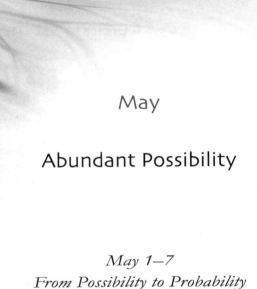

May

Abundant Possibility

May 1–7
From Possibility to Probability

May 8–13
Mother's Day
The Fertile Abundance of the Divine Feminine

May 14–17
Become It!

May 18–23
Healing Happens!

May 24–31
Memorial Day
It's All About Awareness

From Possibility to Probability

My father was a real pragmatist. He always had a lot to say about how realistic we should be in our dreams and working on something. I think he really believed that being realistic would keep us in the arena of what we could do and would keep us from failing. Possibilities were mere pipe dreams, not hard reality.

The problem with focusing on "reality" was that it kept me from trying anything new, and I learned to play it safe. It also guaranteed that the probability of anything new or truly creative breaking through was basically zero. I have since learned that focusing on something as being possible is much more likely to open up a space for something new. Focusing on what's possible moves us toward the achievement of a breakthrough and makes it much more likely that we will actually accomplish something completely new, different, or better than what we had before.

Man often becomes what he believes himself to be. If I keep on saying to myself that I cannot do a certain thing, it is possible that I may end by really becoming incapable of doing it. On the contrary, if I have the belief that I can do it, I shall surely acquire the capacity to do it even if I may not have it at the beginning.

— Mahatma Gandhi

SPIRITUAL CONTEMPLATION: When are you such a realist that it keeps you stuck in what you don't want? In what areas are you afraid to explore what's possible?

AFFIRMATION : I now am open to possibilities that improve my chances of accomplishment and achievement.

The Shape of Our Acceptance

Daydreaming or wishful thinking about having a more fulfilled and abundant life is not enough. We must imagine that it is actually possible for us to experience. Imagine the kind of life you would truly like to have, then notice where the "yeah buts" or ideas of limitation creep in. Notice where there is lingering judgment or a sense of something being unreachable. These are the boundaries of the mold, the shape of your mental acceptance. Every time you say, "I just can imagine . . ." you are defining the shape of your life.

How much life, abundance, goodness, truth, and beauty can we mentally entertain—this is the measure of our possible experience, this is the mold of acceptance. The Infinite fills all molds and flows forever into new and greater ones. It is the unborn possibility of limitless experience. We give birth to it.

— Ernest Holmes

SPIRITUAL CONTEMPLATION: Entertain a new idea about some area of your life. Imagine the possibility of it. Feel into its size and shape. Experience yourself in it. Create the mold of your desire into a mental acceptance of its reality for you.

AFFIRMATION: I expand my mind into new possibilities. I entertain them as my own reality. I accept that I truly can have a more abundant and fulfilling life.

Breaking Open to a New Idea

The only way things can change is if we allow them to change. Nothing will be new if we keep doing things exactly as we have always done them. This means our thoughts, behaviors, attitudes and/or actions may need to change. Can we imagine that possibility?

SPIRITUAL CONTEMPLATION: What if we imagined the possibility that we really are SPIRITUAL BEINGS having a human experience, and that this is our true identity? What story would we have to give up? What limitation would we have to let go of? What false belief that keeps us safe would we need to release? How would we walk around in the world differently?

A thought, even a possibility, can shatter and transform us.

— Friedrich Nietzsche

AFFIRMATION: I allow the possibility of my true identity to shatter all limitations and transform my idea about myself.

Dreaming the I-Am-Possible Dream!

When my son finally moved completely out of the house and I found myself alone, I began dreaming of a place to live, just for me. I loved to imagine some really cool place that was close to everything but still had woods and trees everywhere. I spent time dreaming of a two-story condo that I wanted to call my own.

Without leaps of imagination, or dreaming, we lose the excitement of possibilities. Dreaming, after all, is a form of planning.

— Gloria Steinem

In the meantime I started looking. I looked for over a year, and just kept being disappointed. At one point I wondered whether my dream was simply not possible. Maybe it's impossible to find what I was looking for in my sprawling, flat, overbuilt metropolitan city. But each time that I was confronted with this thought of impossibility, I turned around and claimed that nothing is impossible for the Law to manifest. All I needed to do was stay committed to my dream. I truly believed that the I AM that I am would attract to me exactly what I was dreaming. Today I live in a beautiful two-story condo, close to everything, with woods and a creek all to myself right outside my backdoor. Who knew it even existed within six minutes of my workplace? I may simply have dreamed it into existence!

SPIRITUAL CONTEMPLATION: Where has "impossible" taken up residence in your life?

AFFIRMATION: Nothing is impossible to the Infinite Power and Presence of Life. That Power and Presence is moving in my life today!

Dwelling in Possibility!

How often do we feel like we are stuck, trapped, or unable to imagine that things could be different than they are, whether they are bad or simply okay? It can leave us feeling barren or depressed—how can we break out into something new?

A joke found in an 1899 *Punch* magazine that had been donated to Harvard University by the Pulitzer family offered a look at the "coming century." A genius asked, "Isn't there a clerk who can examine patents?" A boy replied, "Quite unnecessary, Sir. Everything that can be invented has been invented." How laughable is that today, with everything that has happened in the twentieth and twenty-first centuries in virtually every field of endeavor.

> *I dwell in possibility.*
> — Emily Dickinson

We live in an Infinite Universe, which means there is an abundance of possibilities in every situation. It isn't a lack of possibilities that keeps us stuck—it's only the imagination to dream them up and the will to execute them. We worry about consequences, and failure, and the impact on our life. Yet the only way for things to change, is for them to change. It all starts with knowing that we dwell in an ocean of possibility!

SPIRITUAL CONTEMPLATION: Is there an area of your life where you feel stuck or trapped? Have you tried everything or run out of ideas and you just can't figure out anything new? This means there is a whole host of possibilities you have not yet entertained out of fear or unwillingness. Begin to list all the possibilities, no matter how silly or fearful they seem. This is the first step.

AFFIRMATION: I dwell in possibilities. I allow my imagination to soar and my mind to roam in the field of many options.

May 6
Divine Emergence

Only a change in consciousness can bring improved conditions. If there is an area of struggle in your life, then consciousness must be lifted above the human condition in order to live in the abundance that life is. Fighting the situation doesn't bring freedom; the battle just energizes the disorder by feeding it your energy and keeping it more alive. Liberty comes by shifting your consciousness and seeing the larger picture. What is known within out-pictures in your life and contributes to the world. Take the evolution of the Divine out of the hands of the world by returning to God the authority for the emergence of Spirit in your life.

Spirit reveals truth right where the picture of error is. Let me hear thy word.

— Joel Goldsmith

But a different perspective isn't about what it can do for you and your family alone. Rather the degree of spiritual abundance that you achieve in your life is measured by what you give back to the world, quickening the abundance of freedom for all. When you leave this world you take nothing but the qualities of your being with you. What's the big deal about how much you can possess or control if you leave it all behind? If you are a place of spiritual flow, then the battle for conditions won't be your thing because you are free in your ability to shift the causation in consciousness to something larger.

SPIRITUAL CONTEMPLATION: Do you hold a quarter so tight you can hear the eagle scream? What conditions would you like to stop holding on to so tightly with the battles in your consciousness? What larger picture of the abundant flow of life could replace what you are struggling with?

AFFIRMATION: A larger, more abundant vision emerges in my consciousness to share with the world!

Soul Versus Ego

The ego and the soul struggle continuously for control of your life force. When you're young and hungry, the calls of this world are very strong—the ego flexes its muscle for domination while the soul is often gagged and bound in the closet. The ego has its place and benefits in life but it should not be the lead voice. Somewhere along the path, whether early or late in life, spiritual maturity kicks in and you begin to listen to the call of your spirit, release it from its chains, and allow it to lead. The ego takes the backseat at this point in your life and learns to take its directives from your spirit.

> *I equate ego with trying to figure everything out instead of going with the flow. That closes your heart and your mind to the person or situation that's right in front of you, and you miss so much.*
>
> — Pema Chödrön

You move from needing to have facts, evidence, and assurance, to listening to your intuition. Your controlling mind cannot play a part in the realm of the mystical and mystifying side of your intuitive self. It was not created for such adventures and doesn't have the skill set. As such, it is not happy and works hard at attempting to pull your soul back to earth. Why does it do such things when it too loves the beauty it sees? But the day will come when it must acquiesce to the guidance from your higher self. When that day of alignment comes, your power upon this earth will have been multiplied.

SPIRITUAL CONTEMPLATION: Where is your well-meaning ego getting you in trouble? Where do your higher soul observations need to lead the vision for your life?

AFFIRMATION: The clarity of my soul vision leads my life!

May 8
The Fertile Abundance of the Divine Feminine

A powerful tradition of the Divine Feminine found around the globe is that aspect of the sacred that nurtures growth, health, and increase. This is the powerful urge in all creation that is fertile and lush, an urge that manifests as a world luxuriously teeming with life. She has many faces and names, but in each one is the recognition that the Divine Feminine is a presence that fosters abundance in all its forms.

Lakshmi is the Hindu goddess of wealth, prosperity, fertility and power.

— Aimee Rebekah Shea

Lakshmi is the consort of Vishnu, the preserver. Thus fertile abundance is coupled with the preservation of good stewardship. The lovely, verdant land of our life must be "husbanded" in the classic sense of the term, tended and carefully cared for so that it may yield all the bounty it has to offer. This is true at every level—in our minds and thoughts, with our heart and emotions, in our worldly affairs, health and wealth, as well as in our spiritual disciplines.

SPIRITUAL CONTEMPLATION: Are you managing your life in a way that is actually squashing your luxurious, creative fertility? Allow yourself to experience and express through song, dance, or drawing, the fertile lushness of your own Divine Feminine.

AFFIRMATION: I invite in the Divine Feminine to nurture and grow my abundance in luxurious and creative ways.

It's Not the Teacher

The human heart is much too small to contain the love of God—a realm where you are immersed in an ocean of the Divine whereas personal love most often comes with conditions and limits. When you're working with a powerful teacher, counselor, or doctor who seems to know you in a deeper kind of way, it's not uncommon for your spirit to get excited. But an intimate stirring of feelings doesn't mean romantic love; rather a Divine touch of unconditional love has entered your soul. It can become easy to want to transfer those feelings to the one who seems to have awakened them. Divine Wisdom operating within and between the two can close the gap of separation and support the emergence of something greater. An experienced teacher has been to this intimate and illumined place before and knows the feeling is part of the healing power of love and doesn't take it personally.

A student confided in Suzuki Roshi that she had tremendous feelings of love for him, and that it confused her. "Don't worry," he said. *"You can let yourself have all the feelings you have for your teacher. That's good. I have enough discipline for both of us."*
— Buddhist Story

As your relationship to within is activated, your soul will hold mastery over your thinking. Your celestial discernment shifts to being a receiver of the gifts of grace, and you more easily integrate the mystical into your life without being swept away. The Power felt in the presence of a master can take you to the very boundaries and beyond what you have humanly known was possible. But remember, it's not the teacher; rather it's what is going on inside of you that's beyond your senses that you'll want to come to know more intimately.

SPIRITUAL CONTEMPLATION: Have you ever had a teacher, counselor, or doctor see you in a way no one else has and awakened an appreciative love within you? How did that finally settle down? How has that experience and insight served you to this day?

AFFIRMATION: All love leads me to a greater experience of God's love expressing as me!

May 10
Learning to Listen

Spiritual maturity often looks like allowing some of the values and attitudes you hold as truth to die. When you become set in your ways and loath to expand, often something must come along to shake you from your calcification. It's hard to let go of an overprotective, hovering nature, but if you listen for too long you will not develop

A great many people think they are thinking when they are merely rearranging their prejudices.

— William James

your gifts of expression and strengthen the explorer within. How will you retrieve your intuitive nature if you remain in familiar territory? How will you learn to strengthen your resolve in what you intuit if you never take a stand for the newly seen?

If you dishonor your emerging side, you'll lose confidence in the new, leaving you behind and feeling alone. When the invisible inklings are no longer heard, there is a dying inside as the light goes out. Yet this dying could be the very catalyst that launches you into hearing the new voice of inner knowing. As you learn to honor the inner directive again, a confidence will return with eyes that see and ears that hear beyond the physical evidence. Only humans question their intuitive side—all other creatures of this world listen to their inner self and its guidance.

SPIRITUAL CONTEMPLATION: Have you recently said to yourself that you should have listened to your intuition? What inner promptings are you not listening to?

AFFIRMATION: I trust my inner directives!

Trusting in the Moment

Our mind needs reassurance. It wants to know how it will all work out. What's going to happen? Mostly it wants to make sure we are safe! This is not a bad thing, but it keeps us fretting and worrying unnecessarily. The fundamental reassurance we have is that Spirit is moving through us as the wisdom and intelligence of the Universe. We have the assurance that the Universal Law uses our intention as the mold for the end result. If we are fixed on the "what" of our goal—not the "how will we get there" —we are present to what there is to do in this moment.

> *You do not need to know precisely what is happening, or exactly where it is all going. What you need is to recognize the possibilities and challenges offered by the present moment, and to embrace them with courage, faith and hope.*
>
> — Thomas Merton

The Universal Law will take every action of ours and mold it into a step in the direction of our end result. Our job is to step boldly onto the path and take each step with the confidence and courage that the knowledge of spiritual truth gives to us. As we follow the path, the Wisdom and Intelligence of Spirit guide us toward the end result. This is the dance of faith. It is the certainty that gives our soul reassurance and quiets the worry of the mind.

SPIRITUAL CONTEMPLATION: When have you walked in the present moment with faith and courage, knowing that your way was assured, even though you didn't know how it would all turn out? Did it turn out okay? How can you apply this in your life today?

AFFIRMATION: I release my need to know how! I stay focused on my goal and trust I am guided in the action of the current moment.

May 12
The Power of a Positive Attitude

When we decided to move and expand our Spiritual Center, we didn't know how we were going to accomplish it. It took us over a year to find a new location and then to negotiate the lease. During that time it was easy for people to get discouraged because it seemed so difficult to find what we wanted. Yet each time something didn't work out, I reminded us all to stay focused on the vision of our new home. The possibility of growth and expansion of what we had envisioned was so clear, but how it was to come about, no one knew. If we had faltered along the way, we would not have finally found something that suited our needs, even though originally it wasn't exactly what we thought we were looking for.

It's the possibility that keeps me going, not the guarantee.
— Nicholas Sparks

Knowing that we are living into the possibility of Abundance and a fulfilled life does not mean that everything we want is guaranteed to work out how we expect it to. It does mean that as we continue to move forward with a positive attitude, we are much more likely to create or discover an outcome than if we quit along the way.

SPIRITUAL CONTEMPLATION: How do you maintain your positive attitude and expectation for good, even when it doesn't appear to be manifesting?

AFFIRMATION: I stay committed to my vision of an abundant and fulfilled life. I move forward with a positive attitude. I expect good from everything I encounter.

Liberation from the Past

Imagining a possibility really does mean that it doesn't matter how it used to be done. Yes, things can be learned from the past, but we don't want the past to limit the future. Whether it's things as simple as creating new holiday traditions when our children grow up and get married, or things as complex as creating a new business model for a sustainable future, it's so easy to say it's never been done before. This means we don't have to put in the effort to try something new. We don't have to feel the discomfort of moving into the unknown. We don't have to let go of the "way it's always been done."

The one thing that is constantly and consistently true about a human, physical life is that it is constantly changing. We can resist this and cling to what we know. Or we can embrace change and know that we are always guaranteed of another possibility. If we want things to be different, we have to let go of the old and embrace the changes that let in the new.

I have an almost complete disregard of precedent, and a faith in the possibility of something better. It irritates me to be told how things have always been done. I defy the tyranny of precedent. I go for anything new that might improve the past.

— Clara Barton

SPIRITUAL CONTEMPLATION: Is there something in your life you are holding on to because you're afraid that a change might be worse rather than better? Where are you allowing the past to limit your future?

AFFIRMATION: I know that Spirit is always moving through me to express more life, more love, more wholeness, and joy. I release any fear about letting go of the past. I know I move toward a more abundant and fulfilling future!

You Are So Much More!

Although it's a myth that we use only 10 percent of our brain-power, it is true that we don't necessarily use all of our creativity, focus, and energy to achieve what we set out to accomplish. We can procrastinate, talk ourselves out of it, get bored, tired, or simply be undisciplined in our approach. We can undermine ourselves with negative self-talk while gathering evidence from past experiences and other people that it most likely won't work. That's a lot of brain-power we're using!

If we all did the things we are capable of doing, we would literally astound ourselves.
— Thomas A. Edison

Imagine now that we use all that same brainpower to do it now, talk ourselves into it, keep ourselves motivated, make sure we get the rest and sustenance we need, and stay focused and disciplined. People do this all the time, and they accomplish amazing things, not because they have more brainpower or capability, but because they are using all their resources in a positive manner in support of their dreams. Even people with demonstrable "handicaps," whether physical, mental, or emotional, are astounding themselves and others with what they can achieve and accomplish. What an inspiration! We are each completely capable of accomplishing so much that we would amaze ourselves.

SPIRITUAL CONTEMPLATION: What do you most regularly use your brainpower on during the day? In the evening? On the weekends? In your spiritual practice?

AFFIRMATION: I am capable of so much more because I am more than any limiting thought or false belief that I have. Yes, I can! Yes, I will!

Become It!

Somewhere along the line I realized that wanting something, affirming for something, or praying for something wasn't enough if I wanted to create long-lasting growth in my abundance and overall life experience. I learned that I could demonstrate immediate fulfillment of a specific need for the moment, but I still kept re-creating my overall life, over and over again, in the same familiar patterns. I realized that I had to become different, not just demonstrate a momentary experience, if I wanted a more fulfilling life.

Trust yourself. Create the kind of self that you will be happy to live with all your life. Make the most of yourself by fanning the tiny inner sparks of possibility into flames of achievement.

— Golda Meir

I started working on becoming the kind of person who has or does that which I wanted to experience. I worked to become someone who has healthy relationships, for instance. This meant that I had to actually become healthy in my relationships; I had to learn to act in a healthy manner. I couldn't just affirm for a healthy partner or relationship—I had to become it myself. This is true in every area of my life. In learning to become someone who takes care of himself physically, for example, I have had to actually see this was possible for me. Then I worked to believe that I am that!

SPIRITUAL CONTEMPLATION: What kind of Self do you want to become?

AFFIRMATION: I am someone who . . . (fill in your own statement).

Who Am I?

Walking in the mountains, communing with nature, I am reminded that God, Spirit, Life, is all that I am. Every bit and part of me is that Divine Reality made manifest in a self-conscious being. But, I am not all that God is. There is a transcendent reality, a mystery so vast and deep, beyond my comprehension, that is the whole totality of the ONE. I can never know all of IT, but It knows all of me. This is a powerful understanding that Ernest Holmes states as "the highest God and innermost God is one God." What does all this mean about you, your identity, and God's Reality?

Since God is infinite, the possibility of man's expansion is limitless. Therefore evolution or unfoldment is the eternal process through which Being passes into becoming. This does not make man God nor does man create God; but man at any and every level of consciousness is, at such a level, a manifestation of the original Mind. As a drop of water is in the ocean, and in its essence is like the ocean, but still never is the whole ocean; so man is in God, partakes of the nature of God, in essence is One with God, but never is God.

— Ernest Holmes

SPIRITUAL CONTEMPLATION: Give serious and careful thought to today's quote: How does it expand you and your identity?

AFFIRMATION: I am in and of God. I partake of the nature of the Divine Reality; therefore I am a limitless Being.

Intuitions of Infinity

Intuition is the doorway to the Divine. It's not just a hunch or a gut instinct: intuition is our inner knowing, our inner connection, with the very impulse of Life that is moving in, through, and as us.

As we open our inner awareness to a greater reality, it is immediately present to us. We must become still and quiet within ourselves—and listen between the gap of the voices in our mind and the emotions in our body. There we find the Source, the ground of all being, the infinite Presence. It has been waiting there all along. You've always known it. Trust your intuition as it opens the door to a limitless reality.

> *God speaks when we listen. God is there when we open the door. And when we listen, there is a response from something greater than ourselves that is the infinite Person, the limitless Possibility. God speaks wherever and whenever we listen to our Inner Voice.*
>
> — Ernest Holmes

SPIRITUAL CONTEMPLATION: Simply sit and be aware of your inner awareness. Who is aware? What is this awareness aware of?

AFFIRMATION: I open my inner awareness to the Presence of the One. I listen as It whispers to me of Divine Reality.

There's More Than What You See on the Outside

Spiritual awareness is recognizing the Infinite Essence in and through all things—the knowledge that there is only One life and that life shows up in all expressions. In contrast, materialism is dependent on drawing to it what it thinks it needs, on something showing up from the outside. There is a significant difference between trying to get what you think you need, as opposed to aligning with the grace of God knowing that all you need will be provided. A materialistic consciousness would say he needs five hundred dollars to get a ticket from San Diego to New York, whereas a spiritually-minded person is open to the grace of God taking care of all things since It is all things. Manifestation in this case could be five hundred dollars for a ticket, but it also could be a friend needing a companion to go to New York and paying for you to come along. Or someone giving you their frequent flier miles, a lift, or a train ticket. A variety of options that are all part of the Infinite disappear when you specify exactly how it has to be provided.

A dream is the bearer of a new possibility, the enlarged horizon, the great hope.

— Howard Thurman

With the belief in the way being shown beyond what you think is best, your options are opened to a greater capacity of action fulfilling your desire. The spiritually-aware know that the visible comes from the invisible, and form from the unformed with consciousness serving as the sculptor. So if you have a pain in your body and the doctor tells you to take something for it, it could work well particularly if you believe it to begin with. But a spiritually-minded individual knows there are options with God and what is first presented may be only one of many alternatives that Spirit can use to alleviate dis-ease since it's about wholeness and not symptoms.

SPIRITUAL CONTEMPLATION: Where do you fall prey to thinking your way is the only way in which your desire must be fulfilled? If there is room in your awareness, what other options are available to you?

AFFIRMATION: I am spiritually minded in seeing the answers in my world!

Beyond the Confines of Your Body

Have you ever left the confines of your physical body and observed the world from a point other than from the perspective of your own eyes? It's as if you've popped out of your sleeping body and are able to be instantly where your awareness takes you. To do so feels like you are actively conscious while dreaming. You can be either a passive observer of the unfold-ment taking place before you or an active participant with interactions that are mostly reflective of your own beliefs and conceptual state. Actually, whenever you close your eyes and begin to sense and imagine, you've left the confines of your body.

> *Dreams are true while they last,*
> *and do we not live in dreams?*
> — Alfred Lord Tennyson

Whether you travel to other ethereal realities or just daydream, your thoughts are guiding your experience. Imagine your sacred place in nature and instantly you're drawn there. Then as you bring your thoughts back to your body, immediately you're back behind your eyes resting comfortably. This is an exercise that transcends typical time. It's an experience of directing your mind, your self-awareness, to be outside of your apparent body. Maybe between awarenesses you will hear the sound of static as if between radio frequencies, or maybe it's just your brain checking in to see if you're still there, but let it alone because you're in a valuable state where your thoughts have full power to deliver you to your intention. Stay clear and focused and you will see with eyes not of the body.

SPIRITUAL CONTEMPLATION: Close your eyes and allow your aware-ness to take you somewhere other than in your bodily perception. Pay attention, work on clarity, and focus within that imaginal state until you decide to pop back into your physical form.

AFFIRMATION: I am a boundless expression of the Infinite!

May 20
The Argument for Wholeness

It's always nice to pray when all is well. But often we pray when we're concerned about a condition. On this level you have to deny belief in the conditions and replace them with the spiritual truth. You aren't attempting to change anything, but through prayer you raise your awareness to the next level, which is communion with God. The realization of God from a higher place dissolves the illusion of the lower physical senses. All error is part of the hypnotic trance operating in the realm of belief. Once you separate the belief from your consciousness and return to the Divine realization, there is no room for otherness.

> *The argumentative method of treatment is a series of affirmation and denials, for the purpose of building up in the mind of the practitioner a state of realization and acceptance.*
> — Ernest Holmes

Your personal spiritual work is to realize that Spirit is all there is and is appearing as you. It is to bring your consciousness into the alignment of the wholeness and perfection that already exists. Prayer doesn't bring God into your experience because God is already there, but this doesn't do you any good if you don't realize it. So when you know the truth that is already you, you'll be set free. Prayer knows that truth. It's that progression of consciousness moving from having faith in your beliefs to having faith of God, which has no opposites, no duality. Give yourself a mind treatment until you no longer have to remind yourself of the spiritual truth that God is in and through all. And it's Spirit's good pleasure to give you the kingdom.

SPIRITUAL CONTEMPLATION: What beliefs don't you want anymore? Allow your awareness to catch a greater spiritual realization that will lift you above the hypnotic trance of limitation. Rest in the knowingness that God is all there is and allow that realization to out-picture as your life, now.

AFFIRMATION: I know God is all there is to my life!

Healing Points of Pain

A key component in the healing process is giving up the need to know why something happened to you even though your mind wants an explanation to figure out who or what to blame. The challenge here is that true healing is the realm of your heart and soul. A logical justification to totally enlighten the mind for the experience of victimhood is not possible when it takes spirit, not reason, to transform the deep wounds. Your healing does not depend on your finding and understanding the missing piece to your puzzle of pain. Hunting for a scapegoat will keep you engrossed in the past. Get over that neurotic search.

The doctor of the future will be oneself.

— Albert Schweitzer

Keep your focus in the now so that grace can enter and transform. Your outside may not change but within is something that is always ready to lift you beyond the point of pain. There is no guarantee where you will arrive as you walk the path of your healing journey, but one thing is for sure, the crisis will change you. The challenge of healing will compel you to learn how to surrender and trust. You'll be called by your heart to forgive, and forgiveness is a spiritual rather than a logical decree. It may never satisfy the mind but in matters of healing it's love that prevails, not rationale.

SPIRITUAL CONTEMPLATION: Where are you struggling with understanding a point of pain in your life? What if you were willing to give up the mind's involvement, the need to know why and how, or anything else your egoic self is demanding, and instead surrender to the loving intuitive direction of your heart?

AFFIRMATION: I give up my need to know why and surrender to my wholeness now!

Healing Happens

When your consciousness is filled with the Spirit of the truth, not just the law of truth but Spirit itself, healing happens. Friends will reach out to you for healing prayer, and although they may think you are the conduit for the healings, you don't actually heal anyone. Instead you remove horrendous conditions from people's lives, or get their bodies working harmoniously again. Your only responsibility is the spiritual realization of the Omnipresent God expressing through Its perfect creation. You are called upon to feel and know that the Living Presence is alive and well at the very center of the condition you are looking at.

We do not need magic to transform our world. We carry all of the power we need inside ourselves already.

— J. K. Rowling

Your job is not to change your friend's thinking. Your responsibility is to feel, see, and know the truth so clearly that there is a responsiveness in her. It doesn't matter what the condition may be— its only cause is a belief that something other than God can exist. When the Spirit in you is so vibrationally alive, it activates a sympathetic resonance in another. You live, move, and have your being in the heart of God, and so does your friend because Spirit is omnipresent. We are all connected, so there's no need to send your awareness anywhere because it's already there. Your conscious union with the Divine opens you to the activity of Spirit, which brings healing in and through all.

SPIRITUAL CONTEMPLATION: Sit with the thought of Spirit's Omnipresence and see how far it will take you. Does it take you from here to another city and possibly beyond this world as you connect with multidimensional possibilities?

AFFIRMATION: I am the activity of the God Realization!

Mind as Body

Mind is the substance of matter and as strange as it might seem, it expresses as your body. Your consciousness is the invisible action appearing as your body, your organs, and your movements. For instance, your mind sends a message to your hand to wave and it waves. Your mind says shake hands and you watch as your hand reaches out and shakes another's hand.

Grasp and it grasps, let go and it opens up. How does it do that? Is the hand intelligent? No, but it has intelligence just as every cell of your body has intelligence that responds to mind.

You can outdistance that which is running after you but not what is running inside you.
— Rwandan Proverb

What's the difference between the cells of your hand and the cells of your liver, your thyroid, your lymph nodes, or your heart? They're all different parts of the same body operated by the same cellular intelligence under the same operating system. Don't let these guys pull mutiny on you and tell you how to act and feel. You're in charge of your body! Tell it how to behave and don't let it talk back to you.

SPIRITUAL CONTEMPLATION: Where do those little cells of your body gang up on you as they attempt to tell you how it should be? Reclaim authority over your body and tell the intelligence operating at the cellular level what your expectations are. Move your hand a few times and see how it responds to your mind's direction. Rotate your foot around a bit and see how it responds to the direction you give it. Now take that same kind of authority and tell your body what to do.

AFFIRMATION: I now reclaim the authority over my body!

May 24
Availability or Quantifying

Working on the side of a mountain, cutting a path, and moving rocks and trees can leave you parched and thirsty by midafternoon. Your mind and body become hyperfocused on something wet to quench your dryness. How delightful when your beloved shows up with a bottle of water for you! You wouldn't tell her that you'd prefer lemonade, and would she please take the water back, would you? She'd probably throw it in your face and tell you to get your own. No, you'd be filled with joy and relief, filled with a gratitude for an answered prayer for something cool to drink.

Would that I were a dry well, and that the people tossed stones into me, for that would be easier than to be a spring of flowing water that the thirsty pass by, and from which they avoid drinking.

— Kahlil Gibran

When you thirst for Spirit as much as you do for a glass of water on a hot summer afternoon, you stop quantifying how God is *supposed* to show up in your life. You become available to how Spirit *does* show up in your life. Too often people send back the answer to their prayer because they don't think it looks like what they want. Stop telling God how to show up in your life and recognize how God *is* showing up. Life supports you wherever you are on your journey, whether in the wilderness or a temple. All you need is ever available if you can give up quantifying how it's supposed to be and instead be aware of how it is showing up.

SPIRITUAL CONTEMPLATION: When have you turned down the gifts of God and missed life's answers to your prayers? When have you said yes to life's offering that didn't look like what you were looking for and it turned out far better than you had imagined? Is there something in your world right now that is presenting itself to you to say yes to?

AFFIRMATION: I am grateful for Life's gifts!

Beyond 3-D

There is a sense of excitement when you go to a 3-D movie. The moment you're given the special glasses to wear, you know you're in for a different kind of adventure. The minute the movie begins, the images on the screen pop and leap out at you, creating an intensity of surprise. As you become immersed in the visual and audio experience, the illusion feels real.

Meditation can be like putting on those 3-D glasses. Life becomes clearer and more real, and pulls you beyond the three-dimensional world. You are immersed in a new way of multidimensional seeing. You are given access to

> *A mind that is stretched by a new experience can never go back to its old dimensions.*
> — Oliver Wendell Holmes

understanding the interconnectedness of what is before you and unfoldment is slowed down for a richer comprehension. This meditative lens needs to be kept clean the same way that greasy, buttery-popcorn fingerprints must be wiped from 3-D glasses. It's necessary to keep your filters of consciousness cleansed so you're seeing through pure, unadulterated awareness. It's common to attempt to make sense of what pops out from the meditative screen into present perceptions, but sometimes this new dimensional adventure is just meant to rest in your boundless soul without explanation. You don't always have to know why or how—just notice what's playing out before you. It will be interesting as to how that gets integrated into your consciousness.

SPIRITUAL CONTEMPLATION: Where would it be beneficial to clean the lenses through which you look at the world? What insights do you perceive about a particular situation that would be best to keep to yourself and just notice more that is being communicated?

AFFIRMATION: My meditations reveal to me multi-dimensional insights to my world!

May 26
To Egypt and Back Before Breakfast

Sipping your morning coffee while checking your e-mails, you might notice an invitation on your screen to look at other places on the planet. So you click on the earth map and find yourself zooming in on the great pyramids of Giza. Suddenly it's as if you are standing on the apex of the greatest archeological find on the planet, rubbing sand from your eyes as you tour this ancient and exotic land, all before breakfast. What an adventure technology now offers: the ability to open your eyes and see the world as you've never before had the opportunity to.

Everything you can imagine is real.

— Pablo Picasso

Something even more marvelous than technology is your ability to turn within and travel in your awareness to these mythical lands. In your meditative states you can return to a time when the pharaohs ruled those lands and Karnack's temple of pillars was bustling with life. You can climb the passage to the king's chamber, lie down in his sarcophagus and be initiated into the high priesthood. The mystery of the Sphinx can be revealed to you. What an adventure, indeed! Often we forget that this is a possibility, that meditation can open our eyes to see the universe like never before. The beauty of inner dimensional travel is that we don't need an Internet provider because we are always connected.

SPIRITUAL CONTEMPLATION: Where on the planet would you like to visit? Take a trip there on the earth map. Then close your eyes, open your heart, and see if your subjective can deliver you into the energetic activities of a heightened time for that location.

AFFIRMATION: I am boundless!

Prayer Has Nothing to Do with Getting

Contrary to popular belief, prayer has nothing to do with getting your Higher Power to do something for you. It's a state of becoming receptive to a greater wisdom than you presently perceive as your reality. When you quiet the concern chattering in your brain, in the stillness Grace can enter your awareness. Allow your prayer to be a time when you silence your mind and commune with the All Knowing and receive that transference so all that proceeds from the mouth of God become your words of expression.

> *Prayer is not asking. Prayer is putting oneself in the hands of God, at His disposition, and listening to His voice in the depth of our hearts.*
>
> — Mother Teresa

It's in proportion to your relationship with the Omniscience that Truth imparts itself through you. This is not an activity of your memory but something that emerges from within, lifting you above your desire to change things and speaking from a Divine seeing. Your personal sense of "I" dissolves, and you become a beholder of the truth. In this realization, you understand that Spirit hasn't withheld anything from you and that what you're looking for is already established for the awareness of the one praying. Your abundant good has already been given because that which is Infinite cannot withhold anything. Give up the need to get and allow your sense of Oneness with the Absolute to be your prayer.

SPIRITUAL CONTEMPLATION: Give up your need to get, and connect for no other purpose but to establish your awareness as part of the Infinite expression.

AFFIRMATION: I am the Infinite expressing!

Stopping to Remember It's Accumulative

Meditation is about your connection with the Infinite. There is tremendous value in stopping many times throughout the day for the purpose of remembering. During meditation you open yourself to a state of receptivity; and then just as simply as you opened up, you come back to the present and go about your life. Often it is not until sometime later when, zap, an insight drops into your awareness as if from the sky. It seems magical—almost as if all the meditations from the past week have accumulated, and when you're relaxed and surrendering, contact is realized. You might start your day with meditation, and it serves as nothing more than a pleasant, peaceful moment. Then hours later, when you're focused on the activities of the day, you find you're in the midst of Spirit. What meditation teaches us is that the harder we grasp at an answer, the further we push it away. Contact doesn't seem to come when we strain.

If God is your world, what have you to fear?
— Emma Curtis Hopkins

Spirit can show Itself only when mental activity subsides. The more often you pause and ponder your true nature, the more you practice the presence, and something that doesn't come from your rational mind will enter into your consciousness from the mystical realm. You'll find the word of God being placed into your awareness and through that you'll begin to live by grace. These impartations will carry a harmonizing effect to your world without efforting on your part.

SPIRITUAL CONTEMPLATION: Stop at least once an hour to contemplate the Presence of God. Then notice how the buildup delivers a sense of peace and clarity to you later on or even while you sleep.

AFFIRMATION: I remember and see Spirit throughout my day!

It's All About Awareness

When you learn to trust the Higher Power you realize your thinking is not what makes it reality. You can struggle with this realization or relax into it, but thus it has always been. Before time was, Spirit was and is, and always has been, I am. Your thought is not the power; it's not what makes something true. It's an avenue of awareness. You can see that someone is wearing purple or turquoise, but your thought isn't going to change what they have on because it's just an avenue of your perception. You don't make Spirit so—it's your awareness of what is so that allows the power to flow through your life.

Whatever may be the tensions and the stresses of a particular day, there is always lurking close at hand the trailing beauty of forgotten joy or unremembered peace.

— Howard Thurman

Make sure you start your day with a conscious realization of your oneness with your Higher Power, your Abundant Good. If you can't bring Spirit into your awareness at the first waking moment before being bombarded by the rest of the day, when will you get around to it? Do you not want to be aware of Spirit walking with you every step of the way throughout your day? It is in proportion to your mindfulness of the Presence that God is available every moment of every day and when you feel the Presence, you are never alone.

SPIRITUAL CONTEMPLATION: Where are you missing the perception of the Divine Presence in your life? How could a clearer thought be an avenue for an enhanced awareness of an out-of-balance issue of your day? Remember to start your day with a Divine connection.

AFFIRMATION: I start each day with Spirit on my mind!

May 30
Memorial' Day

Memorial Day is a time to remember those men and women who have died serving our country. Although decorating the graves of the fallen has long been a part of the rituals of war, Memorial Day officially began during the Civil War when Congress established it as a day of tribute to America's fallen as well as a day of national prayer for lasting peace. Today in the busyness of life, we still pause to remember and appreciate those who gave their life for what they believed would bring us a better way of living.

Regardless of the circumstances of the battlefield, the cry of the soldier remains the same— God help me.

— Anonymous

During this Memorial Day, as you and your friends and family enjoy the beginning of summer with cookouts at the beach, park, or backyard, remember those families who have an empty seat at their table. Remember those young men and women who once occupied those seats and gave the ultimate sacrifice so you could enjoy this moment in your life. Remember—and in the silence of your heart, pray for lasting peace.

SPIRITUAL CONTEMPLATION: Make sure to pause today and open your heart to those who gave the ultimate sacrifice. Send out some love and say a prayer for lasting peace.

AFFIRMATION: I know peace prevails on this planet in my lifetime.

The Divine Feminine

The Divine Feminine appears to be awakening in the collective consciousness once again. There is a rising in the understanding of the interconnectedness and sacredness of all life. It's out-picturing in the birthing of new technologies that will save the earth, a growing understanding of the importance of harmonious resolution, and a higher understanding of equality for all life. The feminine brings a healing, nurturing, creative balance to the issues of life.

Love risks everything, and asks for nothing.
— Rumi

There is an emergence going on in the holistic field of the body/mind and sacred physical practices for integration of soul into form. A union of apparent opposites seems to be taking place between the inner and the outer, scientific and mystical, matter and form, intuition and knowledge. This sacred marriage is activating the global heart of humanity, which feels justice and equality will unite this world better than domination, exploitation and the implementation of "my-way-over-yours."

You are being called to use your intuitive self to feel the truth beyond what is being pumped through the corporate media outlets of one-sided perspectives. You are being invited to know a greater picture that only the aware observer can truly see. Be careful not to give your power away to the storyteller when there is always so much more not being told. Stop the inane chattering in your head and listen with the heart that can understand more than words can describe. It's said, "Where the Spirit of the Lord is, there is liberty." When you are free enough to open to a higher wisdom, it will interpret itself at the level of the experience in which you find yourself. It will appear in ways you would never expect.

SPIRITUAL CONTEMPLATION: What stories, where you don't perceive a harmonious way out, are you getting caught up in? Sit, be quiet, invite a greater picture to emerge, and remain open to the unexpected.

AFFIRMATION: I trust my intuitive sense!

June

An Abundance of Leadership

June 1–7
Moving Life

June 8–14
What? Do You Think I'm a Mind Reader?

June 15–23
Father's Day
Are You in Integrity?

June 24–30
Living with Uncertainty and Ambiguity

Every Step Is a Miracle

When you start a new adventure, whether it's launching a new business venture, going off to college, or taking the trip of a lifetime, there's often a celebration at both the beginning and the completion. Congratulations are in order for the business, the college degree, and your safe passage from travel. And rightfully so! Where the celebration is often overlooked is all the steps in between those two milestones. You live your life between those two bookends, and every step you take is significant yet hardly noticed. Why wait until it's all over to celebrate life when every minute of every day is a miracle in action.

> *I ask not for a lighter burden, but for broader shoulders.*
> — Jewish Proverb

SPIRITUAL CONTEMPLATION: Where in your life would it be good to take a moment to celebrate your steps? Then celebrate yourself now!

AFFIRMATION: I honor every step I take as significant!

June 2
Spiritual Balance

Each and every person is a perfect spiritual being! This is profound Truth. It is equally true that we are all uniquely imperfect in the way we express our perfection. There is not one person who has it all together or will never make a mistake. Relaxing into this truth makes us better friends, partners, employees, and leaders. When we don't expect perfection in outcome but see it in each other, a powerful, creative, and open space is made in which it is a joy to work and live together.

Failure is good. It's fertilizer. Everything I've learned about coaching, I've learned from making mistakes.

— Rick Pitino

Spiritual Balance means living in harmony with your inner perfection and your outer imperfection. It is seeing your wholeness, while having compassion for your imperfections. It is seeing this same truth in every person we work with or live with. Spiritual Balance is knowing that the Divine is breaking through the human, bringing Heaven on Earth, right here in every person's life!

SPIRITUAL CONTEMPLATION: In what areas of your life do you expect perfection from yourself? Where do you fall short? How have you inflicted this on others? What would be another way you could look at this?

AFFIRMATION: I learn and grow from every experience. I nurture others as they learn and grow. I no longer try to be perfect nor do I expect perfection. I try to be authentic and do my best instead.

There are all sorts of theories to explain why whales beach themselves. One of the reasons, other than sickness, is that they become disoriented while chasing food. Whales eat extremely small food, large amounts of it, but small nonetheless. These giants of the sea can be lured to their death by something very small compared to their size. They are left stranded on the sand to die because they've sacrificed their vast power by chasing something so small.

Human Intelligence is like a Blue Whale. Both are powerful though nowadays almost extinct.

— Anonymous

Be careful not to become disoriented by chasing something so insignificant that it sidetracks you and you find yourself marooned on a barren beach gasping for breath. It's often the little things that trip us up. When those little things demand too much of our attention, big challenges can surface because we have withdrawn our awareness from the fuller picture of our purpose and have lasered in on the microscopic. We need to bring our awareness back from the energy drains so we're not lured out of our element.

SPIRITUAL CONTEMPLATION: What little things pull you offtrack and drain the energy from your life's purpose, leading you toward the possibility of being marooned?

AFFIRMATION: My pursuits expand my awareness!

June 4
Perfect, Whole, and Complete

We've been taught that the whole is greater than its parts. But have you ever stopped to think about your importance in that equation? Have you ever realized that you are part of the whole and without you it would be incomplete? You are necessary, important, and valuable in order for the Divine to be fully expressed. So stop searching outside yourself—get quiet and listen to what's going on inside. As you come to recognize your true identity, judgment and criticism will fall from your world because what you see is a projection of you. You'll be freed from your bondage and join in leading the world away from restrictions and limitation and toward joy in abundant expression.

Individuality is only possible if it unfolds from wholeness.
— David Bohm

Conscious unity with the Whole puts you in the effortless flow. Being a conduit for life enriches and awakens you to the Now Moment as you realize wholeness is not your next stop. That's right, wholeness is not where you are going. It can only be experienced where you are because there can never be anything missing in Wholeness. All your love, wealth, health, blessing, dharma calling, and success are already available to you where you are right now. Whatever challenges you might be facing, remember that you are part of Wholeness and nothing can be missing. Everything is already perfect, whole, and complete, and your only responsibility is to realize that in every situation to support your abundant walk through life.

SPIRITUAL CONTEMPLATION: Where in your life do you feel something is missing? Sit down, get still, and contemplate what it means to be part of the whole.

AFFIRMATION: I am perfect, whole and complete right now!

June 5
Moving Life

A passionate youth, ready to take on the world, once said, "Lord, give me the strength to change the world." At middle age he realized he hadn't transformed the world, or even a single soul, and he changed his prayer to "God, give me the grace to change all those who come in contact with me and I shall be happy." But then as an old man, he realized how foolish he had been, and his one prayer became "Lord give me the blessings to transform myself. If this had been my prayer from the beginning, I would not have wasted my life." When you realize the difficulty in transforming your own life, then you understand the challenge in attempting to change another's.

> *You must be the change you wish to see in the world.*
> — Mahatma Gandhi

The more you evolve, the more you become an instrument for the evolutionary process to unfold. If you want to be an agent of change, you must be the change you are looking for. If you want to lead, you must continue to evolve. If you become stuck, even though you may be a success, the world will pass you by. You must remain receptive to new ideas that seek to birth themselves through open-mindedness to what is next for your life's expression. You either grow—or die—because the world you live in doesn't stand still.

SPIRITUAL CONTEMPLATION: Where in your life have you evolved lately? Are you ambiguous or explicit with this answer? Where would you like to see some change in your world? Is your answer general or precise?

AFFIRMATION: I am courageous in my ever-evolving life!

Fasting from the Negative

Ramadan, which comes from the Arabic and means scorching heat or dryness, is a time for deepening spiritual connection with Allah and reflecting on one's life. During the ninth month of the Islamic calendar, Ramadan is a time of intensive worship and generosity, a time to purify one's behavior and express selfless acts of good. Ramadan is not merely a holiday, but an opportunity to gain by giving up, to prosper by going without, and to grow stronger by enduring weakness. It is a time of grace and forgiveness.

There is an unseen sweetness in the stomach's emptiness. We are lutes. When the sound box is filled, no music can come forth. When the brain and the belly burn from fasting, every moment a new song rises out of the fire. The mists clear, and a new vitality makes you spring up the steps before you.

— Rumi

One of the pillars of Islam is fasting in order to help develop self-control beyond the demands of the body. This ability to resist earthly desires creates an unparalleled closeness with Allah. The fast is not merely of the body, but also of the soul. As you progress through the month-long fasting from sunrise to sunset, you intensify the awareness of God in your life, taking you to a higher spiritual experience. Part of the intention of this fast is to align you with the pain of others and walk in their shoes as a reminder of the blessings in your life that you take for granted, thus opening you to a greater expression of generosity.

SPIRITUAL CONTEMPLATION: If you were to do a daylight fast, what human desires other than food would come to your awareness, asking for you to look at them with greater clarity? In noticing the pangs of hunger, what blessings do you realize you have in your life that you've been taking for granted? Where are you being called to express greater generosity?

AFFIRMATION: I fast from the negative and respond to the call of Spirit in my life.

What About the Committee?

Working with others can be challenging—whether on a volunteer team, a work group, or managing employees. Yet working with others allows us to multiply the effectiveness of our work in ways beyond what any one person can accomplish. Years ago I hated working with committees; it was simply easier to do it myself. And I knew that it would get done right! But oh boy, was it exhausting. Now, there isn't much that I wouldn't tackle with a group of minds and hearts, rather than just working by myself.

I've learned to go with the flow by relaxing into the Divine Presence and Power of Life as It moves through each person in the group. I now love to trust the unfolding process of life toward greater life—because I always know a better outcome and more abundant result are assured. Pushing harder or doing more isn't the answer. It's so much healthier, and much more fun, to allow Spirit to work through you and through others for the greater benefit of all.

Your body has something in the neighborhood of 40 trillion cells—quite a consulting committee. Call on it when you're confused or undecided. Relax quietly and ask your body what it has to say.
— Victoria Moran

SPIRITUAL CONTEMPLATION: Where are you holding on to doing it yourself? What do you believe would happen if you trusted others to get involved? Could you find a new belief?

AFFIRMATION: I allow myself to go with the flow, knowing that as I listen to others, and others listen to me, we are making the larger Reality of Spirit present in the conversation.

June 8
Grist for the Spiritual Mill

Grist is any grain that was brought to be ground at the mill. Because the miller always received a portion of it in payment, he would grind any grain, no matter what it was. Thus he always benefited from whatever was ground. Likewise, every activity, mistake, challenge, and opportunity is grist for our spiritual mill.

Every moment of our life, spiritual opportunities abound! Every activity is an opportunity to learn, grow, or practice. Every conversation, every action, every choice is an opportunity to come from our center and bring the Divine into the moment. Ask yourself, "What do my spiritual values, principles, or practices tell me to do right now?" This will allow you to grind the grains of your uncertainty and unbelief into the fine flour of faith and understanding.

- *With bare attention consume your impurities.*
- *Take whatever comes down the pike.*
- *Everything is grist for the mill.*
- *Not "this" or "that" but "whatever."*
- *Keep giving up your story line.*
- *All of life is a meditation cushion. It's all meditation.*
- *You are the fire and fire doesn't burn itself.*
  — Ram Dass

SPIRITUAL CONTEMPLATION: What am I resisting right now that is actually grist for my spiritual mill? How can I bring this idea to my workplace or business?

AFFIRMATION: Everything is grist for my spiritual mill!

Unable to See the Truth

Resistance to change plagues all evolutionary processes. It's easy to get locked into seeing things a certain way and become unable to see something differently even when the evidence is there. Galileo challenged Aristotle's gravitational theory that things will fall to earth at a rate depending on their size by simultaneously dropping two objects of different weights off the Leaning Tower of Pisa. They landed at the same time, but the observers couldn't see that because of their fundamental beliefs. Despite the physical

It's not what you look at that matters. It's what you see.
— Henry David Thoreau

proof, they continued to hold on to the old thinking. Giordano Bruno correctly substantiated the Copernican model of heliocentrism by showing that the sun was just another star moving in space and Earth was just a planet in its orbit. He was tried for heresy by the Roman Inquisition and burned at the stake in 1600.

Resistance to change will always attempt to halt progressive development. Even the most educated can have a tough time with shifting to the next gear. It's important to validate what has brought you to your present point and be willing to let go in order to improve and move forward into the abundance of what's next. You won't become what you are intended to be while remaining what you are.

SPIRITUAL CONTEMPLATION: Are you so happily attached to a position and habit that you are blind to the current information pointing to your next step? What is your concern about making a shift?

AFFIRMATION: I see and embrace the emerging Truth!

June 10
Understanding Tomatoes

When you plant some tomatoes and they don't seem to be growing well, it would be odd to blame the tomatoes. Most gardeners would instead explore the reason the plants don't seem to be doing well. Maybe it's not enough water, or the soil doesn't have enough nutrients, or possibly the plants are not receiving enough sun. Master gardeners don't sit there and berate the tomatoes. So when there are issues with people in our lives, why is it so easy for us to blame them? Accusations don't bring about blessings, nor does manipulating or arguing with someone create joy.

Anger will never disappear so long as thoughts of resentment are cherished in the mind.

— Buddha

What is the alchemic process? It's the same as working with tomatoes: we must analyze the situation. What is prompting a person to behave like that? What is causing a nation to act in the manner that is painful? Care enough to take extra time to explore with a loved one what's going on. This kind of love and show of understanding will be felt, and the circumstances just might change. You might find that people can communicate a bit more clearly than a tomato.

SPIRITUAL CONTEMPLATION: What area of your life could use some clearer understanding? Bring love and caring to your understanding and see what might be revealed.

AFFIRMATION: I care enough to understand what's going on in a tough situation.

There's Another Way

Sometimes in the process of decision-making, you see your point of view as the only option. But being fixated on only one way doesn't feel right—it will stir your insides and obscure your inner vision for a new kind of seeing. If instead you were to step back, you might easily notice there is an opposite perspective to yours. And observing from an even higher perspective, you'll come to see a third option that is often overlooked: the middle way between the two conflicting opposites. Having a higher perspective is how you'll find the way through your inner obstacles in situations like negotiating with your teenager without either giving in or making him wrong.

It takes two sides to fight, but a third to stop.
— William Ury

As you adopt a higher perspective, pray first for guidance. Then remember to separate the person from the issue at hand. Don't defend your position but invite the other's criticism and counsel. Allow him to share his story, emotions, and concerns as you listen and acknowledge him. Then focus on your common interests rather than the problem. If you are willing to stay in the conversation without making the other person wrong, this approach will bring a shift and another way than was not previously known.

SPIRITUAL CONTEMPLATION: Find an area of your life that could use some fresh observation and find the middle road.

AFFIRMATION: I now see another way through!

What? Do You Think I'm a Mind Reader?

Have you ever driven at dusk and have someone almost plow into you? They honk at you, you honk at them, a few less than kind words are mumbled, and you drive away with your heart pounding. Then while you are stopped at the next intersection, the car across the way flashes its lights at you, and you realize that although you've been able to see where you were going, others could not see you because your headlights weren't on.

Did you ever stop to think, and forget to start again?
— Winnie the Pooh

Trouble brews when you are absorbed in your self-conscious awareness with the subjective assumption that others know what you are thinking and expecting. You must communicate where you are, whether you're driving, cocreating or cohabiting. Not everyone is a mind reader so be clear in communicating what's going on because even if it's perfectly clear to you, it's not to the rest of us.

SPIRITUAL CONTEMPLATION: What are some of the results you created by assuming others understood you when they didn't? What have you learned about clearer communication?

AFFIRMATION: My light shines bright for all the world to see!

Facing It Head-On

People describe me as someone who is willing to have the hard conversations. I have learned that this is the only way to resolve things or actively move them forward. Yes, someone may get mad. Yes, my hands sweat and my heart beats fast. Yes, it can be very uncomfortable and nerve-racking. Yes, I may not know how it will turn out.

However, avoiding pain and not dealing with difficult situations or people do not make them go away. It only makes things worse. Avoidance just keeps you stuck and allows things to fester. Facing the challenge, dealing with what is, and speaking about what is going on, may be painful in the moment, but it will get you to the other side. Trust this Truth: put on your big girl panties (or big boy boxers) and discover the healing and growth available to you, and the beauty and peace on the other side.

> *The best way out is always through.*
> — Robert Frost

SPIRITUAL CONTEMPLATION: Is there something in your life you need to face head-on that you are avoiding? What will you do to move through it?

AFFIRMATION: I am willing to walk through the fire of engagement to get to the other side of communion and resolution. I know that I don't walk through anything alone.

Hear or Deny

It sometimes seems easier to keep your head buried in the sand than to look at what's going on around you. When you pretend not to see it, it's not a reality, right? Wrong. It may not be your reality or yours to deal with in this life, but compassion will keep you from needing to make others who are hurting wrong in their experience. When pain is proliferating in a certain sector, it's good to know God is in the midst, because It's omnipresent and if you want, leave it at that. But denying and making another person wrong by jumping on a bandwagon of attack for something you haven't experienced is a questionable approach to living in love and understanding.

I think the core criterion is the social awkwardness, but the sensory issues are a serious problem in many, many cases of autism, and they make it impossible to operate in the environment where you're supposed to be social.

— Temple Grandin

When something that is wrong in the world reaches epidemic proportions, only then does it finally catch our collective attention—whether it's the housing bubble, autism, media control, or our disregard for the environment. The energy that moves upon the collective of humanity will have its expression until we stop denying what's going on and start coming together around a new idea. There is no large or small in the mind of God, or as Hermes put it, "As above, so below; as within so without." Compassionate hearing and conversations are in order for those who may be harbingers of a new insight to a way of being.

SPIRITUAL CONTEMPLATION: Where can you be compassionate with your understanding in an area where your beliefs want to make another wrong?

AFFIRMATION: I hear more deeply!

Oh Yeah!

How can you be grumpy with a smile on your face? Change the way your body is and you will change your feelings. When you're upset, try clapping your hands and jumping up and down a bit. Shake it out of your body, breathe deeply, and see how change can come over you in an instant. If you've just hit a grand-slam home run to win the seventh game of a world series, you wouldn't mope around with your head hanging low and looking at your feet, would you? No way. Your hands would be in the air and with a swagger in your step you'd show how hot your stuff is.

Don't take yourself too seriously. Know when to laugh at yourself, and find a way to laugh at obstacles that inevitably present themselves.

— Halle Berry

We hear so much about "change your thinking, change your life," but sometimes the body and mind just feel heavy and it's tough to get them to behave. To get out of that state when you're feeling down and tense, consciously change what's gotten into your body. Go outside in the fresh air and get your blood pumping by doing an impersonation of Rocky's victory dance at the top of the stairs.

How would you feel if you'd just won the lotto? What would make you jump for joy and hoot and holler? Movement impacts your body's chemistry. Sometimes you just have to let your motion help shape your emotion.

SPIRITUAL CONTEMPLATION: What would be a joyous, abundant scenario for you? Play it out in your mind, let it get into your body, move around with it, and feel how your mind's state has changed.

AFFIRMATION: My body is now filled with joy and happiness!

June 16
Status Change

There was once a blind girl who didn't like herself because she was blind. She was bitter, and despised all people except her boyfriend who was always there for her. One day she told him, "If I could just see the world I'd marry you." Then it happened, someone donated a pair of eyes to her, the transplant was

Character cannot be developed in ease and quiet. Only through experience of trial and suffering can the soul be strengthened, ambition inspired, and success achieved.

— Helen Keller

a success, and she could see everything, including her boyfriend. "Would you now marry me?" he asked her. But when the girl looked at him and saw that he was blind, the sight of his closed eyelids was just too much for her. She hadn't expected that. The thought of looking at them the rest of

her life was just too much for her to bear, so she said no, and he left in tears. Days later he wrote her a note: "Take good care of your eyes, my love, for before they were yours, they were mine."

When your status changes, do you change? Do you use life situations as an excuse for your poor behavior? Life's dynamics reveal your true character. People and circumstances don't make you act in a way you are not; they uncover the content of your character. Do you like the manner with which you conduct yourself when your world swirls?

SPIRITUAL CONTEMPLATION: Take a look at a time when your response to a circumstance elicited a behavior you are less than proud of. Choose a manner of behavior you would prefer to respond with next time that button gets pushed, and impress it on your subjective.

AFFIRMATION: I respond to life's dynamics from a high place.

Lost Touch with the Divine Touch

The indigenous peoples have lived for thousands of years in harmony with nature and the Divine expression. They have listened to their intuitive hearts more than the logic of their heads. Their philosophy has been about living in touch with the rhythms of life. But as importance shifts from the intuitive to the measurable realm of form, the very fabric of the love and reverence that held it all together appears to now be one of material mindedness. Corporations are now endowed with the rights of a person, yet there is no heart or soul to con-

When a man moves away from nature his heart becomes hard.

— Lakota

nect them with the Infinite. The link with the rhythm of life that our indigenous ancestors developed for guidance has been severed for the imbalanced filtered facts that support personal positions.

It's time to return from our sense of separateness to the revelation of wholeness and the Divine touch in all and remember that God is the reality of our heart and soul. The Divine at the center of our being is at the center of all being. When we are in communion with that which is all things, we then naturally live in balance with all that is. We remember in our heart and soul that we are part of one global family.

SPIRITUAL CONTEMPLATION: Have you lost touch with the internal connection by doing something that is out of alignment with your heart and soul? How can you return to the Divine touch?

AFFIRMATION: I live in touch with the Divine expression.

June 18
Staying Present in the Midst of It All

It has been proven that we don't actually multitask—rather we shift quickly back and forth between various things. But unfortunately we usually don't pay attention to any one of them really well, and over time this becomes frustrating, and our efficiency and effectiveness go way down. Rather than trying to do too many things at once, do each thing well while it's there in front of you. Once you focus, you will find yourself moving into the zone of perfectly balanced concentration and attention where things seem much more effortless.

Forget multitasking; find the beauty in doing one thing at a time.

— Unknown

This is moving in the flow—living in Grace—being in the zone. Allowing each activity, person, or decision to fully engage you until you move on to something else creates a more balanced experience of work and life when things are all working and unfolding easily and effortlessly. This is the way Spirit operates as you in the world: by being present in the moment, fully present.

SPIRITUAL CONTEMPLATION: How much multitasking do you try to do during a day? How does it feel when you focus on just one thing? How can you be more present with what's in front of you?

AFFIRMATION: I am present with what is right in front of me. I do not try to do two or more things at once. This way I allow myself to BE as Spirit in every aspect of my life.

June 19
Are You in Integrity?

My favorite definition of integrity is "the state of being whole or undivided" in the same way the hull of a ship has absolute integrity. Each sheet of metal, each rivet, each plank is so completely integrated that they have become one, whole, unified structure. Integrity isn't about living by someone else's moral code or behaving perfectly. It's about being wholly in alignment with yourself or with your purpose. This is just as true for a team or business.

Anything that has integrity holds its shape.

— Buckminster Fuller

We often speak about being "perfect" from our spiritual perspective, but this perfection is not a flawless or static state. It's not something you achieve or attain. To be "perfect" is to be whole and complete, just as you are . . . right now! You are wholly and completely yourself—you cannot be anyone else. When you bring your whole self into everything you do, operating in alignment with your purpose and values or those of your work, then you are in integrity!

SPIRITUAL CONTEMPLATION: Am I in integrity or am I trying to be perfect? What activities do I still need to bring my whole self to?

AFFIRMATION: I am wholly myself. I bring all of me—my values, my spirituality, my strength and my skills—to everything I do. This is the unique way Spirit is showing up as me!

June 20
Children of Light

The summer solstice, which is the longest day of the year and the shortest night, has been celebrated across all cultures and locations. Symbolic of fire and the source of all creation, the sun has been a central theme in the cosmic stories of spirituality from the time of the Great Pyramids of Egypt and the monoliths of Stonehenge.

There is an earthly sun, which is the cause of all heat, and all who are able to see may see the sun; and those who are blind and cannot see him may feel his heat. There is an Eternal Sun, which is the source of all wisdom, and those whose spiritual senses have awakened to life will see that sun and be conscious of His existence.

— Paracelsus

It is written, "As within, so without"—what out-pictures in the world of physical form is a reflection of what comes from within. This is why so many ancient cultures such as those of the Essenes, Hindus, Sumerians, Egyptians, the First People of North and Central America, the Inca, and the Maya, all referred to themselves as the "Children of the Sun" or "Children of Light."

As a child of the light, take some time today to allow yourself to be sourced from within and recharge, for the night will return to bring the balance of the yin and yang, light and dark. Celebrate the sun so you may remember it in those times when it is not as high and strong, and know there is something All Powerful within you that can be called to shine at any time.

SPIRITUAL CONTEMPLATION: Find a place to sit outside in the sun today. Allow its life force to penetrate your body and allow your mind to connect you in consciousness with your ancestors who came before and felt this same sunlight on their bodies. As the cells of your body respond to the light, how does your spirit respond in this moment of recharge?

AFFIRMATION: I am a child of the light!

Moving Around!

Flexibility is an attitude and state of mind. It is required as we continually are confronted with faster and faster changes in our world. We can truly appreciate diversity if we are flexible enough to hear other people's perspectives or try out new ideas. There are many ways to keep ourselves in the habit of being flexible rather than rigid. A significant way is through the body.

Sitting all day in front of your computer, driving everywhere, and then sitting at home in front of the TV, all cause your body to become rigid and inflexible, which can also create inflexibility in your psyche. It's important to find lots of different ways to move your body. Have fun with it! Take dance lessons, learn to golf, swim, or do yoga. More flexibility in your body creates more openness in your life.

I think there is a big and significant difference between being a leader and being a manager. Leaders lead from the heart. You have to be analytical and flexible. Flexibility is one of the key ingredients to being successful. If you feel like it's difficult to change, you will probably have a harder time succeeding.

— Andrea Jung

SPIRITUAL CONTEMPLATION: Where am I rigid in my thinking or attitude? Where in my body is this rigidity reflected?

AFFIRMATION: I move easily. I bend gracefully. I am flexible and open, in mind and in body.

June 22
Passion to Play

It's the bike and not the books that teach the child how to ride, for we learn by actually doing rather than just reading and thinking about it. Going for it teaches us more than staying at home calculating the pros and cons of our next move until all possibilities have passed us by.

We don't stop playing because we grow old; we grow old because we stop playing.

— George Bernard Shaw

You'll never learn how to swing until you pick up the baseball bat, and even if you strike out, you'll have a better understanding of how to swing. You have to get moving from where you are, even if you haven't mastered that home run swing quite yet. Life is your coach and helps you develop your passion to play at the highest level. Stop looking with your doubting, judging mind and let your adventurous spirit out to play—you'll get better at whatever you are doing with some practice and experience. When you step out of the house, your next experience will take you where you need to be, even if it's a bumpy road. Life will offer you what you need in order to bring forth your gifts from within.

SPIRITUAL CONTEMPLATION: Are you too much of a perfectionist? What is keeping you from trying until you become better with time? Where do you need to get out of your head and onto the field?

AFFIRMATION: I trust my progression in life.

Playing It Safe?

Hiring a new employee, starting a new business, or taking on a new position, all are wonderful opportunities ripe for adventure. How many times do we approach them, however, with a cost/benefit or risk analysis mind-set? How often do we hear or say, "Well, the way we've always done it is . . ."? Yes, sometimes doing it the way it's always been done is necessary—in things that are very repetitive and need to be exact. However, most things beg for reinvention and new possibilities.

Life is a grand adventure, or nothing.

— Helen Keller

What if we approached each new opportunity as an adventure, as something that takes us right to the edge of our comfort zone and grows us in ways we hadn't thought of before? An adventure creates openness and brings in new ideas. It invites us to rely on something beyond what we know, and to step out into this new possibility.

SPIRITUAL CONTEMPLATION: Where is the adventure in your life? Where are you playing it safe?

AFFIRMATION: I step out into new adventures without fear. I walk with Spirit in Faith!

Are You Making Room for Something a Little Bit Unexpected?

According to Vedanta, there are only two symptoms of enlightenment, just two indications that a transformation is taking place within you toward a higher consciousness. The first symptom is that you stop worrying. Things don't bother you anymore. You become light-hearted and full of joy. The second symptom is that you encounter more and more meaningful coincidences in your life, more and more synchronicities. And this accelerates to the point where you actually experience the miraculous.

— Deepak Chopra

Welcome serendipity into your life and invite coincidences to happen by getting out of the ruts of your routine. Go to a new place, try a new dish, take a new road, talk to a new person. These all allow greater room for Spirit to play more fully with you in your life. Support others in creating space for serendipity by becoming more present to the coincidences that happen in the workplace and in group activities. By actively naming them and calling them out, you invite the creativity to flow. Don't be surprised at the magic that starts happening!

SPIRITUAL CONTEMPLATION: What was the last serendipitous happening in your life? How do you see coincidences operating in your workplace? Can you make room for more?

AFFIRMATION: I make welcome serendipity. I invite powerful coincidences to flow in my life and at my work. Everywhere I see Spirit in action through these unexpected events.

Are You Asking for Help?

Overcome obstacles by reaching out for help. Negotiate detours in your life by learning the way from others who have traveled before you. You do not need to face anything alone. Pray with someone, talk to a friend, find a support group, lean into your community, and reach out to Spirit. There is always a helping hand and heart within reach.

The healthy and strong individual is the one who asks for help when he needs it.

— Rona Barrett

SPIRITUAL CONTEMPLATION: Where are you not asking for help? What holds you back?

Asking is the beginning of receiving. Make sure you don't go to the ocean with a teaspoon. At least take a bucket so the kids won't laugh at you.

— Jim Rohn

Asking for help does not mean that we are weak or incompetent. It usually indicates an advanced level of honesty and intelligence.

— Anne Wilson Schaef

AFFIRMATION: I ask for help knowing it is readily available. I trust Spirit to support me in every way.

Uncertainty and Ambiguity

Oftentimes as we feel called to do some great work in the world, it comes without great clarity or definition. It's as if there is this mysterious impulse within that would have its way with us—we are just not sure where it will lead. In our era of facts and science, we don't like this uncertainty. We want to know where we are going, and what's going to happen along the way before we will even set out.

The mark of a mature, psychologically healthy mind is indeed the ability to live with uncertainty and ambiguity, but only as much as there really is. Uncertainty is no virtue when the facts are clear, and ambiguity is mere obfuscation when more precise terms are applicable.

— Julian Baggini

This mystery is the Divine calling you beyond everything you know. It is a dark, organic, and seemingly empty road. Yet this is the path of potentiality, ripe with possibility. Do not be afraid of the unknown. Let it embrace you like the soil enfolds the seed. This is the fertile womb of creation. This is something you can be certain about—that you can trust the womb of creation to birth whatever seed you have planted. This is the only way to get any place new.

SPIRITUAL CONTEMPLATION: Are you comfortable with uncertainty? Can you live with ambiguity? Do you know what you are certain of that you can count on?

AFFIRMATION: I count on the Universal Power and Presence as I live in alignment with spiritual principles. I am not afraid to be uncertain as I let the process unfold.

The Place We Come From

Organizational development theory and change management systems are beginning to realize that there is an interior space within each individual, and within a group, that is the space from which people function in the world. If we are not conscious of this space within us or this space between us, we will never know what's lurking in that blind spot. Sitting in the still-

ness, in silence by ourselves or in a group, helps us to become aware of this "inner place." The ancients used the practice of meditation for this very purpose.

The success of our actions as change-makers does not depend on What we do or How we do it, but on the Inner Place from which we operate.

— Theory U

Meditation is a discipline for strengthening your spiritual muscles of intention, focus, and awareness. It's also an opportunity to simply "be" and enjoy your own company. Meditation allows you to center within yourself and contemplate/experience the qualities and Presence of Spirit. Even five minutes a day will make a difference.

SPIRITUAL CONTEMPLATION: Have you taken the time to sit in the stillness today? Do you sit in stillness and silence with those you work with on a regular basis? How could you accomplish more of this?

AFFIRMATION: I quiet my mind and still my senses that I may become more aware of the inner place within me and the inner place between us.

Where Is Your Source?

God is the Source of everything. It is also what everything is made out of. Therefore, money is simply God in a form that we can see, a way of making God's action of abundance visible. Everything we need to prosper our business is present. We focus on the service we provide or the activity we do with as much good intention and effort as we can. We know that our business is the activity of the Divine Mind moving in the world. We realize that neither our customers, nor the economy, nor the government is the source of our Good, nor the hindrance to our success.

I lift up my mind and heart to be aware, to understand, and to know that the Divine Presence I AM is the Source and Substance of all my good.

— John Randolph Price

In the downturn of 2008/2009 I worked with business owners who were seeing their markets dry up and their fellow competitors close. We didn't focus on the problems and issues; we focused on the fact the Spirit is the Source of all Good. We spent time knowing that the Universal Law always responds to the intention of success, sound business practices, and a willingness to stay positively focused. We declared that the business would survive and ultimately thrive. In every case this was so!

SPIRITUAL CONTEMPLATION: What or whom are you making the source of your success other than Spirit? Who do you think has more power than the Universal Power and Presence of the Source of all?

AFFIRMATION: I let go of seeking for the source of abundance and success anywhere other than in Spiritual Truth and Reality. I use the Universal Principles and Laws for the benefit of my business.

An Abundance of Intention

Everything begins with intention. This intention isn't just a passive thought; it is an actively living, fiery movement in the belly and in the heart. It is a movement in consciousness that is directly chosen and committed to without thought of retreat or inaction.

Who do you intend to be? How do you intend to behave? What intention are you holding about this moment, conversation, or project? What is your intention at work, around your business, or in your relationship?

Begin there, and then let your speaking, thinking, and doing be in alignment with your intention. This changes everything.

When you left the house today, you had the intention of putting clothes on and you did. You didn't try to put your pants on today. You simply put them on. The same has to hold for all of our intentions. We don't try to be more loving partners. We make the intention, and we act on it.

— Patch Adams

SPIRITUAL CONTEMPLATION: Where am I only giving lip service to my intentions? What active intentions am I willing to set and to model for those around me?

AFFIRMATION: My intention is an active movement in my life. I align myself with my intentions knowing Spirit supports me every step of the way.

An Abundance of Leadership | Living with Uncertainty and Ambiguity

To Promote or Not to Promote

Muhammad Ali, the master of self-promotion, once said, "If you even dream of beating me, you'd better wake up and apologize." Having an aversion to promotion is one of the biggest obstacles to being a Masterful Manifester. How can you possibly build a successful business or represent one if you aren't willing to tell people about it? When you were little, maybe you were told not to toot your own horn, but if you don't, no one else will. You may have the best the world has to offer, but if no one knows about it, what good are you doing humanity?

I am the greatest.
I said that
even before I knew I was.
— Muhammad Ali

All successful leaders are great advocates because they must inspire a captivating vision for people to want to be part of something that hasn't yet taken form. Do you really believe that what you are sharing is valuable? Then why wouldn't you tell others about it? If you had the answer for cancer and didn't promote it but waited for those who were suffering from it to be clairvoyant enough to intuit you have what they need, you'd be either really shy or crazy. When you don't believe in yourself, others don't either. But if you have an answer, you must share it because it's your responsibility to let the world know about it.

SPIRITUAL CONTEMPLATION: Have you had something good to share but for one reason or another you withheld? How did that make you feel? When did you have something good to share and you did? How did that make you feel?

AFFIRMATION: I am comfortable sharing what I believe in!

July

Plenty of R&R

July 1–7
Independence Day 4th
Slow Down!

July 8–15
A Soul Spa Day

July 16–22
Boxed In

July 23–27
What's Distracting You?

July 28–31
Catching Flies

July 1
Going with the Flow

A Taoist story tells of an old man who fell into the raging rapids of a river headed toward a perilous waterfall. Observers were left breathless as they watched his limp body get sucked over the falls. Certain he was a goner, they were truly amazed when he emerged downstream unfazed by the event. People asked him how he managed to survive. "I adapted myself to the water, not the water to me. Without thinking, I allowed myself to be shaped by it. Plunging into the swirl, I came out with the swirl. This is how I survived."

Don't go around saying the world owes you a living. The world owes you nothing. It was here first.

— Mark Twain

Are you able to go with the flow of life and deal with the swirls and eddies of your world so you can emerge on the other side otherwise unfazed? In the river of life there are rapids and rough patches and if you attempt to fight them you'll discover they have a power about them that is all-consuming. But if you allow yourself to be part of the flow, you'll become one with the turbulence. Nature isn't going to change her ways for you. Give up the rigidity of thinking the world is going to accommodate you. Have faith that all will work out in the Divine flow.

SPIRITUAL CONTEMPLATION: Where are you fighting the flow in your life? How do you get defensive when you can't muscle your way through a situation? Where would it be a good place to adapt yourself to the living water of life?

AFFIRMATION: I am one with the flow of life.

A Bench in the Woods

I spent a summer cutting a path up the side of a mountain, clearing the brush, and lining the deer trail with rocks. Near the top is a lookout spot from which you can see three lakes side by side, the biggest one right in the center. On this lookout I placed a bench for the adventurous wanderer to both meditate from and enjoy the view. Made of aluminum it can weather the seasons for years to come, but what's interesting is, I still couldn't help but wonder if someday its legs might collapse from the natural elements of oxidation when someone sits on it. Now isn't that silly? Rather than considering all the incredible, insightful, meditative moments that bench is waiting to deliver, I'm polarized to a potential problem that may or may not materialize somewhere in the future.

The power of imagination makes us infinite.
— John Muir

Do you likewise rob yourself of the gifts of the universe by focusing on potential problems? Do you see what might go wrong rather than enjoy the present good? Do you tell yourself it's wise to be aware of all the issues that might plague the experience, which keeps your head in the negative potential rather than the abundant joy of now? Why waste your life in friction when you can live in joy? Choose to feel the joy and take that with you everywhere you go.

SPIRITUAL CONTEMPLATION: Where are you focusing on the negative and denying the joy of now?

AFFIRMATION: I live in the abundant joy of now!

July 3
Slow Down!

I grew up listening to Paul Simon's "Feeling Groovy" and loved his message to slow down. We've all heard the admonishment, "Stop and smell the roses!" The question is—are we listening? It always seems like there's one more important thing that needs to be done before the day is over, so I often feel like I'm pushing right to the last minute. Then when I do get home, ready to relax, sometimes I just collapse and escape. Unfortunately this means I'm missing the life I am in the process of creating.

Slow down and enjoy life. It's not only the scenery you miss by going too fast— you also miss the sense of where you are going and why.

— Eddie Cantor

This year I made an agreement with myself that I would find a new rhythm. I practice walking more slowly, having longer conversations and shorter meetings. I work to have regular breaks in my day and in my week. All this slows me down considerably. Surprisingly it doesn't make me any less productive or effective. Actually the opposite. In the meantime, I'm rediscovering things I like to do, places I like to go, and people I like to spend time with. My life is much more fulfilling and I'm feeling way more "groovy" than stressed. How would it be if you decided to do the same thing?

SPIRITUAL CONTEMPLATION: Are you moving too fast? What can you do to slow down?

AFFIRMATION: I slow down and enjoy the ordinary moments of my day. I am present to the beauty and wonder of life!

No one—neither an individual nor a nation—wants to be told what to do. Being free trumps being good or bad, and freedom allows you to be influenced by both and able to make real choices between the two. Freedom is a foundational principle of your spiritual expression. Don't abdicate that freedom and be who you are not in order to be accepted. Instead of getting caught up in being told who you should be and how you should express yourself, claim your independence and just be who you are.

A little rebellion now and then is a good thing and as necessary in the political world as storms in the physical.

— Thomas Jefferson

You cannot be free within, however, while you ignore the injustice and lack of freedom outside yourself. There are still those who are enslaved without rights or respect. Discrimination, whether because of race, income, gender, or sexual orientation, is still prevalent. So let's be grateful for the concept of freedom and independence that was cast in 1776, but also be aware that the fight for freedom from oppression, whether from the outside or from within, requires continual awareness and action.

SPIRITUAL CONTEMPLATION: Celebrate your freedom, then become aware of where you may feel oppressed. What are you going to do about that awareness?

AFFIRMATION: I declare my independence from all oppression in my life.

Too Full for God

Have you unknowingly kept away the very thing you were looking for? Ever recognize that the harder you push for an answer, the further it seems to retreat from your awareness, like that word on the tip of your tongue. The more you attempted to grasp it, the more elusive it became. Have you ever been so convinced of how difficult something was going to be that you couldn't do anything at all? This paralysis is actually a great opportunity to chill out and allow yourself to open to the abundant good all around you that's looking for a portal of entry.

What could I say to you that would be of value, except that perhaps you seek too much, that as a result of your seeking you cannot find.

— Hermann Hesse

If your time is filled with seeking, where's the space for the wealth of the Divine to pour forth Its blessing? And where can this blessing find a home? If you want an abundant life of joy, harmony, and health, rather than efforting from sun up to sun down, just STOP. Love, good friends, and the freedom to enjoy them are here for you now! The answer you are looking for is inside you, and the love you are looking for is the love you must give. So the next time you are too tired and too stressed to make things happen, your body's telling to you to take a break. You've become too full of yourself and have forgotten to leave the door open for God to come visit.

SPIRITUAL CONTEMPLATION: When do you struggle to make things happen and take the fun out of the experience for those around you? Where do you get so consumed with your perspective at how tough it is that you forget there is already an answer that can ease your stress? Relax, go play, and let God back in.

AFFIRMATION: That was easy!

Vortex of Wonder

Going-to-the-Sun Road is an engineering marvel of road building in Glacier National Park. Hairpin curves overlook tremendous drops into the valley and rivers below, while towering peaks above cast shadows and waterfalls onto the road. The best and easiest way to experience it is via a red shuttle, but many visitors choose to use their own cars, so the road is gridlocked with vehicles. Hiking trails are crowded with the human footprint, which puts pressure on wildlife, like the amazing, sure-footed, white mountain goats. Close encounters with them are often the talk of the trip, yet because of the traffic and crowds these extraordinary experiences are diminishing.

If you are losing your peace in your quest for peace, you are not on the road to peace. The road to peace is peace.
— Alan Cohen

Sometimes in life you find an extraordinary place but you then return to it so many times that it loses its wonder and mystery. Or maybe social media makes it into a commonplace cultural event—a happening that everyone now knows of, talks of, and writes about . . . and for you, this rubs the shine right off. It's become a cliché and people continue showing up late for a party that's long over. What once enthralled you may still be incredible, but it doesn't give the same gifts that it did when it was something you and only a handful of people enjoyed. When the crowds converge, it may just be time for you to find another vortex of wonder.

SPIRITUAL CONTEMPLATION: Do you have a special place that has lost its magic, but you keep returning? Is it time for you to expand the possibility of a new and vibrant place in consciousness or on earth to feel the magic again?

AFFIRMATION: I know when enough is enough without making anything wrong.

July 7
Opening to Wonder

The endless round of our ordinary lives can dull our ability to see beauty and feel wonder. This is one of the reasons why traveling can be so amazing. Because we see things that are new, we are invited to look with new eyes. When I climb a mountain in the Alps I am in awe of the grandeur, and when I sit in a temple in Bali I see spirituality in a whole new way. When I walk through a German forest I am enfolded in the land of my ancestors. When I sample the wares in a French market I am treated to a host of fresh flavors and a riot of colors. Each moment invites me to stay open, be present, and really SEE life in all its beauty.

The real voyage of discovery consists not in seeking new landscapes, but in having new eyes.

— Marcel Proust

This is like looking at life with the eyes of a child, or *beginner's mind* as the Buddhists call it. By bringing wonder, adventure, and the desire for discovery into how you view the world, you become open to a new way of seeing it. This invites you to find where Spirit is trying to break through and where love is lingering, waiting to be noticed.

SPIRITUAL CONTEMPLATION: What invites you to open up and see life with new eyes? How can you build more of this into your life?

AFFIRMATION: I am open to the wonder and beauty of life. I see how Spirit shines through it all.

Taking Time—Making Time

Take a break from the busyness and the hurry. Have a quiet chat over coffee, an afternoon to yourself, a weekend away, or an all-out vacation.

SPIRITUAL CONTEMPLATION: Are you making and taking time, to rest, renew, and refresh? Have you planned your vacation? Schedule some break time with friends.

You shouldn't feel guilty about taking time for yourself. Every so often, everyone needs to give themselves a big ol' bear hug and treat themselves to some TLC.

— Sean Covey

AFFIRMATION: I take time away for myself to rest, rejuvenate, and renew.

July 9
A Time to Relax

It can be a busy, hectic world, yet in the midst of it all, it is so important to stay relaxed. Tensing up makes things only worse and causes us to miss opportunities. But mostly it means we don't bring our best self to whatever is going on. Tension literally restricts the flow of blood and oxygen in our bodies, which is a perfect metaphor for what it does to us energetically and in consciousness. Everything becomes contracted and restricted.

> *The time to relax is when you don't have time for it.*
> — Sydney J. Harris

Stop and breathe. Step back for a moment. Unless someone will die or the world will come to an end, you actually have thirty seconds . . . one minute . . . possibly even five, to get centered and release some of the tension. This immediately opens you to the flow and brings you to be present. The perfect time to do this is when you don't think you have the time. Because that's when you need it the most!

SPIRITUAL CONTEMPLATION: When do you most need to take a moment to relax? How will you remember?

AFFIRMATION: In the midst of tension, I stop, I breathe. In that moment Spirit is present in my awareness and I move forward easily.

A Soul Spa Day

Take a soul spa day. Connect with the universe through the beauty of nature. Relax with quiet music and heart-opening conversation. Rejuvenate your soul, refresh your heart, and ease your mind through gentle, spiritually uplifting activities.

Aaaaahhhh! You deserve it!

I thank You God for most this amazing
day: for the leaping greenly spirits of trees
and a blue true dream of sky; and for everything
which is natural which is infinite, which is yes.

— e. e. cummings

SPIRITUAL CONTEMPLATION: What is your favorite kind of soul-nurturing day? Plan one today!

AFFIRMATION: I take the time to nurture my soul. I take the time to rejuvenate my heart.

Take a Brain Break

An evening at home watching a movie with a loved one can be a very special time. How fun to be in the comfort of your surroundings, cuddling and conversing as you get lost in the adventure before you. It's beneficial to pause from the busyness of your demands and give your brain a break. Surrendering the weight of responsibilities for a couple hours is just fine. When you're done with the pause, you'll find all your concerns still waiting for you to pick up where you left off. So don't fret about recharging; you owe it to yourself and all you are responsible for to take care of your body, mind, and soul.

I saw that my image was changing or fading. One of the reasons for taking a break from clubs was to be missed —not forgotten.

— Sammy Davis Jr.

SPIRITUAL CONTEMPLATION: What stories do you tell yourself that keep you going nonstop? If you were to honor yourself by giving your brain a break from all that bombards it, what could you do today for a few hours that would give you a breather from some demands of your world and recharge your soul?

AFFIRMATION: Frequently I let go of the demands of my world to recharge my body, Mind and Soul!

Work Hard—Play Hard

Work can be fun and enjoyable, and even have elements of play; however, we are at work to work—not to goof off, talk on the phone, read FB, chat with friends, or try to do as little as possible. So work hard, not as in struggle and suffering, but as an effort toward accomplishment.

On the other hand, and just as important—play hard! Take time to play, be silly, laugh out loud, and do frivolous things that are not sensible. Having fun is another way to rest. Do something completely different from your normal routine—break out, be free!

When you play, play hard;
when you work,
don't play at all.

— Theodore Roosevelt

SPIRITUAL CONTEMPLATION: How do you like to play? When do you take time to play?

AFFIRMATION: I make time for play. This brings balance and joy into my life.

July 13
Too Much Sitting

Have you ever thought about all places you sit through the course of the day: at the breakfast table, in your car, at your desk, on a couch in front of your TV, on a chair in front of your computer. Do you spend the majority of your day sitting rather than being active? And if you sit in one place for too long, you just might feel your back, hips, shoulders, or neck crying painfully— *Enough!* Sitting for more than half your day is just not the best thing for your body, which wasn't designed to be idle a majority of the time. Lack of movement is unhealthy. Even if you are fast paced and hyperproductive, you still could be living a sedentary life.

Our nature consists in motion; complete rest is death.

— Blaise Pascal

Spirit is about flow. Regeneration doesn't take place in stagnation. Rest is important but so is movement. Are you on your butt, or your feet, more than half your time? Are you reading this on the treadmill, or a couch? How about doing a moving meditation or a stand-up meeting? If your work is not physical, how can you build some physical activity into your day? Can you stand at your computer or park your car farther from the door? Did you take a stroll this morning or were you just too busy to care for your vehicle— your body?

SPIRITUAL CONTEMPLATION: How can you adjust your life to get some more motion into your body?

AFFIRMATION: I honor my body!

Having It All

"You can have anything you want. You just can't have everything you want all at the same time!" I found a great deal of comfort in this revelation in the years I was raising a child, and working full-time at a job I loved, and volunteering at our national organization. But I also wanted to travel, get my PhD, and write a book. Whenever I found myself frustrated with all the things I wanted to do but couldn't at the time, I remembered that I had decided to make raising my child a priority. My time was already maxed out, and if I was going to enjoy what I already had, I needed to keep myself from becoming exhausted and overcommitted.

> *You can have it all.*
> *Just not all at once.*
> — Oprah Winfrey

Now that my son is grown, I've written my third book and traveled, and I'm considering going back to school. It's always just a matter of priorities. Although the universe is infinite, we manifest our life in a finite space/time continuum. Everything here takes time to experience. So yes, we can have anything we want, right now! We just have to choose what to focus on and make it our priority. Remember, this doesn't limit you. It actually allows you to fully engage in your current reality while knowing you can choose something else in the future.

SPIRITUAL CONTEMPLATION: What are you carrying around as a "want" that simply isn't a priority right now? Are you trying to be and have and do too many things all at once? What are your priorities now, this year, this time, in your life?

AFFIRMATION: I can have anything I want right now.
I choose wisely, and create a balanced healthy life.

The Creative Juices

Creativity is inherent in the Universe. It is in the Nature of Spirit to create—all of creation. It is in the nature of life to create—new life, new ideas, new forms. You are made in the image and likeness of Spirit; you are Life made conscious. Therefore, it is in your nature to be creative.

You may have come to believe that you are not creative. This is not true! You may not be artistic, but you are creative. Every time you imagine a new idea, think of a solution, or try something different, you are being creative. And that's how things change. Exercise your creativity every day!

Creativity is just connecting things. When you ask creative people how they did something, they feel a little guilty because they didn't really do it, they just saw something. It seemed obvious to them after a while.

— Steve Jobs

SPIRITUAL CONTEMPLATION: What kinds of activities express your creativity? Art, new ideas, puzzles, solutions, decorating, baking . . . where do you express your new ideas?

AFFIRMATION: I co-create my life with the Universal Principles through my new ideas. I am Creative.

Meaningfulness Matters!

You are here to manifest the glory of life as you! Cultivating meaningful work gives you a place to give your gift and shine your light. Don't just go to a job. No matter the tasks, find the purpose and the gift that your work is to others. Large or small, you can always make a contribution that matters.

Our deepest fear is not that we are inadequate.
Our deepest fear is that we are powerful beyond measure.
It is our light, not our darkness, that most frightens us.
We ask ourselves, who am I to be brilliant, gorgeous, talented, fabulous?
Actually, who are you not to be?
You are a child of God.
Your playing small does not serve the world.
There is nothing enlightened about shrinking so that other people won't
   feel insecure around you.
We are all meant to shine, as children do.
We were born to make manifest the glory of God that is within us.
It's not just in some of us; it's in everyone.
And as we let our own light shine,
   we unconsciously give other people permission to do the same.
As we are liberated from our own fear, our presence automatically
   liberates others.

— Marianne Williamson
A Return to Love

SPIRITUAL CONTEMPLATION: Are you manifesting the Glory of You?

AFFIRMATION: I am here to make manifest the Glory of God—at work, at home, in my life.

Boxed In

Was there a point in your growing up that the fire of your self-expression went out? When was your joy to dance through life extinguished—your knowing that you are a creative expression in manifesting art or business magic, enchanted relationships, or abundance? The singing stopped, and you put your paints and pens in the closet with the canvas of life aching for your attention again. You once were poetry in action, then the fire went out. You put away your dancing shoes and got cleaned up so you could be acceptable, fit in, and make a living.

Every Child is an artist, the problem is staying an artist when you grow up.

— Pablo Picasso

Question anything that causes your life to diminish or breaks your spirit, like antagonistic pressures that box you into some inferiority complex. Remember, you don't have to remain in that corner or closet. Be careful not to fall prey in this weakened state to false enhancements or to accept your less than glorious life. A soul that has been repressed will often seize upon some poor choices in order to escape the pain. It's easy to forget the Divinity that resides within you and has chosen you as Its vortex of expression. You can break the mesmeric trance, "not by might or by power," but by understanding and remembering who you are—and going out to play again.

SPIRITUAL CONTEMPLATION: What can you do to let your creative expression out from the closet? Do it today.

AFFIRMATION: I am poetry in action.

Being Yourself

This statement by Churchill was my favorite as a teenager. It continually reminded me that I don't have to be perfect, it's okay to make mistakes, and all I really ever need to do is give it my all. I also discovered that this meant I had a lot more opportunities, and many more cool things happened to me than most of my peers. I was simply willing to try! I learned that if I have the courage to try, somehow the universe will conspire to support me.

Success is not final, failure is not fatal: it is the courage to continue that counts.
— Winston Churchill

So now I say to you: You are more supported than you know. The entire universe is designed to assist you in becoming all you want to be, and to live a life of meaning and purpose. God's dice are always loaded, and they're loaded in favor of more life, love, peace, abundance, and joy. Let all that support lift you through the past and into your greater yet to be!

SPIRITUAL CONTEMPLATION: Where are you holding back or not moving forward out of a fear of either success or failure?

AFFIRMATION: I am here to be me, Spirit as ME. I have the courage to be me. I am no longer afraid.

Finding a New Idea

Creativity comes in all forms—solving a business problem in a new way; looking at a situation from a different perspective; trying out a unique way to talk about something. These are all ways you are creative!

Limited and negative thinking will never create abundance and joy. Turn your thinking to universal spiritual truths. Focus on them as much as you can while thinking about what you want to have different. You are always co-creating with the universe, so try a new thought, a different perspective, or a unique point of view. This is how you create something new in your life!

No problem can be solved from the same level of consciousness that created it.

— Albert Einstein

SPIRITUAL CONTEMPLATION: What problem are you trying to solve with old solutions? What entirely new, spiritually grounded idea can you try?

AFFIRMATION: I stand on Universal Truths, finding new ideas and a different perspective. This brings new solutions to the challenges at hand.

The Rummage Sale

One common cultural sign of our day is found on telephone poles with its arrow pointing down the street to the nearest rummage sale. What you'll find there is a crapshoot; you might stumble onto a gold mine, or a bunch of nothing. Yard sales are actually a wonderful rotation that creates abundance and good feeling. One person's junk can be another's treasure. Sellers are happy for a few extra bucks and a good home for their items, and buyers are happy because they get a good deal on a new prize. Rather than ending up in the landfill, a piece finds new

> *Everything I buy is vintage and smells funny. Maybe that's why I don't have a boyfriend.*
> — Lucy Liu

life and appreciation in a new environment. Everyone is blessed in this exchange. (Just be sure to get there early or the good stuff will already have been picked through and on its way to a new home.)

In addition, walking through the slew of stuff sprawled out for the picking can be a journey back in time, filled with recollections and smells triggering lost memories, each piece with its own mysterious history. Most important, circulating and repurposing what once had value in your life is a great way to create space for what is to be new in your world. Letting go and making room is an important spiritual practice. So stay healthy, take some deep breaths, drink lots of water, and clear the clutter.

SPIRITUAL CONTEMPLATION: Circulate some of your old treasures that have lost their value in your world. Watch the joy you bring to others and notice how good it feels to be a blessing with that which blessed you.

AFFIRMATION: It's a joy to share my treasures with others.

July 21
Come Back to the Present

We humans are time travelers—we get lost fantasizing about the future or are taken hostage by our thoughts of the past. The present is the place of impartation and creation. So sit down with a freshly brewed cup of coffee and relish the aroma. Sip and appreciate the complexity of flavors. This is possible only in the present moment.

> *Pick the day. Enjoy it—to the hilt. The day as it comes. People as they come . . .*
> *The past, I think, has helped me appreciate the present— and I don't want to spoil any of it by fretting about the future.*
> — Audrey Hepburn

If you're caught up in yesterday's news, or tomorrow's to-do list, you're not here in the present enjoying your cup of coffee. Yes, plan for the future but don't get lost in it with anxious thoughts. Worry is a waste.

Sometimes you might look down and wonder what happened to that cup of coffee because it's gone and you don't remember drinking it. Your life is like that. The accelerated pace you live in requires that you come back to the present; otherwise you'll look around and it will be gone. The kids will have been raised, the body won't be quite as nimble, and retirement will be in your thoughts. Being present to enjoy a cup of coffee is an important practice in escaping the prison of the past and the lure of the future. Allow that cup to be a spiritually grounding experience teaching you to be fully appreciative to enjoy the abundance of your life in this now moment.

SPIRITUAL CONTEMPLATION: Take a good amount of time to be fully present with that cup of coffee.

AFFIRMATION: I am fully present in the here and now.

Too often we don't make the effort to really push through on accomplishment. We think that if something isn't easy, somehow it isn't meant to be. In our instant gratification society, if we can't look it up in fifteen seconds or buy it in a minute, we can become easily frustrated. Yet we are here to enjoy the creativity of our life and the power of the creative force as it moves through us.

Happiness lies in the joy of achievement and the thrill of creative effort.
— Franklin Roosevelt

"Sustained effort" and "trying too hard" are two completely different things. Trying too hard causes you to stop being aware of what's going on, and you end up feeling like you're pushing the river. Sustained effort, however, is simply consistent, persistent attention to the issue, so that forward progress becomes unavoidable. It's like the difference between racing up the mountain and arriving exhausted and spent, or climbing the mountain while enjoying the progress and arriving ready to take in the view and savor the accomplishment.

SPIRITUAL CONTEMPLATION: Am I giving up too easily because it "feels hard"? The question is—is it worth doing and doing well?

AFFIRMATION: I know that spirit supports every effort I make to express my creativity and purpose. I am not easily deterred from my goal. I press on in confidence and joy.

July 23
Distracted or Focused

In some cultures, an elephant walking through open marketplaces is as normal as a curious dog. The only problem is his exploratory trunk that reaps mayhem, knocking over whatever it smacks on its way to pilfer a few pieces of fruit. Knowing that an elephant's trunk is naturally restless and undisciplined, a wise owner has learned to

You can't depend on your eyes when your imagination is out of focus.

— Mark Twain

give his pet a few pieces of bamboo to grasp in his trunk to settle him with purpose and bring focus. No longer distracted by bananas and goodies, the elephant is now able to walk through the bazaar like royalty. In much the

same way, circus elephants normally swing their trunks from side to side and would create a path of havoc when they parade through town. But instead, they have been trained to hold one another's tails, which keeps them occupied.

Your mind without discipline or focus is similar to the curious, snooping elephant trunk swinging all over the marketplace looking for something sweet. There are many intriguing distractions that can and will easily sidetrack you because your mind is inquisitive and can find all sorts of interesting tangents to get lost in. Use your affirmations to reduce distraction from all the interesting expressions calling for your attention in the marketplace of life. Like the elephant's bamboo, your affirmations will keep you calm and centered rather than scattered all over the place.

SPIRITUAL CONTEMPLATION: Where are your thoughts getting distracted by energetically depleting concerns? Create a short positive affirmation that focuses your awareness, allowing you to walk like royalty through the bizarre offerings life has to show you.

AFFIRMATION: I walk with focus through the bizarre offerings of life.

What's Distracting You?

Lion tamers go into cages with their whips and sometimes a pistol at their side to put on a good show, but a stool is the most important prop of their trade. When the trainer holds the stool by its seat and thrusts the legs at the face of the lion, it's said the wild animal attempts to focus on all four legs at once. This creates a paralysis that confuses, overwhelms, and incapacitates the beast, rendering it more docile.

For fast acting relief, try slowing down.

— Lily Tomlin

Have you ever been overwhelmed by piles of e-mails waiting in your inbox, phone calls needing to be returned, meetings necessitating your planning, staff wanting a moment of your time, bills needing to be paid, and family longing to be with you? When your to-do list gets too long and you're overloaded with demands for your attention, you can feel incapacitated by the sheer number of tasks awaiting you. It's time to prioritize. Get help from someone you trust to figure out which tasks you can delegate, those you can dump, and which ones you must address. Always remember that the number one thing is to start every day with a few minutes of quiet time and connect with your Life Source. Making this your daily practice will help you to focus and be more energized which will, in turn, help you to accomplish more.

SPIRITUAL CONTEMPLATION: Prioritize your to-do list of tasks. Identify the ones you must do, and do them, and dump or delegate the others, but do it now so it's not hanging over you.

AFFIRMATION: I am focused!

Temper

A Zen story tells of a student who came to his master for help in ridding himself of his violent temper. The teacher asked the young man to show him his temper because it sounded very fascinating to him.

A quick temper will make a fool of you soon enough.

— Bruce Lee

"But I don't have it right now," the student replied.

"Well then," the teacher mused, "bring it to me when you do."

"But I can't bring it just when I happen to have it," the student responded. "Anyway, by the time I got it to you, I'd surely lose it again."

The master gently placed his arm on the student's shoulder. "In such a case it seems to me that this temper is not part of your true nature. If it is not part of you, it must come into you from outside." The master took another moment to think. "What I suggest is that whenever it gets into you, beat yourself with a stick until the temper can't stand it another second and runs away."

Do you allow yourself to be possessed by emotions to the point of losing who you are by behaving or saying things you wouldn't typically say? You are the guardian of your consciousness and the gatekeeper to the influence of your own behavior. Don't give that power away to something outside of you.

SPIRITUAL CONTEMPLATION: What takes over you that isn't part of your true nature? The next time it arrives, you might want to try a master teacher's direction, and see how long it takes to beat it out of yourself before you fall on the floor in laughter.

AFFIRMATION: My true nature shines through all the ways of my world.

July 26
The Willingness to Feel

We call them negative feelings because we don't like to feel them—vulnerability, grief, sadness, depression, loss, and pain. We often work very hard to avoid them by distracting ourselves, drowning them out, or covering them up. We use TV, food, sex, shopping, social activities—any kind of addiction. But the problem with not feeling our feelings and trying to avoid our unhappiness and pain, is that we can't selectively numb out. It's like taking a general anesthesia: we stop being able to feel anything, which means we also can't feel our joy, bliss, love, or peace.

I spent a lot of years trying to outrun or outsmart vulnerability by making things certain and definite, black and white, good and bad. My inability to lean into the discomfort of vulnerability limited the fullness of those important experiences that are wrought with uncertainty: Love, belonging, trust, joy, and creativity to name a few.

— Brene Brown

Rather than numbing out, we must become resilient to the bad times and learn to become comfortable with the discomfort. Negative feelings are important parts of the human experience. There is something to learn, or grow from, or practice in every situation when these feelings are present. Remember that feelings aren't forever—they come and go like waves on the ocean. Everything changes, ebbs, and flows. Only Spirit is forever.

SPIRITUAL CONTEMPLATION: What do you do to allow yourself to feel your feelings? Which ones do you try to avoid the most?

AFFIRMATION: I have the strength and courage to feel my feelings. I allow them to ebb and flow like the waves upon the shore. Spirit is the steady, ever-present shore upon which my feelings are released.

Where's the Dump?

What if, instead of taking his garbage to the curb, your friend came and dumped it on your living room floor? Now that would catch your attention! You wouldn't put up with his garbage in your house, and you'd probably remember that invasion for some time. Now think about those people who dump trash in your mind:

Life is always richer when we're not playing who we are, but being who we are.

— Sir Ben Kingsley

gossip, sarcasm, put-downs, attacks, complaints, inebriated slurs, and doomsday fears. It's not that these people are necessarily bad folks—it's just that they themselves have become trash dumps and that's all they have to share. But as much as you'd like to see their world filled with joy, it's not your mission in life to take out their trash. You hang out with trash and you're going to stink.

Dumpster diving is not what you were created for. Instead of sifting through other people's trash, try looking to the spiritual truth of who you are. What are you allowing into your consciousness? You may offend your friends by not being their dumping ground but it's time for your life to be richer than trash. Give up being the garbage collector. You've been created for your own unique expression, but being a repository for other's junk only burdens you with what you're not. Be who you are.

SPIRITUAL CONTEMPLATION: Who has been dumping in your world? What can you do to end that?

AFFIRMATION: I am keeping my mind clean for God to express as me!

Have you ever stopped to think about the word *club?* It can mean a weapon, or an organization with members. It's interesting to note that a club is a way to keep someone out of the "in" group, but its exclusivity is equally as seductive and powerful in keeping someone in. If you use the club to keep others out, you'll soon find the club keeping you trapped in. When you stop believing that the grass is greener on the other side of the fence, no matter how desirous the club members make it sound, the grass will be greener where you water it, so bring your focus home.

> *The grass is always greener over the septic tank.*
> — Erma Bombeck

A while back a couple of farmers were conversing about the mouse problem in their area. One of the farmers shared how his hay was fouled by mice and his cattle wouldn't eat it. His neighbor suggested he fence off the fouled hay, which he did. The next day the farmer went outside to find his cattle reaching through the fence eating the hay they wouldn't touch the day before. Exclusiveness, elitism, superiority, snobbery are all an invisible fence that makes what's on the other side seem greener and deserving of the club. But is it really?

SPIRITUAL CONTEMPLATION: When have you been seduced to want to be in "the club"? When in, what did you do to help perpetuate its exclusivity? When have you wanted out of a group dynamic that you couldn't easily free yourself from? What was the imaginary club that was ready to bop you if you were to proceed? What did you learn about yourself from these experiences?

AFFIRMATION: I see Spirit right where I am.

Compassion and Openheartedness

Compassion means to breathe with another. It is neither empathy nor sympathy, as it isn't about feeling another's feelings. Rather it is the ability to walk beside others with a helping hand, without falling into the hole with them. Compassion is openhearted clarity—it is being able to stand witness to the human experience with recognition and understanding. By experiencing compassion in this way, we become more gentle and forgiving of ourselves. This, in turn, allows us to do the same toward others.

We are called to be strong companions and clear mirrors to one another, to seek those who reflect with compassion and a keen eye how we are doing, whether we seem centered or off course . . . we need the nourishing company of others to create the circle needed for growth, freedom and healing.

— Wayne Muller

This is what we create within a loving, supportive group of friends and spiritual community. We come together with compassion for each other's fears and foibles, while being able to see the truth in each other. This is the greatest gift we can give.

SPIRITUAL CONTEMPLATION: How comfortable am I to simply be with and walk with another's fear or pain without having to fix or change them? Can I simply sit and be a benevolent presence without jumping into judgment or control?

AFFIRMATION: I open my heart to the human experience while staying firmly grounded in spiritual truth. I am compassionate and present with those around me.

How can we consider ourselves a part of one human family if we can't embrace the cultural differences of our brothers and sisters around the planet? How can something fresh ever get in if we stay closed to new experiences? Being open to embrace others' expressions is part of the expanding spiritual journey of Oneness. When the question of difference and separation stirs in your awareness, it's a Divine invitation to consciously draw the circle of love and inclusivity wider. Put your hands together over your heart and then open your arms. Feel your heart widen, your mind open, your soul-expanding energetic circle widening—and welcome newness.

Spirit has placed the Stamp of individuality upon Itself and called it you.
— Ernest Holmes

Loving unconditionally means valuing diversity. Are we able to put aside the bias of the world we grew up in and get to know people of a different social identity from our own before we make up our mind about who they are? We all have biases, and our behavior out-pictures those beliefs whether they're subtle or not so subtle. We must be careful not to get caught in creating an otherness, for we all belong to one human family and we all bring a unique piece to the Divine tapestry of humanity.

SPIRITUAL CONTEMPLATION: What privilege or bias did you grow up with that is still in your subjective? Anything that just came to mind is still there. Is it possible that what you call your intuition is actually a hidden belief still influencing you? What reasons keep you from getting to know someone whose orientation toward life is different from your own?

AFFIRMATION: I see God's expression in all people!

Catching Flies

Using manipulation and aggression in order to force someone to see your point or change his mind may get a response but it won't create any kind of long-term connection. Many times my father got instant obedience from us girls in his moment of anger, but we paid no attention to what he wanted when he wasn't around to yell at us. On the other hand, my mother's willingness to discuss, understand, and explain made us want to please her and helped make our lives more pleasant and easy. Father was vinegar—Mother was honey.

It's easier to catch flies with honey than with vinegar.

— Unknown

Love blooms between two people in any situation when the invitation to connection is present in their heart. Rather than blame, shame, guilt, or anger toward another, we might try quietly and truthfully to share our needs, feelings, and choices with each other. When we do this, we let our eyes meet in softness and presence. Then the alchemy of love works its magic and transforms anger into understanding, and separation into connection.

SPIRITUAL CONTEMPLATION: Do I spread more honey than vinegar? Am I willing to openly share my feelings and needs?

AFFIRMATION: In challenging conversations I share openly. I listen with an open heart. I seek to understand and to connect.

August

The Vibrations of Abundance

August 1–7
Say YES to Life

August 8–14
Cultivating Beginner's Mind

August 15–21
Beyond Wishing

August 22–31
Learn from the Past or Repeat It!

August 1
More Than You Can Imagine

As long as you hold on to the side of the pool you won't learn how to swim. As long as you lean on a crutch, you won't learn how to run. And you won't know God and the peace and security of the Infinite as long as you refuse to surrender to Spirit. When that part of you that knows there's something more starts calling to you to let go—let go. Because there's way more out there for you to express than you could ever begin to imagine.

I can do nothing of myself; I do not seek my own will, but the will of the one who sent me.

— John 5:30

You'll feel the nudging in the quiet of the soul and realize that this call manifests not by your might or power but through the Spirit. Spirit is not a power to be used against anything because it is everything. Spirit is a creative, sustaining expression of life, always expressing through available outlets, of which you are one. This wellspring can use you, but you cannot use it. When you surrender and align with the One and Only Power, all form that took expression under your own personal power is washed away in the affluent flow of the Divine. Stop seeking God to rescue you from some specific situation. Rather, choose to come into harmony with the greatest gift of all—God Itself. You'll find you are secure in the flow of more than you ever thought was possible.

SPIRITUAL CONTEMPLATION: Allow your imagination to conjure up as much good as possible for yourself. Sit in that good feeling for a while. Now open up to a vision of an even greater good to fulfill what is possible for you. What can you do now to start moving in that direction?

AFFIRMATION: More abundant good than I can imagine is now coming into my experience!

Living in Answered Prayer

One day a woman spoke up in class and shared that she had been praying (doing Spiritual Mind Treatment) for two years in order to find her perfect partner. But her partner had still not shown up. This really concerned her, until she realized that she was not at all ready for this perfect someone that she had described in her journal. She recognized that she herself had some cleaning up and growing to do before her perfect person would actually be attracted to her or want to be in a relationship with her. The true benefit of her two years of treatment/prayer work was her own growth. She first had to become the kind of person that she wanted to be with. This realization allowed her to stay completely focused in her faith and know that she was living in answered prayer, even though it was taking time.

> *Never let anything cause you to doubt your ability to demonstrate the Truth. CONCEIVE OF YOUR WORD AS BEING THE THING. See the desire as an already accomplished fact and rest in perfect confidence, peace and certainty, never looking for results, never wondering, never becoming anxious, never being hurried nor worried.*
> — Ernest Holmes

Sometimes a demonstration is years in the making. During that time, you are becoming the person who you need to be in order for that demonstration to manifest. Do not give up! Allow yourself to be grown by the process as you move in the direction of your dreams.

SPIRITUAL CONTEMPLATION: What are you praying for that you are being impatient about? How is this process helping you to grow?

AFFIRMATION: I know I am living in answered prayer, no matter how long it takes. I am willing to grow and change as part of the Universe bringing about my answered prayer.

Say Yes to Life!

Practice saying "yes!" The Universe is always saying yes to your most deeply held thoughts and beliefs. The power of the Universal Law is that it says yes and only yes. Just as the Universe is saying yes to you, what if you said yes back? What if you simply said "yes!" to every possibility or opportunity, rather than worrying about the "what if . . ."? Saying "yes!" is a powerful spiritual practice for creating miracles in your life.

Find a way to say yes to things. Say yes to invitations to a new country, say yes to meet new friends, say yes to learn something new. Yes is how you get your first job, and your next job, and your spouse, and even your kids. Even if it's a bit edgy, a bit out of your comfort zone, saying yes means that you will do something new, meet someone new, and make a difference. Yes lets you stand out in a crowd, be the optimist, see the glass full, be the one everyone comes to. Yes is what keeps us all young.

— Eric Schmidt

SPIRITUAL CONTEMPLATION: In what situations do you have an automatic or unconscious "no"? How would your life expand, which opportunities would arise, if you said yes more often?

AFFIRMATION: Life says yes to me! I say yes back to Life!

The Principle of It All

How do you raise the vibration of your life to create more abundance than you currently attract? One way is to apply spiritual principles to your life rather than just the beliefs of your childhood.

A spiritual principle is a description of changeless reality. It is something you know is true about the nature of reality or the way the universe works according to spiritual laws. It can also be a quality you attribute to Spirit, the Divine, and God. In any situation, remembering a spiritual principle and applying it to your thinking helps you move into alignment with reality in such a way that your life is lifted and transformed.

A spiritual principle, as well as your intuition about reality, never has fear or limitation attached to it. It is always an expansive, life-affirming, creative possibility. It may seem challenging because to live according to a spiritual principle

What we all need is a better understanding of the principles at the very foundation of Being, of the spiritual character of God, and especially of the omnipresence of the spiritual principles. Then we need to understand our relation to these spiritual principles and what we have to do to make them operative in our mind and affairs.

— Charles Fillmore

may be outside of your comfort zone or your current experience, but it in itself is not inherently fear-based or limiting.

SPIRITUAL CONTEMPLATION: What spiritual principles do you reach for most often to help you move through challenging situations?

AFFIRMATION: I raise my awareness and my vibrational rate by applying spiritual principles to my thinking.

Can You Let Go?

Surrendering to the Divine sounds like the right choice every time, but it's extremely hard to trust enough to let go to life. It's no real surprise that most people fearfully fight their way through the world rather than allowing themselves to be swept up into the Divine embrace. Can you release your prayers, let go to love, and trust perfect unfoldment, or do you keep sticking your nose in the situation to make sure it's going the route you have mapped out for it? Are you like the camel that sticks his nose under the tent in order to see what's going on, and in the process pulls the whole thing down? Surrendering to your Higher Power is the definitive sign that you've entered a consciousness where you are willing to be fearless and faithful in your trust of Divine Guidance.

Everything I've ever let go of has claw marks on it.

— David Foster Wallace

Releasing the need to control the outcome opens you to the mystical pulse that can lift you into happenings that defy logic. Releasing your grasp tells life that you're ready for something more than you already know. Rather than stopping at the end of the road of the known, leave your doubts and denials behind and find the courage to go into the wilderness, embrace the mysterious, welcome the unknown, and dance in the dark. Your Divine partner is ready to take your hand and guide you beyond whatever abundant good you thought was possible.

SPIRITUAL CONTEMPLATION: Where are you having difficulty surrendering to grace leading the way? What good could actually happen if you loosened your grip?

AFFIRMATION: I trust in Divine Guidance to direct my ways.

août

The Presence in It All

When I feel stressed or shut down, my favorite thing to do is walk in the woods. Simply being in the quiet and hearing the wind in the trees help to settle my soul. Without all the demands of life pressing in on me I notice that my Spirit expands. In that moment I begin to look around and see life with awe and wonder again. A beautiful leaf, an intriguing gnarled tree, a tiny flower, or the racing clouds remind me that I am part of something vast and filled with Love and an explosion of Being. This completely shifts my state of consciousness, raises my vibrational rate, and alters how I see everything.

Open your heart and mind to the Presence of the Divine. Court the beloved by seeing it everywhere and in every being. Notice the squirrel—that's the Presence. Listen to the wind—that's the Presence. Gaze into another's eyes—there's the Presence as well. Smile, and the Presence smiles in return!

The Divine Presence is already what you are, and It contains the possibility of all joy in living. You should not entertain any thought that would limit your experience of the good life. There is nothing in you that can separate you from the Divine Presence . . . The greater possibility of knowing the Love of God, increased joy of living and greater good in your life is yours for the accepting.

— Ernest Holmes

SPIRITUAL CONTEMPLATION: What do you do to commune with the Presence? When are you most aware of the Presence?

AFFIRMATION: I open my heart and mind to an awareness of the Presence.

Divine Love Raises the Vibration

Being love is the most powerful way to change your vibrational rate. Love is the highest frequency there is, and when you bring it into your heart or into any situation you immediately begin to raise the consciousness around whatever is going on.

Imagine that you are the conduit for the love of the Divine to be shared in the world. Are you acting as if that is true? Is there any place or situation, or with any person, where the conduit seems blocked or closed? Practice being the love in your mind, in that situation, with that person. Now you are an intentional conduit of Divine Love, and you are raising the vibration around whatever you focus on.

When we let the love that is within us go out to the God who is in all people and the Divine Presence that is in all things, then we are loving God with all our heart and with all our soul and mind because we are recognizing that the Spirit within us is the same Spirit that we meet in others. This is loving our neighbors as ourselves.

— Ernest Holmes

SPIRITUAL CONTEMPLATION: Are you Being Love when it comes to your finances and money? At work or on the job? Paying your bills? Making your tithe? With everything having to do with your abundance?

AFFIRMATION: I bring love, I am Love, as I engage with everything having to do with my abundance and prosperity.

Criticism Can Sting

Criticism can sting. If it comes from a coach or someone who is committed to assisting you, it can be insightful; otherwise, it can hurt. Not everyone will celebrate your good fortune, so don't take it personally when people take shots at you. And don't sink to a level lower than theirs in an attempt to prove you are right and they are wrong. Shake it off, keep going, and remain in your joy. Walk away from other people's negative opinions of you and don't allow them to take up one more moment in your mind.

If people are talking trash about you, you walk away, but don't go on the gossip circuit and fan the flame. Let it die, because what comes out of their mouths and their behavior is a reflection of them. You don't need to put others in hell in order for you to be in heaven. Don't waste your time by wondering what people are thinking and saying about you. Don't waste your creative, artistic energy by being distracted by someone else's misinterpretation of you. Not everyone is going to be your cheerleader, but your fate is not finalized by what they say. Your destiny is a result of what God put in your heart.

> *It feels like the more I'm out there in the public eye, the more criticism I get. You need to have confidence— that's what it takes to walk out there and sing a song in front of a huge group of people.*
> — Gwen Stefani

SPIRITUAL CONTEMPLATION: Where have you buckled to criticism and denied your greater expression? Where are you now questioning your gifts and talents and looking outside for validation? How would bringing forth that which is within you serve you better at this point than listening to the naysayers?

AFFIRMATION: I create from the inspiration from within me.

August 9
Loving Life!

Stop focusing on what brings you down. For years I used drugs and alcohol to avoid feeling my feelings. But then after getting sober I spent years skirting around depression. One day I realized that I spent an amazing amount of time hashing over everything that wasn't working in my life. I was constantly having conversations in my head with people who weren't even in the room, trying to get them to be different or change how they behaved. My mind was filled with criticism and judgment.

I have found that if you love life, life will love you back.
— Arthur Rubinstein

Then I had a child! Watching this precious being learn about life, look at the flowers, and gaze at the stars reminded me of the beauty of life. Every time he asked me to play or simply to sit and snuggle on the couch, I moved into a timeless state of wonder and joy that was truly a blessing. The more time I spent loving being with him, the more I began to enjoy other parts of my life as well. Because I was too busy dreaming up fun things for us to do, I didn't have time to be in that constant state of depression and judgment. My son taught me how to love my life in a whole new way. And I discovered that Life started to love me back in a whole new way as well!

SPIRITUAL CONTEMPLATION: Are you loving your life? Notice the places of beauty, the people of kindness, and the opportunities for self-expression in your life. Seek out the pleasant moments and the things that bring you joy. Count the ways you are growing and all the gifts you are giving.

AFFIRMATION: I love my life! My life is filled with Joy, Beauty, Laughter, and Love. I focus on all the good in my Life and see how abundant and blessed I truly am.

Jumping to Assumptions and Leaping to Conclusions

Jumping to assumptions and leaping to conclusions can be hazardous to your health. You could easily fall into the rut of thinking you know what's really going on, but you could be completely inaccurate! Not only that, you could actually just be projecting your own thoughts and feelings onto someone else or the situation, rather than seeing it clearly or with Spirit-centered eyes. This is true whether you are thinking about a person, a situation, the state of your abundance, or the world in general.

It's always better to ask, discuss, and explore whatever you think is going on, before acting on it. If you must jump to an assumption and leap to a conclusion, why not assume the best and conclude that everything will work out okay? This will keep you from projecting your unhealed past or triggered emotions onto the person or situation.

Out of damp and gloomy days, out of solitude, out of loveless words directed at us, conclusions grow up in us like fungus: one morning they are there, we know not how, and they gaze upon us, morose and gray. Woe to the thinker who is not the gardener but only the soil of the plants that grow in him.

— Friedrich Nietzsche

SPIRITUAL CONTEMPLATION: When have you leaped to a conclusion that was unhelpful and untrue? When have you jumped to an assumption you later discovered was just a projection of your own stuff?

AFFIRMATION: I release any need to make assumptions or jump to conclusions that are negative. I see with the positive eyes of Spirit's Love and assume that abundance and good will abound.

August 11
A False Sense

It was on this date in 2014 that Robin Williams took his own life, joining the likes of Whitney Houston, Seymour Hoffman, and Marilyn Monroe. The human psyche alone is not strong enough to carry the longed-for-desire of the masses without eventually buckling under the pressure. Substances can give a false sense of coping that, when abused, create a dependency that ultimately leads to one's self-loathing and demise.

You have this idea that you'd better keep working otherwise people will forget. And that was dangerous.

— Robin Williams

It is only in the soul's growth and strengthening that you'll be able to handle the projections of others. Your urge to express life through the arts, gifts, talents, and passion will help you develop the skills to handle the energy of abundant success. Success excites not only your soul but the cellular level of your body as well, and through its expression you will become more alive than you ever knew was possible. This natural high is intoxicating, though it cannot be sustained and you must learn how to come down and integrate back into life. The genius expression must be carefully integrated if not mentored into the balanced human experience if the deliverer is to survive.

SPIRITUAL CONTEMPLATION: How do you come down from your natural highs without crashing?

AFFIRMATION: I am balanced in my life's expression.

The Pull of Opposites

Sometimes rushing to resolution is not always the best answer to a situation. Living your spirituality can often bring you face to face with conflict between what you believe and what the world presents to you. It's natural to want to resolve that conflict, particularly in our microwave, hurry-up society. But sometimes, living in the pull of opposites is a powerful way of being. Instead of racing to a solution, sit yourself calmly in the question to bring a different way never perceived before.

Whatever this new way may be, it comes as a surprise because you never thought of it before. It emerges

The paradox is the source of the thinker's passion, and the thinker without a paradox is like a lover without feeling: a paltry mediocrity.

— Søren Kierkegaard

because you were willing to sit in the tension of opposites and not battle to get rid of it immediately. It is a spiritual skill to trust the mystery of not knowing and believe that a greater abundant good is present. It is loving the sun and the moon, the yin and the yang, the ebb and the flow without choosing one over the other. By sitting fully present you will discover a new way.

SPIRITUAL CONTEMPLATION: Where do you feel the pull of opposites creating inner conflict for you? Let go of your desire to have it immediately handled and sit with it to see what surprising insight that tension has to present to you.

AFFIRMATION: I see a greater way emerging in the midst of the pull of opposites.

The Mirror of Your Life

I remember when I learned that the physical world of my life was like a giant feedback mechanism. If I wanted to know what I was thinking and believing, all I had to do was look at my life. It was like looking into a mirror, and I really didn't care for this idea at all! Surely most of what I didn't like about my life was because of those other people and what they were doing! I had a really difficult time taking responsibility for the messes in my life and the ways my lack-filled and limited thinking was perfectly mirrored back to me.

You are either attracting or repelling according to your mental attitudes. You are either identifying yourself with lack or with abundance, with love and friendship or with indifference. You cannot keep from attracting into your experience that which corresponds to the sum total of your states of consciousness. This law of attraction and repulsion works automatically. It is like the law of reflection —the reflection corresponds to the object held before a mirror.

— Ernest Holmes

Eventually I realized that taking responsibility isn't about blaming or shaming myself. Rather it's simply noticing that my life reflects back to me the quality and state of my habitual thinking: how much attention I'm paying to what isn't working in my life and how much of my intention is focused on what other people are or aren't doing. As I began to change where I placed my attention, things in my life improved. As I began to focus my intention on my own life, I began moving in the direction of my dreams.

SPIRITUAL CONTEMPLATION: Where you place your attention and intention is what the universe mirrors back to you. Attend to those things that are working and to those that you desire. Remember, a mirror is blank until something stands in front of it. What are you placing in front of the mirror of your life?

AFFIRMATION: I pay attention to where and how things are working in my life. I focus my intention on contributing greater good into life. I love what the mirror of my life reflects back to me!

Cultivating "Beginner's Mind"

When my son turned fourteen I was reminded of my own teenage years when I was sure that I knew everything! I thought my parents were unbelievably stupid and didn't have a clue. As I watched my son go through that same phase, it made me smile to realize that the older I have become, the less I'm completely certain about. At fourteen I was freely dispensing advice; now I'm not always sure I have that kind of clarity for myself, let alone someone else. Sometimes, however, teenage arrogance can harden into a closed mind of certainty in adulthood. I've seen it when I've been afraid to experiment with ideas, or let things unfold without knowing where they're leading. I much prefer to know for sure.

Beginner's mind means having an attitude of openness, eagerness, and freedom from preconceptions when approaching anything. Beginner's mind is actually the space where the mind does not know what to do. It is that delicious state when you are sure of nothing, yet completely fearless, totally available to the moment.

— Nithyananda

Yet what I have come to learn through my spiritual awakening is that Life is a series of opportunities that invite us to be present in each moment and accept the gift of possibility. There is something so profound when we savor the prospect of coming to each moment, each event, each person, completely fresh and new—when we allow ourselves to live in beginner's mind without judgment or expertise. Let yourself be surprised as you discover how good life can be with an open mind as well as an open heart!

SPIRITUAL CONTEMPLATION: In which areas of life are you closed to new ideas and possibilities? What do you want to bring your beginner's mind to?

AFFIRMATION: I see myself with beginner's mind. I see my life with openness and eagerness, free of false perceptions and judgments.

August 15
The Bull

Do you know people who are like a bull in a china shop in that they're so out of touch with what is actually happening that they just bull their way through? Their conversations are so full of their stuff that it seems they've forgotten to listen to the discussion at hand. They come from their egoic-self, not their soul, though their head is quick to tell you they are all heart. Their recommendations come from what they think is better, but they totally miss what is best.

A student asked Suzuki Roshi why the Japanese make their teacups so thin and delicate that they break easily. "It's not that they're too delicate," he answered, "but that you don't know how to handle them. You must adjust yourself to the environment, and not vice versa."

— Shunryu Suzuki

Love means being in sympathetic vibration with your environment—not dominating or exploiting it, because love is a communion that allows true connection to happen. If someone or something is not like you or what you are accustomed to, that doesn't mean you must change it to fit your patterning. Wisdom comes when you are able to step outside your position, see how you match up, and decide whether or not you can handle the teacup.

SPIRITUAL CONTEMPLATION: Where are you butting heads in your life? How can you adjust to the environment, or do you even want to?

AFFIRMATION: I am able to connect in the various environments I find myself.

August 16
The Need to Pay Attention

Too often you can spread yourself too thin rather than going deep with what you know and do. When you're cooking, it's easy to get distracted and turn away from the pot cooking or oven roasting. But forgetting to keep an eye on the fire can leave you with nothing but a scorched pan and fodder for your composter. Mistakenly thinking it will go on without your attention is flawed, especially as the fire goes out or the smoke begins to rise. When you take your awareness off what calls to you, you lose.

Keep all of your eggs in one basket but watch that basket closely.
— Warren Buffet

Without your care, your grand ideas, your heart's desires remain uncooked, even if you put some initial energy into getting them started. Without your watchful eye, dreams can go askew. You must nourish and weigh in on the progression of what you've set in motion. The fewer pots on the fire, the less chance you have of missing the signs that need your attention.

SPIRITUAL CONTEMPLATION: Where are you spread too thin in your life? How can you bring more of the pieces of your life into one caregiving basket so you can stay on top of what is valuable to you?

AFFIRMATION: I bring all that is near and dear to my heart into my watchful care.

Point of Transformation

A boat, a horse, a train, a car, a jet, or maybe even astral projection—they are all expressions of the spiritual idea called transportation. The Infinite must move through a filter in order to take some kind of form. You are that filter, that point of transformation, and no matter what may be happening in your life, a part of your awareness can always tap into the ever-available Omnipresent, Omniscient, and Omnipotent Spirit with its revelation of where you are. It is this kind of realization that can translate the God quality into an appropriate expression.

Somewhere, something incredible is waiting to be known.

— Carl Sagan

Spirit is present within all that is possible in this instant. When donkeys were the main mode of transportation, people were grateful for them, though at the same time the possibility of a rocket ship was always available. What kept it from manifestation was that the current filters of perception were not yet able to embrace that concept. Only to the degree that you are a conscious realization of the presence do the blessings manifest. You are never bound by the present condition because there is a higher possibility waiting to move through your filters of awareness. Gratitude for a raft can open you to the possibilities of an ocean liner. But until you enter the plane of a spiritual quality or idea, you are not the filter for what is next in that particular expressive flow. There is so much more wanting to be known. Where are you saying, "Come through me"?

SPIRITUAL CONTEMPLATION: Knowing that your future unfoldment is waiting to be known now with all its evolutionary ideas, what spiritual quality would be good for you to meditate on to uplift an area of your life? Spend some quiet contemplative time with that quality and witness its evolution of possibilities available to come through you.

AFFIRMATION: Spirit now finds expression through me.

What Words Are You Using?

All of creation begins with a word. The way in which we co-create our life with the Universal Power is through our intentions, which we frame by the very words that we use. Ernest Holmes reminds us that "in the integrity of one's own conscious self, each person's word is a seed which is already impregnated with Divine life, and all we are doing in prayer is nurturing this seed. We do not make the seed grow; we let it grow! The great Power is always near, ready at any time to help, but we must use It according to Its own nature, in harmony with Its Law."

In the beginning was the Word, and the Word was with God, and the Word was God.
— John 1:1

There is such power in your words! Every word you speak is a seed planted in consciousness. Pay attention to the words you use and what you spend your time talking about. This is a good indication of what you believe, and what will play out in your life experience. Be very mindful of your words!

SPIRITUAL CONTEMPLATION: What words and phrases do you habitually use that are actually limiting and contrary to your spiritual beliefs and the life you want to lead?

AFFIRMATION: I consciously use only those words that are in alignment with Spiritual Truth, the Power of the Universe, and the Presence of Love.

August 19
Singing the Song of Life

The song of life is forever singing, through all of creation. This song is singing through you. Do you hear it? The melody of your joy glides over the rhythm of your days, sustained on the bass notes of faith. This song pours forth from you whenever you feel most alive. This is the song of Abundance, Joy, Peace, Wholeness, and Love! Let life's song resound in your thoughts, words, and actions.

Since God is infinite, our expansion is progressive and eternal. No matter how much good we experience today, the Infinite has more in store for us tomorrow. We should joyfully look forward to this expansion with enthusiastic anticipation. The march of Life is not dismal, but a song of triumph.

— Ernest Holmes

SPIRITUAL CONTEMPLATION: How much of life's joyous and abundant song do you sing on a daily basis?

AFFIRMATION: The Song of Spirit is singing in my heart, from my lips, and in my life, praising the abundance and joy of Spirit that is everywhere.

Living at the Frequency of Vision

How would you describe the overall quality of your life—adventurous, plodding, meaningful, dull, fulfilling, stagnant, full, or empty? How would you like it to be? When you describe the life of your dreams, not in terms of form, but with descriptions of feelings, you are describing the frequency or vibrational rate of your life. At what frequency does your vision vibrate?

A philosophy of life:
I'm an adventurer,
looking for treasure.
— Paulo Coelho

Now you must keep your eye and heart trained on your vision. Stay focused on the end result. Don't become confused by the twists and turns of the path. Simply continue moving in the direction of your dreams. Eventually, you will get where you are going. The path really does lead toward complete alignment with your vision, where you regularly live at the level of the frequency of your dreams.

SPIRITUAL CONTEMPLATION: Describe the feeling/tone/vibrational frequency of your vision. How close are you to living at that frequency on a regular basis?

AFFIRMATION: I choose to live my vision. I don't let anything get in my way! My life is lifted to a higher vibration.

August 21
Beyond Wishing

Claim your prosperity, abundance, and joy! Wishing and hoping for them simply aren't enough. Begin with realizing and knowing that you live in an abundant universe—this is a good place to start.

If, then, we believe God is substance, God is food, God is shelter, God is happiness, God is life, and we wish to enjoy and experience that life which God is, we must claim for ourselves everything that we claim for God. For we and God are one. The mind by which we think is God.

— Ernest Holmes

Knowing that you are part of that same universe is the next step. The final step is to claim the abundance in consciousness, accepting it in your mind and heart as true for you. You make this claim because you now sense and feel what the Master Teacher Jesus reminded us: "The Kingdom of Heaven is within." You are already in and a part of this Abundant universe. Now stake your claim to your experience of your birthright!

SPIRITUAL CONTEMPLATION: What helps you feel the Abundance of the Universe? How do you sense yourself as part of this same Abundance? Is there anything that keeps you then, from claiming that this abundance is also yours?

AFFIRMATION: The Universe is flowing with Abundance. I am a part of it all. I claim my place and my abundance in this ever-flowing River of Life.

Amber Waves of Grain

If you have ever seen golden wheat fields, you know what the song "America the Beautiful" is describing. The summer wind rippling across a golden valley of wheat looks like waves on a lake of gold, and you are surrounded by abundance that is ripe for the harvest. As you watch four combines moving abreast across the massive fields, don't you feel a sense of appreciation to the farmers of our land who provide such a main staple for so many?

Observing this kind of abundance fills the soul with such a love for how well nature provides for us. Truly, we live in a world of plenty and we are provided for: from the moment the seed is planted in the fertile soil, then watered, cared for, and harvested;

> *O beautiful for spacious skies,*
> *For amber waves of grain*
> *For purple mountain majesties,*
> *Above the fruited plain!*
> — Katharine Lee Bates

loaded into trucks, stored in silos, moved to manufacturers, and processed into its various forms; packaged and trucked to the store and finally placed on the shelf. When you partake of a meal, stop to remember the elements of nature, from the sun to the clouds filled with rain, that created what you are about to eat. Give thanks as well to the myriad of individuals and their diverse skills that got this food to your table. And whatever you do, don't forget to kiss the cook.

SPIRITUAL CONTEMPLATION: While sitting at the table before your first bite, close your eyes and think of all the people, from the farmers, to truckers, and grocers, and the cook, as well as the elements of nature that created this meal. Be thankful for the abundance you live in.

AFFIRMATION: I live in a beautiful world!

In the World

Your intellect and emotions are great gifts, but it is just as important to pay attention to this world in which you walk, for your body and the physical Universe are great gifts as well. Something about living in your body and the physicality of life allow the Divine to become more real. Take a bite of the most amazing orange, sweet and juicy, and you partake of Life. Follow a winding trail through the woods onto a bluff with a spectacular view, and you gaze upon the Beloved. Feel your muscles move and enjoy the strength in your body as you stride purposefully down the road, and you sense the power and presence of Spirit.

I believe the world is incomprehensibly beautiful—an endless prospect of magic and wonder.

— Ansel Adams

Open your eyes, mind, and heart to the beauty, wonder, and simple pleasures of life all around you. Feel yourself in the midst of life, embraced by its joy and sharing in its pleasure. This is what our senses are for—to engage with God in form, God as Creation, and grow your Joyous Abundance in miraculous ways!

SPIRITUAL CONTEMPLATION: When do you most experience yourself as partaking of the manifest body of God?

AFFIRMATION: I live in the manifest body of God. I savor It and am moved by Its beauty. Everywhere I look I see the beautiful and the miraculous.

The Art of Doing Nothing

Wu Wei, which means to do without doing or act without acting, is a powerful idea from the Tao Te Ching. Winnie the Pooh is a master of Wu Wei, as Benjamin Hoff points out in one of my favorite books, *The Tao of Pooh*. Pooh is a master of the Tao and Wu Wei because he simply lets things and people be what they are. He doesn't spend a lot of time trying to figure things out or make something happen. Pooh is much more likely to simply be present to what is, in the moment, and thereby is able to respond from a completely open and present state.

"Rabbit's clever," said Pooh thoughtfully. "Yes," said Piglet, "Rabbit's clever." "And he has Brain." "Yes," said Piglet, "Rabbit has Brain." There was a long silence. "I suppose," said Pooh, "that that's why he never understands anything."

— A. A. Milne

To practice Wu Wei, be like Pooh, which means that any effort you put into something is actually effortless because there is no sense of making something happen, no struggle or emotional hook. You simply are present to what is called for from you in the moment. Then you can enjoy your life with simplicity and experience the abundance that is ever-present.

SPIRITUAL CONTEMPLATION: When are you like Rabbit, clever at trying to figure things out? How would being more like Pooh help your life?

AFFIRMATION: I am simply present to what is. I respond in the moment, without trying to make anything happen. I simply trust that it does.

Bend Like the Willow

Most really, really wealthy people have lost and regained their fortunes more than once. How do they survive these storms of life? I am reminded of Wayne Dyer sharing his experience of living by the ocean through hurricane season: "What is the palm trees' secret to staying in one piece through huge, devastating storms? They bend almost down to the ground at times, and it's that ability that allows them to survive." This flexibility allows the tree to withstand the rigors of life. Storms come and go—the physical Universe is always changing. Even our greatest financial abundance isn't a guarantee that things won't ebb and flow. The question is, can we be flexible in the human experience of this ebb and flow, while still maintaining our rootedness in the Abundance of Life?

The wind does not break a tree that can bend.

— Sukuma Proverb

The tree that does not bend with the wind will be broken by the wind.

— Mandarin Chinese Proverb

One of my favorite mantras is "I bend like a willow in the breeze." This reminds me that even though the winds and storms of life may rattle my branches and flutter my leaves, my trunk is rooted in Divine Reality. Be strong and steady in your faith, yet flexible in your living, and Life becomes a joyous Dance of Abundance with the Divine.

SPIRITUAL CONTEMPLATION: Are you rigid in the face of adversity, or are you able to let things be what they are? Are you rooted in truth in the midst of chaos and change?

AFFIRMATION: I bend and am flexible on the outside while staying firmly rooted in Truth on the inside.

Choose Your Own Adventure

In a fun book series called *Choose Your Own Adventure,* you determine the direction of the story. Each choice leads to an adventure, which leads to another page with other choices, and you travel a path that is entirely of your own choosing. Some decisions can lead to disaster and ruin while others allow you to be the hero. If you reread the story and make different choices at the various junctures, you'll find yourself on an entirely different journey with completely different paths to an alternative ending. You can discover Atlantis, time travel, explore the Amazon, or even search for a black rhino.

> *How people treat you is their karma; how you react is yours.*
> — Wayne Dyer

Sounds like life. You are given choices that bring with them certain consequences. You must decide your next step from the options life presents to you. You have the power to alter your direction at any time if you aren't too caught up in the drama of the story or if you can let go of your insistence on the kind of ending you wish you see. If you can remember that you are the observer of your life, you are free to make new abundant choices and open the floodgates to greater good at any time. But you must remain conscious that you are always at choice and not fall into the drama of it all—even if it makes for a good story.

SPIRITUAL CONTEMPLATION: What paths do you want to stay on in your life and which ones are you ready to alter?

AFFIRMATION: I am conscious of my path choices.

August 27
Light Makes Shadows

Gremlins of old habits are some of the most daunting challenges along the spiritual path. When I illuminate an area in my life where I am not as aligned with Spirit as I would like, I suddenly become aware of how I behave, think, or speak in ways that are counter to the Spiritual growth I declare. It's like a junk-filled basement that you ignore for years until the day you finally grab a flashlight and descend the steps. All sorts of spooky shapes and shadows startle you, until you come close enough to see that they're only a pair of antlers on a box or your grandmother's wedding gown draped over the back of a rocking chair. The very act of bringing in the light has caused these weird, scary shapes to appear. It's not like they weren't there all along. It's just that now you are aware of them.

> *Accepting the lessons and experiences of the past, and taking the best from everything, we should press boldly forward, looking ever for the Truth, and ever ascending higher and higher into the heavens of reality.*
>
> — Ernest Holmes

The same is true when we look at past choices that are hidden in the basement of our consciousness. Being willing to shine the light of spiritual principles into the corners can reveal some pretty scary and startling insights. Yet these truths have been available to us all along. We just have to look at them in the light and see them for what they are—beliefs from our family, behaviors to make ourselves feel more important, and smallness masquerading as a false sense of identity.

SPIRITUAL CONTEMPLATION: What shadowy places and old baggage have been illuminated in your life now that you are living more from the Light?

AFFIRMATION: I know that I am simply illuminating that which has always been there. Now I can see it and release it.

Learn from the Past or Repeat It!

Learning from the past is one of the best ways we can move forward on our spiritual growth. This takes courage and a willingness to see ourselves clearly. Yet the doors that are opened are worth the price.

Once we've really begun to clear out the boxes and baggage in the basement of our past, we can graduate to the Earth School that is currently in session. When we no longer play out old beliefs and false identity, we get to participate in learning in real time. Now, if we are paying attention, our lessons present themselves as opportunities to practice and grow. This is the invitation to choose, consciously in the moment, how we are going to speak, act, respond, or move through whatever is going on right in front of us.

The challenges in life are not here to stop us . . . The challenges are here to help us grow . . . A big enough challenge will bring out strengths and abilities you never knew you had.

— Alan Arcieri

SPIRITUAL CONTEMPLATION: Where in your life are you being invited to practice living from your spiritual understanding and deal with old situations in a new way?

AFFIRMATION: I know that every day and every situation is an opportunity for me to practice living from Spiritual Truth. I enjoy the practice!

It's More Than Learning Lessons

Life forever and ever expands into some greater-yet-to-be, expressing more Joy, more Love, more Peace, more Abundance. All Spirit wants for you is what it wants through you, as you. If there are lessons to be learned, they are really just opportunities for us to realize that the Law of Cause and Effect is playing out in our life. Do we like what we are experiencing? Do we like the outcome of our behaviors and words? If not, it means the Universal Law is providing feedback for us.

You are led through your lifetime by the inner learning creature, the playful spiritual being that is your real self. Don't turn away from possible futures before you're certain you don't have anything to learn from them. You're always free to change your mind and choose a different future, or a different past.

— Richard Bach

We enter Graduate Earth School when we consistently move through our life with intention and mindfulness, and realize that everything is simply feedback for our awareness. Do we like how those words or that action played out? Did they bring more love and peace to the situation and make for more aliveness in others and ourselves? Did they move things forward toward the vision or hold them back out of fear? This awareness allows us to modify our choices and instantly choose something different—say we're sorry or think a new thought or not react to a triggered negative emotion. Our choices are no longer dictated by events and beliefs from our childhood, our woundedness or our fears, but rather are current, spiritually grounded responses to the present moment. Our choice has become a tool that we consciously use in service to live a light-filled, spiritually mature life.

SPIRITUAL CONTEMPLATION: Are you using your choices to live from Spirit and Light—or from the past and your woundedness?

AFFIRMATION: I make healthy choices from the Light of Spiritual Truth.

What's Your Favorite Class?

Do you remember being in school and having one class you really loved? Whether it was music or math, art or science, learning to play an instrument or a sport, it didn't matter. You couldn't wait to get to class, and you loved doing the homework and projects! Remember when learning was fun? You felt stretched and you couldn't believe the cool new thing you now understood or knew how to do.

The world is your exercise-book, the pages on which you do your sums. It is not reality, although you can express reality there if you wish. You are also free to write nonsense, or lies, or to tear the pages. Earth School is in session every day.

— Richard Bach

This is truly what Earth School is supposed to be like. It's not just about cleaning out our baggage, strengthening our mental muscle, and exploring all the ways we experience our sense of separation from Spirit. Earth School is the playground for our imagination to soar. It's about exploring the possibility of all the ways we can experience and express more of ourselves and more of Spirit through us, as us! As we grow in our ability to live in alignment with Spiritual Principles, we allow Love to shine through and Law to make the way possible—and everything we choose supports us, touches others, and adds something beautiful and new to Life.

SPIRITUAL CONTEMPLATION: What are your favorite Earth School classes? Are you going to them regularly or are you living by someone else's idea of what you should be learning and practicing?

AFFIRMATION: I make the time to explore new ideas and possibilities, and express those things that cause my soul to soar.

August 31
Earth School Is in Session

Every day is an opportunity for us to contribute to the evolution of humanity by evolving ourselves. Every choice we make impacts the collective consciousness and becomes part of the morpho-genetic field of our species. Just as we create new grooves of thought in our own brain, so we create habits of thought in our collective brain. Earth School isn't just an individual experi-ence. It's also about our whole species continuing to become who we are meant to be—the place where the Infinite becomes conscious of Itself and experiences and expresses with complete awareness. Our species is in school and we are clearly on all dif-ferent grade levels!

> *The requirements for our evolution have changed. Survival is no longer sufficient. Our evolution now requires us to develop spiritually—to become emotionally aware and make responsible choices. It requires us to align ourselves with the values of the soul—harmony, cooperation, sharing, and reverence for life.*
>
> — Gary Zukav

SPIRITUAL CONTEMPLATION: What grade are you in? How are your choices contributing to the evolution of humanity's consciousness?

AFFIRMATION: I choose wisely and grow joyfully, evolving human-ity to its greatest potential.

September

Abundant Creativity

September 1–7
Labor Day (5th)
Building Up or Tearing Down?

September 8–15
Healing the Breach of Duality

September 16–22
Your Life Is Your Masterpiece

September 23–30
What Slide Are You Looking Through?

September 1
To-Do List

In football just before the end of the first and second half there's something called the two-minute drill when the offense moves the ball down the field with great speed and accuracy. The two-minute drill is also an excellent strategy for much in your day. Ever notice if you have only one important e-mail to write, you might labor over it all day, but if you have several, somehow you tackle them all in a swift and timely manner? How about the week before your vacation? Are you suddenly able to handle a vast amount of work in order to clear your desk and docket? When you have friends or family coming to stay at your house, don't you do chores you've been putting off for months?

It is our attitude at the beginning of a difficult undertaking which, more than anything else, will determine its successful outcome.

— William James

Imagine running your life with this kind of proficiency of swift decision-making and follow-through on a regular basis. Rather than waiting for pressure to prompt you into effectiveness you can choose to live from the abundance of energy that is generated from vision and inner connection. Instead of telling yourself how difficult the task is, open your consciousness to receive the power, the presence, and wisdom now in you, as you, to establish your heaven on earth. Then notice how much freer your mind is and how much more energy you have to direct toward your creative endeavors.

SPIRITUAL CONTEMPLATION: What tasks that beg your attention have been enlarging in scope since you've been putting them off? Go do them and see how good it feels to have them handled.

AFFIRMATION: I am efficiently handling my to-do list today!

Who Is Going to Teach Him?

A great teacher's monastery once drew students from near and far to learn meditation and the skills of mindfulness. One day a student was caught stealing and was reported to a sage who requested that the perpetrator be kicked out. The teacher disregarded the request. Weeks later this same student was once again caught stealing, and again the teacher chose to ignore the issue. This time the other students became outraged and drew up a petition asking that the thief be expelled. They all threatened to leave if he wasn't. After reading the demand, the wise one called his students together and stated how astute they all were. He confirmed they knew the difference between right and wrong—and he released them all from their obligations at the monastery to go learn somewhere else. "But," he concluded, "this one poor brother who doesn't know right from wrong, he must stay. Who is going to teach him if I don't? He must stay even if all of you must go."

> *The man who strikes first admits that his ideas have given out.*
> — Chinese Proverb

SPIRITUAL CONTEMPLATION: When would it be easier not to have to deal with an uncomfortable situation? Face it anyway.

AFFIRMATION: I follow through with that which is mine to do!

Abundant Creativity | Building Up or Tearing Down?

September 3
There Is Power in the Words

I had the joy of going to a liberal arts college where I had an amazing English professor who completely understood the power of the word. One day in class, he talked about how an author creates an entire world in which his characters play out their life. He described how the narration invites us to step through a window and look inside these life. Somewhere in the lecture it became clear that he was discussing not only the process of writing, but also the way in which we narrate our life. The very words we use and the way we describe things become, he emphasized, a type of window through which we look and ultimately create, the reality of our life.

Herein is the mystery of life. You and I are intelligent centers using the creative word for that which we will constructively or destructively, and that creative word which we use becomes the law unto the thing whereunto it is sent and becomes the concept behind it and projects the thing, creates the thing in our life.

— Ernest Holmes

So you see, your words are the Words of Creation. Pay attention to these words you use, habitually or unconsciously, and how you describe things and people in your life. Is this the way you want your life to look? If not, use different words. Over time, you will see your world conform to the way you describe it. That is the power of your word!

SPIRITUAL CONTEMPLATION: What is the underlying narrative of your life? What kinds of descriptive words do you tend to use?

AFFIRMATION: I pay attention to my words! I use the power of the Word to describe a creative, joyous, abundant life!

September 4
Building Up or Tearing Down?

How many of us were told that we couldn't draw or paint, or sing or write, or dance or throw a ball? On parents' day at my son's preschool, we were shown our kids' art. My son had painted an abstract watercolor, and then had torn strips from another picture he'd painted and attached them all around the edge so they stuck out in different directions. It was truly unique, and his teacher praised his "out of the box" thinking. Clearly his creativity was not confined by the edges of the paper. The following year in kindergarten, however, he was severely criticized for not coloring inside the lines. This was the first time his creativity hadn't been supported, and I watched his out-of-the-box thinking learn to conform throughout the rest of elementary school.

Because there is only one of you in all of time, this expression is unique. And if you block it, it will never exist through any other medium and it will be lost.

— Martha Graham

These kinds of experiences turn into the way we talk to ourselves about our own creativity and our ability to create something new in our life. We end up repeating to ourselves the things we heard from parents, teachers, and friends in school.

Every time your self-talk belittles or berates you, ask yourself, "Is this really true about my deepest, truest, Spiritual Self?" Of course it's not! Ask yourself this question until you can laugh at the absurdity of your self-talk and make space for your real creativity to emerge.

SPIRITUAL CONTEMPLATION: How do you belittle your creativity in your own mind? How do you talk to yourself when you are trying to create or make something?

AFFIRMATION: I am creative. I like how I do things! This is Spirit showing up as ME!

September 5
Labor Day

Now if God can take a break, so can you. Where did this concept come from that says you have to brag about how hard you work and how many hours you put in? The key to prolonged runs of work is to love it, because loving what you do energizes you. If you work forty hours a week from the age of twenty until you're sixty-five—

. . . and on the seventh day, God rested.

— Genesis

excluding two weeks of vacation every year—you'll work 90,000 hours over your lifetime. If you don't love what you're doing, that's a waste of a lot of life. Even if your work is regenerative, it's still vital to your wellbeing to have a breather at least weekly—running yourself into the ground is not a healthy approach to a joyous, abundant life.

Labor Day was first celebrated in the U.S. and Canada in the 1880s and became a national holiday in 1894. What's interesting is that it has now turned into a major shopping day. Does it seem rational that many employees find themselves working harder and longer hours on a day that's supposed to honor the work force? If you find yourself shopping on Labor Day, remember to pause and say thank you to those who are serving you.

SPIRITUAL CONTEMPLATION: Commit some of this day to an extended period of not doing, just being in the recharge mode.

AFFIRMATION: I am worthy and entitled to continual replenishing times in my day, week, and life!

Resistance and Creativity

Resistance is usually based on fear, the need for control, or the belief that our expectations are not going to be met. We can't believe that we are capable of doing or having what our inner knowing is telling us, so we procrastinate or simply avoid doing what needs to be done. These are all forms of resistance.

The habit of resistance closes you down and shuts off the flow, which means you get more of what you don't want and less of what you do. Resistance results in less creativity and abundance in your life. But by letting go of your fear and moving through the resistance, you begin to get a different result. Become a martial arts master in your own life and flow with what is, while trusting your inner wisdom to move you in the right direction.

Resistance is experienced as fear; the degree of fear equates to the strength of Resistance. Therefore the more fear we feel about a specific enterprise, the more certain we can be that that enterprise is important to us and to the growth of our soul. That's why we feel so much Resistance. If it meant nothing to us, there'd be no Resistance.

— Steven Pressfield

SPIRITUAL CONTEMPLATION: What are you in resistance to that you know is exactly the thing you need to be doing?

AFFIRMATION: I am willing to allow life to flow and to move through my resistance.

September 7
Got to Do Something with It

The pictures in a cookbook may look delicious but they don't satisfy the hunger. It doesn't matter if there are five hundred easy-to-follow, step-by-step recipes, unless you actually follow them and cook, you starve. Likewise, you can read all the spiritual books from your local bookstore, quote the hippest philosophers of the day, and be enrolled in the best spiritual classes money can buy, but unless you apply the principles they won't satisfy the hunger of your soul. Whether it's a taste-bud-tantalizing picture or an inspirational spirit-rousing message, it doesn't do you any good unless you do something with the information.

I have learned over the years that when one's mind is made up, this diminishes fear; knowing what must be done does away with fear.

— Rosa Parks

Sometimes it may take a few attempts to get what's on your plate to look like the picture in the book. And it may take some practice to find the nirvana your teachers or facilitators are pointing to. But don't quit in frustration before tasting the delights of your recipes for life. What good is it to have drawers full of spices you never use or shelves filled with books that have no relevance? To walk the talk and not just talk the talk, you have to be willing to make a bit of a mess in your exploration to make the potential become real for you.

SPIRITUAL CONTEMPLATION: What spiritual principles would you like to take off the shelf and put into greater practice so as to demonstrate a more delicious expression of life?

AFFIRMATION: I am able to manifest the pictures of my consciousness!

Whose Fiction?

It's interesting that the story of the West with its romanticized stereotypes of bad guys and good guys was actually developed back East by the book *The Virginian*. Even today its western notions form much of the storytelling about the West. Fortunately, however, some folks chronicled the real story in their memoirs. Books like *Letters from a Woman Homesteader* capture the brutal realities of the western frontier—the loneliness, fear, death, sickness, alcoholism, suicide, psychological struggles, physical abuse, and the brutal removal of the Native Americans from their ancestral land. But not many people wanted to read stories that contradicted the romanticized depiction of the western cowboy, so the true stories became shadows of the fiction that became the reality.

> *Words are like bullets; if they escape, you can't catch them again.*
> — African Proverb

Do you have a reality that isn't really the truth? Do you romanticize an aspect of your life so you can convince others of the story you want them to see while other unattractive actions lurk in the shadows? You might feel alone and abused by life, but you tell an entirely different story to the world, and your friends embellish and perpetuate this heroic version of your life. While it's nice to have the mythical story told, your truth is what will touch people's hearts and make a difference. It's time for your truth to be told. Tell the truth and be seen as a perfect expression of Spirit.

SPIRITUAL CONTEMPLATION: What have you romanticized about your life that is covering your true struggle?

AFFIRMATION: I come from my heart in sharing my truth!

September 9
Trust Is a Choice

Living in trust is much easier than distrust. Believing that the world is for you is a lot simpler than thinking it's conspiring against you. Trust can be difficult, or it can be comforting. It can feel like you're in midair clutching desperately onto a trapeze, or it can feel like you're lying in a hammock that cradles your body softly and securely as you swing above the ground. You can rest in your trust, or you can struggle to hold on to it. Either way, trust is not about being unwise—as it's said, "Trust everyone, but cut the cards." Keeping your eyes wide open doesn't make you any more or less trusting. It just makes you more observant of what is going on around you.

All I have seen teaches me to trust the creator for all I have not seen.

— Ralph Waldo Emerson

How you approach life impacts your experience. Trust that you're eternally supported as you bring forth the revelation of your Spiritual Wholeness, your Abundant Good, God as you. Trust that everything you will ever need is already within you. Choose to feel the comfort of knowing you are wrapped in the ever-loving embrace of Spirit, and that your inheritance has already been given to you and contains all you'll ever need or desire. Then the Divine that appears in your world will provide abundantly in areas near and dear to your heart.

SPIRITUAL CONTEMPLATION: Where are you struggling with trust? With whom could a courageous conversation bring the clarity you are looking for so you can rest in the truth? What action needs to be taken in order for the next piece of your unfolding situation to reveal valuable insight? Or do you need to just rest in the nonaction, trusting in God's action moving in your life?

AFFIRMATION: I trust in God expressing as my life.

Do You Need It All Right
Before It's All Right?

Tired of playing it safe? Here's an inside tip: Everything you do will give you valuable insight to activate the personal power within you. Honoring the creative urge will open you to so much more than staying closed for protection. If you want to be creative, you've got be willing to explore beyond where you've been. Experiencing what you've got and how it plays out in the world is the best teacher you will ever have. You

If you want a happy ending,
that depends, of course,
on where you stop your story.
— Orson Welles

might flub up and fall down but you'll get up, dust off, and learn how to take off for the sky.

Having it all right before it's all right will just keep you grounded. You'll find reasons for not wanting to proceed, but you'll transcend them only when you're in the sky and not on the ground. Every time you allow the creative urge to emerge, it will take you where you need to go. You have to launch from where you are rather than from where you wish you were because you're not there yet—but that's where you're headed. Can you surrender what you hold to be true and choose a newer truth that will set you soaring? The question comes down to whether you're willing to stop playing it safe and instead bring forth your creative urge without self-judgment.

SPIRITUAL CONTEMPLATION: How do you need to have it all perfect before you proceed? What action can you launch now that might move you in a direction that honors your creative urge to express?

AFFIRMATION: I trust life enough to proceed before I know the outcome!

9/11

September 11, 2001, changed America. The new cultural meme that was cast united the hearts of the country in compassion and divided our minds as to what a rational response looks like. Life was never again the same. We were aligned in shock, but rather than terror and fear prevailing because of that day, love awakened. For a moment there was a planetary outpouring of caring that was felt globally and can never be forgotten. Sometimes when a tragedy hits, it's easy to forget there is a choice as to how to perceive the circumstances other than what the majority is feeding you.

No day shall erase you from the memory of time.

— Virgil

If you can move beyond the initial knee-jerk response that attempts to understand why this happened, you will realize that a greater possibility beyond the pain is possible. Life will do what is necessary to get your attention. Often similar, but louder events will repeat their pounding until it is understood and embraced. Whether individually or planetarily, a balance will return. So as you remember the happenings of the day and all of the lives lost, may insightful gifts of higher understanding beyond a one-sided perspective emerge in your awareness.

SPIRITUAL CONTEMPLATION: If two separate symbolic towers in your life had to collapse in order for a single new expression to emerge from the ashes, what two distinctive and separate positions in your life would come down in order for something greater to appear? An example would be like the distinction between the spiritual and the physical being. They are both distinctively separate yet both positions give way to the understanding that spirit and form are one.

AFFIRMATION: I move beyond my single-sided position to understand beyond my comfort level!

May Peace Prevail on Earth!

YOU are an agent of peace. Your words, actions, and presence make a difference. Every time you do not react, but stand in peace and act as a benevolent presence in the midst of chaos or turmoil—you are an agent of peace. Let us join together and BE the peace we want to see in the world!

In honor of those who have given their lives in service,
*   may we have peace.*
In memory of those innocent lives that have been lost,
*   may we pray peace into reality.*
In compassion for those still driven by fear, hate, or greed,
*   may peace awaken their hearts.*
In support of those who work tirelessly for peace and justice,
*   may our prayers make a difference.*
In solidarity with all life, all beings, all people,
*   may we be people of peace.*
May peace prevail on earth, and may it begin with me.

— Petra Weldes

SPIRITUAL CONTEMPLATION: How are you participating in bringing about more peace in the world?

AFFIRMATION: I am peace. I live peace. I bring peace into every situation.

September 13
Strength-Giving Obstacles

Without the resistance of air, an airplane couldn't fly; it would fall out of the sky. It's the resistance of water on the propeller of the boat that propels a boat. If your life were obstacle-free, would you have any traction for forward movement? Obstacles are opportunities for success. Without the dynamics of circumstances, creative tension wouldn't be called into action. Without the desire to move fast, we would not have developed the combustible engine. Without the need for swifter communication, there wouldn't have been computers. Without exile, the world would not know the spiritual leadership of His Holiness the Dalai Lama. The purpose of the obstacle is to call forth from within you that which is greater than that which is in this world.

If you want the rainbow, you gotta put up with the rain.
— Dolly Parton

Your difficulties may stop you momentarily but you are the only one who can stop yourself permanently. Who you are is more important than the difficulty at hand. The circumstance may appear bigger or smaller depending on the consciousness of the one experiencing it. It is the magnitude of consciousness that allows some to come through their financial challenges or life-threatening illness while others don't. There is no large or small in the mind of God.

SPIRITUAL CONTEMPLATION: What difficulties are you facing that have you feeling like throwing your hands up and saying, "Forget it"? Go within and find that inner strength that knows it's greater than anything you are facing and call it into action in your life.

AFFIRMATION: That which is within me is greater than that which is in the world!

Antiquing

When you walk into an old antique store, you can sense stories and histories both rich and sad. As you pick up an item, you can feel your soul's curiosity as to its history and how it ended up here. If it's an authentic antique, it carries with it an emerging story and beckons you to be part of its history.

Like an antique shop, your subconscious is a storehouse of all your history, and is just waiting for you to discover the lost treasures of your soul. These rich and worthy memories of blessed times can enrich you with gifts of strength and courage. Dust off those noble aspects of yourself that somehow went by the wayside and now sit dust-covered in a

> *Remember that the most valuable antiques are dear old friends.*
> — H. Jackson Brown Jr.

corner. Go on an inner exploratory adventure to unearth the rich aspects of who you are that have long been cast off and forgotten. They are just beneath the surface when you begin to poke around. Remember the stories of times gone by that have blessed who you are in this world, and spend some time in memory of your heart with some good old friends. Remember how blessed your life has been and how the now reflects your beautiful history.

SPIRITUAL CONTEMPLATION: Dust off some memories you haven't visited in a while and allow your spirit to go on a recollecting journey. Have any of your soul lessons from that time been forgotten? Is it time to remember them now?

AFFIRMATION: I wisely incorporate the gifts and lessons of life!

September 15
Repeating Your Lessons

A bush pilot flew two hunters into the Alaskan wilderness where they each managed to down a big bull moose. As they loaded up the plane, the pilot explained they had room for only one moose if they also wanted to take all their gear. The hunters objected vehemently, saying that their pilot the previous year had let them take two moose on the same size plane.

When you try to do things, and they will not go the way you want, leave them alone.

— White Eagle

The pilot's ego got bagged and not wanting to be outdone, he acquiesced. Naturally the little plane couldn't handle the load and eventually crashed in the desolate forest. Fortunately the three men survived. As the pilot assessed the plane's damage, one hunter asked the other if he had any idea where they were. "I dunno," he replied, "but I think we must be pretty close to where we crashed last year, don't ya think?"

How many times do you need to repeat your lessons before you get them? What aren't you paying attention to? A higher consciousness requires humility in order to progress. Since Spirit's thoughts aren't your thoughts, entering new territory requires taking the next step from where you are. But if you're busy repeating patterns, you'll just circle and crash in relatively the same place time and time again. Give up your old thoughts and positions and accept the higher possibilities that are emerging. Then you can apply the guidance into action.

SPIRITUAL CONTEMPLATION: What lesson keeps showing up for you with the same disastrous ending? What guidance aren't you adhering to? What might you do differently and get a different result?

AFFIRMATION: I follow Spirit's guidance to glorious new results!

Divine Filters

One day an old woodworker went to his garage to find his favorite chisel. After some time of being unable to find it, he began to suspect that his neighbor's kid had swiped it. After all, he was always hanging around and interested in his carvings. After more thought he became certain it was the kid, especially since the kid acted increasingly more uneasy and nervous around the old man. One day, however, the woodworker discovered that the chisel set had somehow been knocked over and had been behind the shop table the whole time. The magical part of this story is that the kid no longer seemed nervous and uneasy after the woodworker realized that his suspicions were unfounded.

Who you are speaks so loudly I can't hear what you're saying
— Ralph Waldo Emerson

Your mind is a powerful filter and all you perceive must go through the filters of your consciousness. Your attitudes and assumptions about the ones you are with are felt long before you open your mouth. Your true attitude about God is reflected beyond what words you prophesize. It is your desire for something more that creates a sense of separation or leads to the thought that you can be satisfied with something other than the Divine. Let your only desire be to know God, particularly in situations that are pulling you to less than Divine filters of seeing life.

SPIRITUAL CONTEMPLATION: How in the past have you allowed your judgments to get in the way of the truth? How did it feel when the truth was revealed to be contrary to what you believed? Where are you now allowing life's situations to pull you from seeing through Divine Filters?

AFFIRMATION: I am seeing through Divine Filters!

September 17
Already There

A young man once came across a mighty river as he journeyed home. Stunned at its expanse, he stood on its banks and looked across with focused contemplation as to how to cross it. For half of a day he wandered up and down the riverbank attempting to find a way across. Just as he was about to give up,

The grass is always greener
on the other side.

— Proverb

he saw a wise-looking man sitting quietly on the other side. In haste, he shouted, "Oh wise one, can you tell me how to get to the other side of the river?" The wise one contemplated his knotted hands for a while before looking up and down the riverbank and responding. "My child, you are on the other side."

Perspective is a powerful spiritual tool. What if you are already on the other side of your issue but you just don't realize it? Are you one who paces the banks of consciousness ruminating endlessly on your perplexing issue until you've exhausted yourself, only to find that when you give up the battle of the anxiety, the concern has dissolved? What side of the matter do you want to be on—the one of struggle or the one of ease? The perspective is yours for the choosing.

SPIRITUAL CONTEMPLATION: Are there any wide and expansive crossings you are looking at? What if you were on the other side already—what would that mean to your issue at hand?

AFFIRMATION: I realize I am where I need to be!

Your Life Is Your Masterpiece

Don't quit! Don't take no for an answer. Don't let yourself get sidetracked because the first or second thing didn't work out. Stay focused on your destination, even if it takes time. Stay focused on creating the life of your dreams. Stay focused on the spiritual principles and practices that move you into a deeply connected and creative life.

What would it be like if you lived each day, each breath, as a work of art in progress? Imagine that you are a Masterpiece unfolding, every second of every day, a work of art taking form with every breath.

— Thomas Crum

Step out in faith, with determination and persistence. Keep trying new colors and textures as you paint on the canvas of your life. Listen to the song that is singing in your veins and the tune that is whispering on your breath. Trust that the Universe is rearranging everything in your favor, no matter how long it takes! Your life is your masterpiece. Get lost in the process and enjoy being with yourself.

SPIRITUAL CONTEMPLATION: If I live my life as a masterpiece, a work of art I'm creating every day, how might I do and be differently?

AFFIRMATION: I am creating a work of art with my life. It is my gift to God.

September 19
Walk Your Own Path

I love reading new books. I love hearing about new authors and new spiritual places and new techniques for spiritual and personal healing. There is great inspiration in learning about other people's walk and how they got where they are in their spiritual development. Sometimes however, it seems like spirituality becomes a fad, and we have to get on the bandwagon of the next great idea. Occasionally I even feel judged if I don't take the same supplement, go to the same "healer," or do a certain type of practice.

No one saves us but ourselves.
No one can and no one may.
We ourselves must walk the path.
— Buddha

What I've noticed is that it's easy to be influenced by someone else's way of living a spiritual life. It's easy to think if you do it just the way "they" did, you'll reach enlightenment. But your path is your own. You cannot walk someone else's. The Universe is so infinite and so creative that there are countless paths to the Divine. Allow your own revelations to provide direction and inspiration. This is Spirit's illumination in your life. TRUST your own Divine Intuition.

SPIRITUAL CONTEMPLATION: Where are you following a spiritual fad? What does your inner guidance show you as your primary spiritual path?

AFFIRMATION: I walk my own Spiritual Path with God. I invite inspiration from others and my own inner light to illuminate my way.

Recharged

As the long lazy days of summer fade into memories and the sun fights with the winds of change, there is a lingering of what is to fortify you for what lies ahead. You returned from vacation recharged with the energy of newfound excitement for your daily doings. You found a truth within you greater than all that is in the outer world. With this realization has come a newfound freedom that is yours as a guest of this world.

As a guest of life, all has been provided for you including your food, clothes, and relationships. What you owe in return is to be the best conduit

The afternoon knows what the morning never suspected.
— Swedish Proverb

for life to flow through. In order to dwell harmoniously, an occasional adjustment to consciousness is necessary, and taking a break from the routine of the day is an ideal way to get your timing back in place. First adjust your consciousness, and then watch your conditions change naturally. The entire world doesn't need to be transformed; the illumined consciousness of just one person who returns recharged and renewed to his daily world will make a significant difference. And you are that person.

SPIRITUAL CONTEMPLATION: How has the thought of the drudgery of returning to your daily activity robbed your recharge? How can the newfound energy excite you about what you do?

AFFIRMATION: My spiritual recharge is lasting!

International Day of Peace

In 1981 the General Assembly of the United Nations passed World Peace Day—a day dedicated to world peace when all violence is to pause. On this day warring factions are asked to put down their weapons so people can breathe in the air of peace. On this day we educate our youth about peace. The day begins with the ringing of the peace bell at the United Nations headquarters. The bell, which is inscribed "Long live absolute world peace," was cast from coins donated from children around the world as a reminder of the human cost of war.

Peace cannot be achieved through violence, it can only be attained through understanding.

— Ralph Waldo Emerson

Take time in your heart to unite with and support those who suffer from the brutality of war today. Find ways in which you can stop any hostile emotions in your personal expression that might be adding to the collective consciousness of violence. Peace is essential for a foundation of progress and sustainability. The United Nations asks you to help commemorate this day through education and public awareness of issues relating to peace. It's everyone's responsibility to see that future generations do not suffer from the scourge of war during our lifetime. The journey to peace must be traveled together and you can be part of that now. We all have the right to peace.

SPIRITUAL CONTEMPLATION: Pause at noon today and contemplate what peace feels like on our planet and what it means to our human family!

AFFIRMATION: Today peace grows on the planet because of me!

Autumn Equinox

An equinox when the day and the night are of about equal duration occurs twice a year. The word *equinox* comes from two Latin words meaning equal and night. It's a time of balance before the night takes over and brings the coming winter. Although many may want to avoid the dark, if we desire to be in the light we must first face our inner darkness. Spirit is Omnipresent—as fully present on the dark half of the wheel as it is on the light. It's our cultural connotations that have put an out-of-balance onus on the concept of darkness.

He found himself wondering at times, especially in the autumn, about the wild lands, and strange visions of mountains that he had never seen came into his dreams.

— J. R. R. Tolkien

In the New Thought movement, many people would prefer to always skip around in the light of the endless summer, but autumn is the regenerative grounding that makes way for the birth of the eventual new light. Without rest, we would burn out. Without descent there is no ascent. The procession of equinoxes is a common story that has been symbolized throughout time to remind us of the role of darkness and light in creating movement through polarity. The Egyptians had Horus, the god of the sun, battling Seth, the god of darkness. Our ancestors knew the valuable part darkness played in one's evolution and did not superstitiously fear it or ignore it, but embraced it. In the spiritual work of transformation, all things must die before they can be reborn.

SPIRITUAL CONTEMPLATION: Prepare yourself for some hibernation and slumbering this fall. Honor your regenerative time; be willing to go within for a while without guilt or fear.

AFFIRMATION: I welcome the quiet cycle of my life!

Creativity and Spirituality

The creative process and the spiritual path have much in common. Just as the best novelists create their characters from themselves and their plots from personal experiences, Life is constantly preparing you to walk your spiritual path. All that you experience today has its place of value in your tomorrows. Trusting what is before you is perfect preparation for life's coming attractions. Look back and see how far you've come! See how your past has forged you into who you are today. Relax into your Divine Guidance, knowing that tomorrow will be even better!

Every artist dips his brush in his own soul, and paints his own nature into his pictures.

— Henry Ward Beecher

SPIRITUAL CONTEMPLATION: What from your past has provided the most mileage on your spiritual journey? How are you creatively using your past to grow a better future?

AFFIRMATION: I create a joyous future from the things I learn and experience today. I see my past as part of the process of growing. I release all judgment about where I've come from or what I've gone through.

Creating Grooves of Abundance Thinking

All those nasty old ideas that we took on from our families became habitual ways of thinking because we heard the same things said or implied so many times that the ideas became etched into our consciousness. These old habits of thinking were created by negative mantras: "You're stupid," "You can't trust anyone," "Life is hard."

Affirmations, on the other hand, are powerful, positive mantras that can build new grooves in our consciousness and create new habits of thinking. Every time your thoughts get caught in the groove of "not enough," say your favorite mantra (positive affirmation) instead. "There's always enough in God!" or "Somehow, I always have enough, no matter what." But don't say them just once or twice—say them repeatedly so that a new groove is worn in your brain, a new pathway of thought.

> *As a single footstep will not make a path on the earth, so a single thought will not make a pathway in the mind. To make a deep physical path, we walk again and again. To make a deep mental path, we must think over and over the kind of thoughts we wish to dominate our lives.*
>
> — Wilfred Arlan Peterson

When you change your thinking, you change your life. Change your consciousness, the habits of thought, and the Universe instantly begins to support that new way. A new consciousness is the most powerful creative force in the world.

SPIRITUAL CONTEMPLATION: What are your most cherished, habitual limiting grooves of thought? Create a new mantra instead, just five to seven words that you can memorize and repeat constantly for days on end.

AFFIRMATION: I am one with God! I am completely Abundant!

What Slide Are You Looking Through?

One of my favorite teaching analogies to illustrate how we co-create our life with the Universe is to imagine that we are like a slide projector. When we plug our projector into an inexhaustible source, the light is pure and without form. It's the slide that determines what colors and shapes will be shown on the screen of life. We can put in any kind of slide we want—any color, almost any topic, even a black one. The light will project our slide no matter what we choose.

Life is a train of moods like a string of beads, and, as we pass through them, they prove to be many-colored lenses which paint the world their own hue, and each shows only what lies in its own focus.

— Ralph Waldo Emerson

What if you were to put in a slide of Abundance, or a slide of beauty that's tinged with joy and steeped in love? You decide the color and texture of your slides, so pay attention to which ones you choose. Notice how the world looks now.

SPIRITUAL CONTEMPLATION: What's in your slide projector? Are you looking through the lens of fear, the filters of your past, or the picture of the way things "should" be, but aren't? Are you taking charge of your slide projector?

AFFIRMATION: I choose to view life through the lens of Joy and Abundance. I choose to project onto the screen of my life only those things in alignment with Spiritual Truth!

Creativity Begins with Seeing

When we were looking for a new place for our Center, we saw various buildings that might suit our needs but needed remodeling. The last one in particular really caught my eye and imagination. I could visualize the sanctuary and fellowship hall and classrooms for both kids and adults. The others with me saw something completely different, however. They saw a dirty space that had been vacant and accumulating junk and mess for five years. One man's comment was, "I can't imagine how this would work!" But I could . . . and we now have an amazingly perfect place we call our spiritual home!

> *A rock pile ceases to be a rock pile the moment a single man contemplates it, bearing within him the image of a cathedral.*
>
> — Antoine de Saint-Exupéry

What you see is what the Universe sees through your eyes. In every situation, there is something that can be done. Look for the glimmer of hope, the ray of possibility, or the moment of opening, and you will see with different eyes. Even if you don't recognize it right away, know that it is there. It may not seem to be what you are looking for, but without examining the possibilities, you may pass the perfect opportunity by. As you truly see it, you take the first step in your creative process. Then the Universe gets busy creating your reality with you!

SPIRITUAL CONTEMPLATION: When have you seen the completed project even before you started? When have you focused more on what wouldn't work instead?

AFFIRMATION: I co-create my life with the Universe by seeing possibilities and opportunities everywhere. I am creative and open to new ideas and new ways of seeing.

September 27
Focus on "What," Not "How"

"But I don't know how it's going to work out" is one of the most common complaints I hear when I do spiritual coaching. We all want to know the *how* because we think if we know how, then we can fully relax and trust that it will. Often, people don't know what they want and are waiting for the Universe to do something for them. But this is exactly backwards. Our job is to give the Universal Law clear directions by providing the *what* that we want to experience— more abundance, a better relationship, a closer walk with God. Once we've stated the what, the Divine Law knows the how. That's its job. It makes and creates the entire Universe. Surely if this Law knows how to grow babies and giant sequoias and quasars, it knows how to create what you have intended. This is the power of Divine Law.

The term Divine Law is synonymous with the Universal Subjective Law. It is never self-knowing, though it is always self-doing. It knows how to do, but not what it is doing. The soil knows how to grow corn, but not that it is growing corn.

— Ernest Holmes

The Infinite Intelligence of the Universe really does know how to manifest and grow things. Trying to figure out how just keeps you in your rational, egoic mind. Trusting in the Wisdom of Life, however, moves you into a deeper place of inner knowing. So plant the seed, nourish it with intention and faith, and allow it to grow under the guidance of the Divine Law. This is the powerful and joyous way to live.

SPIRITUAL CONTEMPLATION: Where are you blocking your abundance by worrying about "how" it could happen? Have you clearly stated and intended "what" you want to demonstrate?

AFFIRMATION: I confidently declare what I want, knowing that the Divine Law is completely able to manage how to do it. I trust the Universe! I trust Spirit! I trust Divine Law!

Hey, Where Was the Sign?

They've been working on the major highway in my part of town for almost five years now. Although it's been an amazing engineering feat to watch, there also have been lots of lane closures, rerouting, and detours. One day the exit I usually take was in such a different place, I missed it completely—even though I've been using this road for years. I've taken wrong turns, wrong exits, and gotten trapped in one of those "you can't get there from here" loops. I try to follow the signs, but they just aren't always as clear as I'd like. Yet, if I'm paying attention, they are always there.

> *Life is one big road with lots of signs. So when you riding through the ruts, don't complicate your mind. . . . Wake Up and Live!*
> — Bob Marley

Isn't that just like our life? It'd be good if life came with flashing neon arrows that said, "Go this way" or "Stop!" because sometimes the signs seem very small and obscure, and far apart. But they are there if we're paying attention. Sometimes the road tests our faith, and staying the course, especially when we haven't had a sign in a while, can be an act of sheer courage. That's when we need to trust our intuition, follow our direction, and rely on the Guidance of Spirit. We'll know what we need to know, when we need to know it, as we progress down the road of abundance, freedom, and prosperity.

SPIRITUAL CONTEMPLATION: Are you still looking for or waiting for a sign? Could there have been one that you didn't pay attention to?

AFFIRMATION: I pay attention to the signs that Spirit puts along my road. I walk my journey with faith and confidence.

Lessons from Handball

An elementary school playground game called handball teaches kids that the ball returns at the same speed with which it hit the wall. Whether it's hit hard or soft or sliced close to the ground, the ball will return at the same force with which it's hit. The game of handball demonstrates the law in physics that says to every action there is an equal reaction.

For every action, there is an equal and opposite reaction.

— Newton's Law of Motion

This same law is valid for human interactions as well, for when you project anger to those around you, you'll be met with anger in return. If you show generosity to the world, you'll find the world is a very giving place. If what is emanating from your countenance is love, your life will be filled with caring, loving individuals. If you create drama in your life, then your life will give you stories to tell. There is no judgment here—just the inevitable outcome of your consciousness. Change the energy you send out to the cosmic wall, and that change will come back. Play with this dependable return, and practice until you have mastered this game in life.

SPIRITUAL CONTEMPLATION: What's coming into your life that you no longer want? Practice some new energetic send-outs and make the adjustment to your game in order to get the return you are looking for.

AFFIRMATION: I am grateful for the dependability of life that returns what I send out!

If you were to look at your life from a detached observer's perspective, would you find that what you've thought was acceptable isn't really acceptable at all? Have you been putting up with something that depletes rather than enhances? Sometimes a situation is like a leaky faucet whose slow drip gains momentum without your noticing it until a friend asks why you can't turn it off. Or like those gasoline prices that sneak up, up, up, until they hit an unacceptable plateau.

Error is acceptable as long as we are young; but one must not drag it along into old age.

— Johann Wolfgang von Goethe

Is your abundant flow where you would like it? Is your relationship juicy and passionate, filled with mutual support and intimacy, or could it use a bit more attention? Have you given up caring and turned off your desire for a richer experience, and just accepted that this is the way it is? No, that's not the way it is—it's the way you are. You may want things to be different on the outside, but not until you're different on the inside will the outside change. Your internal dialogue that's looping in your subjective keeps you willing to accept mediocrity. Bring awareness to what's no longer acceptable and enhance your inner dialogue by knowing you are worthy and anointed. The time is now. But caution—do this only if you want to enjoy your life more.

SPIRITUAL CONTEMPLATION: Take some quiet time to observe your life from a detached observer's perspective and notice where your life is working well. Now, notice where you accepted things that aren't working as well as your heart would desire because you believed that was just the way they were going to show up in your life. Cancel that level of acceptance and upgrade your creation story.

AFFIRMATION: I am loving all areas of my life!

October

Claiming Abundance

Infinite Abundance

One of my favorite places to camp is in La Push on the wild Washington State coast. The waves are enormous and bring huge logs from Japan or Alaska and wash them up on the beach as if they were mere twigs. When I hike out onto the rocky headlands, I can see the water stretch to the horizon where the blurring of sea and sky invites the idea of infinity. This is how I often imagine the Divine Reality—as a vast, infinite ocean upon which the waves of life play over the surface.

We live in this Abundant Ocean, this Infinite Reality, which is the source of all Life and all Creation. What we see is but the tip of the iceberg. The rest lies below the surface of the world of appearances. Do not be fooled by the storms and waves of life. That which lies beneath is so much more–vast, rich, and deep. Know that you are forever lifted and supported by this Abundant Ocean. This is something you can count on!

> *The truth is that we live in a lavish and abundant universe, in which everything we could ever want or need can be and will be provided to us.*
> — Edwene Gaines

SPIRITUAL CONTEMPLATION: What does imagining the Divine Reality as a vast, infinite ocean teach you about the reality of life and its limitless abundance?

AFFIRMATION: I live immersed in an infinite ocean of Life, Abundance, Love, and Joy!

October 2
Practicing Infinity

See Infinity in the leaves on a tree, in the grains of sand on the beach, in the measureless expanse of space. This same limitless Infinity is true about your life. Release any belief that limits you or others. Court the limitless in your life. Practice Infinity!

In the demonstration of abundance, we seek to realize the liberty of the Sons of God—the freedom whereby God proves His absoluteness. This is done, not by meditation upon limitation, but by contemplating plenty, abundance, success, prosperity and happiness.
— Ernest Holmes

SPIRITUAL CONTEMPLATION: Contemplate all the ways you can see and experience Infinity. Expand your ability to embrace the notion even if your mind can't quite imagine it.

AFFIRMATION: I live in an Infinite and Limitless Universe!

Rosh Hashanah, which means "head of the year," is the first of the Days of Awe—the high holy days in Judaism. Known also as Yom Teruah or the Feast of Trumpets, the sound of the shofar blast reminds people of the importance of reflection during this important two-day celebration of the anniversary of Adam and Eve's creation. It's a time to examine one's life and ask for forgiveness, "teshuvah," for any wrongdoings, to make amends with others, and set an intentional plan to be a better person in the coming year.

> *May you be inscribed and sealed for a good year.*
> — High Holiday greeting

Because this is when God's book is opened and it will be determined whether you will live or die this year, one looks for God's compassion to accept the prayers of forgiveness. People often greet one another with, "May you be inscribed in the book of life and sealed for a good year." Whether you believe in an outside judge—or in self-review and self-forgiveness—it's powerful to know that the new year before you is blessed. Let the heaviness of your mistakes go, and proclaim in your heart and soul your intention to be a better expression of Spirit. May you then hear the trumpets triumphing your proclamation, which has sealed your good in your heart.

SPIRITUAL CONTEMPLATION: When have your behavior and expression been different from what your heart wished you had expressed? Forgive yourself, make amends (if appropriate) with others, and declare your intention to be a better expression of the Divine. Let this vision be sealed in your heart and lived as your life.

AFFIRMATION: I am free to express the higher vision of me!

October 4
It's Been There All Along

Has a friend ever asked you to go into another room and get a book for her? You walk in there with the best intentions, but you don't see it anywhere. You look on the coffee table, the shelves, and search from ceiling to floor only to return to say you couldn't find it.

People only see what they are prepared to see.

— Ralph Waldo Emerson

She sighs loudly, walks into the other room, points to the table and says, "It's right here." You swear you didn't see it, but your friend easily found it because she knew exactly what she was looking for and believed it was there. It was there the whole time, of course, but you didn't see it simply because you didn't believe it was there.

Is your abundance here? You bet it is! It's just a matter of believing it to see it. Your belief controls what you see. You are an ambassador of abundance ushering into form all that you believe is possible. You can choose to think in ways that help you spot and create abundant success instead of missing what's right in front of you. You will find ways to take the necessary action to support that which you see as possible. The strugglers in the world believe life happens *to* them rather than realizing that they are the creators of their experience.

SPIRITUAL CONTEMPLATION: Where do you believe life is happening to you and you don't see other options? If you were to see other possibilities what would you like to see?

AFFIRMATION: I am seeing as God sees!

Life Begins Today

I was in junior high school the first time I heard the phrase, "Today is the first day of the rest of your life." I noticed that for some people this saying became a bit of a platitude, like "Have a nice day," and it lost its deeper meaning. For me, however, it was a clarion wake-up call! Each day is the only day that I can live my life. If I keep waiting for something to happen or change, I could be waiting a long time. This belief has been a cornerstone of my journey in this lifetime, and it has kept me awake to my choices in ways nothing else ever has.

For the past 33 years, I have looked in the mirror every morning and asked myself: "If today were the last day of my life, would I want to do what I am about to do today?" And whenever the answer has been "No" for too many days in a row, I know I need to change something.

— Steve Jobs

"Someday" is today! Today your ship comes in and your life begins. Today you are living in the Light of Truth, the Love of God, and the Infinite Abundant Reality. Don't postpone your well-being until sometime in the future. It is NOW. Practice believing it, accepting it, and trusting it! Claim your good today—now!

SPIRITUAL CONTEMPLATION: "When I . . . then I . . ." keeps you in the future, not the present. Where are you living this out in your life?

AFFIRMATION: My life starts TODAY! I choose my life TODAY! I live a spiritually grounded life TODAY!

October 6
Freedom to Dream

A few years ago I went on a three-month sabbatical in Europe, traipsing around my favorite places and exploring new ones in five different countries. When I first decided to go I wondered how I was going to pay for the whole thing. I was anxious about saving money and how I could go as cheaply as possible. Then I remembered that I live in an abundant universe and Spirit supports my creative dreams. I got up my courage to ask for the money to support my dream of a sabbatical in Europe, and I received so much support that I was able to go where I wanted and do what I wanted without having to worry about money. That is freedom!

If one advances confidently in the direction of his dreams, and endeavors to live the life which he has imagined, he will meet with a success unexpected in common hours.

— Henry David Thoreau

We are free to live the life of our dreams. Money is one of the things that give us freedom. Financial freedom allows us to do more than just pay our bills—it allows us to imagine the life of our dreams and contribute in meaningful ways while expressing our joy and love. Financial freedom comes from knowing that we are completely supported by the infinite blessings of abundance surrounding us right now.

SPIRITUAL CONTEMPLATION: What are you not doing, what dream aren't you following because you don't believe you have the money to do it? How might you begin if you knew the Abundant universe supported you?

AFFIRMATION: I have the financial freedom to follow my dreams! Spirit supports me in every way!

Simple Indulgence

Do you feel guilty about a midafternoon rendezvous with a novel, followed by a nap? Do your e-mail and to-do list whine when you take a moment to recharge? Can you swing from hyperactive to luxuriating without concern that the universe will fall apart without you? When was the last time you took a midday stroll and put all demands on hold just to go and recharge? Exercise is important for your body, but so is a pause from "doing-ness." Let go of what you are attempting to make happen for a while. It may just be what creates the opening for the magic of life to happen.

> *The problem with people who have no vices is that generally you can be pretty sure they're going to have some pretty annoying virtues.*
>
> — Elizabeth Taylor

You lose much value in your life if you deplete your sense of freedom. Whether it's in your world or your head, what have you allowed to chain you to a work ethic that denies you your right to move around as a free person? What underlying beliefs keep you from enjoying simple moments of pleasure in your life? Close your eyes, open your ears, and let God in. You just might find yourself strolling along the beach in the middle of the week smiling from ear to ear as you reconnect with a dear friend you haven't been with for way too long because your plate's been full. How could this time-out be anything but a Divine blessing to you?

SPIRITUAL CONTEMPLATION: Find a simple indulgence and enjoy it.

AFFIRMATION: I say yes to that which nurtures my soul.

Being a Receiver of Good

Where did we get the idea that it's spiritual to be poor? Some people say, "How can I feel good about having money when others have so little?" Really? What good can you do anyone by being broke? Who can you assist by being poor and just another mouth to feed? Not being able to support yourself doesn't feel good because it isn't good. Isn't it a greater blessing to be a masterful manifester of wealth, someone who can help those who are struggling and can give a gift that makes a difference?

Whatever we are waiting for— peace of mind, contentment, grace, the inner awareness of simple abundance—it will surely come to us, but only when we are ready to receive it with an open and grateful heart.

— Sarah Ban Breathnach

We've all heard that it's better to give than receive, but if you don't have anything to give, that's a moot point. Giving and receiving are both valuable and necessary, for if you're not receiving you can't be giving. Forget the concept that it's more spiritual to be poor. God is an abundant God and we live in a rich universe that is forever seeking to flow through us. So get on with being a receiver of good. The world awaits your contributions of the heart.

SPIRITUAL CONTEMPLATION: How have you denied someone the gift of being able to give to you? How did it make you feel when you attempted to give to someone and they turned down your offer? When have you seen the joy in someone's face when he gave you a gift?

AFFIRMATION: I am a good receiver!

Accepting Your Abundance

All you need is already available in consciousness from the very fabric of Being. There is enough and more than enough already! I remember the first time I heard this—my whole being leapt in agreement. Something within me knew that this was true. As I began working with this idea, I began demonstrating new and better relationships, financial prosperity, and joy in my life. And then all of a sudden I realized that it began to feel almost "too" good. I noticed that part of me was walking around waiting for the other shoe to drop, for something

> *The mold of your acceptance is the measure of your experience.*
> — Ernest Holmes

to go wrong. Really, could it be this good? It was stunning for me to realize that I believed I could experience only so much joy and love and prosperity before I worried that it was more than I deserved or could possibly have.

Learning to accept all my good was a powerful practice. It was easy for me to see that others could, even should, have wonderful, joyful, prosperous lives but somehow I left myself out. So I began working on simply accepting my good. Every time something wonderful came about or I felt a deep rush of gratitude, I would affirm "I accept my good!"

SPIRITUAL CONTEMPLATION: Are you having trouble accepting your good? When and how do you wait for the other shoe to drop?

AFFIRMATION: I accept my good! I accept my good! I accept my good!

Your Abundance Robs No One!

Sometimes we have an unconscious belief that it's more spiritual to be poor than wealthy. We might also believe there is only so much good to go around, and if we have all that we desire, somehow we are robbing others of their good. We know that in the physical universe things do, in fact, run out. But in the reality of the Infinite nothing can ever run out—there is always enough abundance, in whatever forms are available to us today, to fulfill each and every one of our needs and our inner desire to express a fulfilling life!

The kingdom of God is at hand. The riches, power, glory and might of this kingdom are yours today. You do not rob others by entering into the fullness of your kingdom of joy, your kingdom of abundance. But you must recognize that all people belong to the same kingdom. You merely claim for yourself what you want the Divine Spirit to do for everyone.

— Ernest Holmes

So go ahead, claim your good! Wake up and announce that you are heir to the Kingdom, and child of the Infinite Presence, deserving of all the Life, Joy, and Freedom you can imagine. Then know that this is true for each and every person on the planet. Let's claim it for everyone today!

SPIRITUAL CONTEMPLATION: When do you hold back, thinking you have to take from others in order to have your abundance? How often do you realize that everyone deserves and can have all the good you desire for yourself?

AFFIRMATION: I claim enough abundance for myself and for each and every person, right now, today! I know my good does not take away from anyone else. There is enough of Spirit to support and supply all of creation!

The Affluent Flow of Life

The key to receiving is being alert and available. Practice being a conduit for flow. How are you with what you have? Do you question how long your good is going to last before it runs out or the other shoe drops? What you want is a consciousness of believing this is just the beginning. This manifestation of good is a seed of the greater yet to be, for as you plant your good, more good grows for you. Let your actions reflect your level of trust in the ever-expanding universal good. If you withhold and pull your good out of circulation, its value diminishes. If you agonize about protecting what you've accumulated, you are not free. Abundance is freedom.

> *The biggest human temptation is to settle for too little.*
> — Thomas Merton

You want to be in the flow which is endless and everlasting. When you comprehend this, your anxiety simply dissolves. The joy of living is not in embracing what you have, but what you enjoy, and aliveness comes from being in the flow. What good is it to be so tight that you shut yourself off from what's fresh and vibrant? Let go of all resistance—loosen that grip, relax, and surrender to the affluent flow of Life. Make yourself available to the Divine currency that ever replenishes Itself as you.

SPIRITUAL CONTEMPLATION: Do you find yourself holding tight with concern of losing something, when what you really desire is the endless replenishment of your good? Try doing some seed planting of your good by giving some of what you value to someone else.

AFFIRMATION: I am now in the affluent flow of life!

Yom Kippur

Yom Kippur is the most important holy day of the Jewish year. It's the Day of Atonement when one atones for the mistakes of the past year. On Yom Kippur, it is said that the judgment is entered and sealed in God's book; therefore this is the last day to show in our heart the reconciliation between us and God. It's a day spent in prayer getting as close to Spirit as humanly possible. Imagine if we worked to heal transgressions, mistakes, and inappropriate expressions the moment we recognized them instead of waiting for a future resolution? What would our world look like if we spent time daily having closeness to our higher Power?

Who can say, "I have purified my heart, I am free of sin"? There is no man on earth so righteous that he never sins! Cast away the evil you have done and get yourself a new heart and a new spirit.
— Proverbs 20:9

Yom Kippur is a strong reminder to clean up our blunders and accept apologies that others offer us. What's more important—a vendetta kind of consciousness whose angst eats away and consumes our energy and inner real estate, or a clean space for the Divine to show up with new blessings to add to our expanding abundant good? The power of atonement is profound and life changing. Let it live in us all our days.

SPIRITUAL CONTEMPLATION: What do I need to heal in me that's creating a distance from God, thus keeping me from being a clearer expression of the Divine?

AFFIRMATION: God and I are one!

Flow Versus Fear

Love and fear simply cannot live in the same place at the same time. Fear is nothing more than negative faith, which is faith that something bad will happen. Recognizing that Love is present, that the Power and Wisdom of Spirit are always available, and that nothing is too big for God, this awareness casts out fear. Love is the faith that something good will happen.

Living in Abundance is more about where you are coming from than what material goods you have. Step into the abundant flow of the Universe and realize that your good is at hand. Trust Spirit to support you, and then notice all the many unexpected ways you are supported, guided, lifted, and loved. Do not let your fear stop you from moving in the direction of your abundance!

Affluence is about being in the flow. Fear creates constriction and contraction. Fear will be neutralized when you turn and face it, and see it for what it is. Courage allows you to face your fear and walk through it. Remember that you are supported, guided, and surrounded by the strength and wisdom of the Loving Power of Life Itself. Everything you need is at hand.

— Eric Butterworth

SPIRITUAL CONTEMPLATION: Where am I allowing fear to stop the flow of abundance?

AFFIRMATION: I do not let fear stop the flow of my Abundance. I allow love to open all the channels for the flow of abundance in my life!

October 14
Poverty and Spirituality

Ernest Holmes writes in *The Science of Mind* that "the word 'poverty' usually conveys to our minds the idea of a money shortage, but actually the word means the lack of any good thing. Poverty is the very antithesis of abundance, and abundance of good is necessary to human happiness. It is only as we experience good that God is expressed through us. The more completely we realize good—in all of its manifold expressions of health, wealth, and happiness—the more completely do we express God; that is, the more does God become personified through us."

Both prosperity and poverty are states of mind. If we desire to erase the thought of poverty we must go back to the thought of prosperity, an affirmation of the allness of Good, the source of which is God.

— Ernest Holmes

Too many of us as we become immersed in a spiritual path unconsciously take a "vow of poverty." Embedded in our cultural consciousness is this notion that you can't be rich and spiritual. Yet the Master Teacher reminds us that we are to have life and "have it more abundantly." Expressing our life in whatever form it takes is the way in which Spirit operates in the world. Being poor simply limits the Divine Expression. Vow to live from the Abundance of the Universe, to demonstrate prosperity in your life, and to share it every chance you get!

SPIRITUAL CONTEMPLATION: Do you believe that to be spiritual you have to be poor or turn your back on material enjoyment? What would be your "Vow of Prosperity" instead?

AFFIRMATION: I vow to receive, manage, and share my wealth as a joyous expression of Spirit's abundance!

Self-Discipline Is a Form of Freedom

There is such a paradox in the notion of discipline and freedom. In our instant gratification society, we chafe under the idea of disciplining ourselves. We think, somehow, that it means lack or limitation or deprivation. So we buy everything and anything we want, when we want it, thinking that this means we are "being abundant." The problem is that going into debt or using a credit card when we don't have the money to pay for something is living in an abundant future, not an abundant present. The result is that buying on credit creates debt in our present.

This burden of debt actually limits our feeling of abundance. Being disciplined with our money is good stewardship by using our resources wisely once they are in our hands. This does not mean that we limit what is coming in through all the many channels and ways the Universe supports us. It does mean we are thoughtful about it once we have it, not from fear, but from care. This creates a powerful opportunity for spiritual practice and spiritual discipline. The paradox is that the result of this discipline is true financial freedom! Now everything that comes in is available to use in the way we choose, not obligated to mountains of debt.

Self-discipline is a form of freedom. Freedom from laziness and lethargy, freedom from the expectations and demands of others, freedom from weakness and fear—and doubt. Self-discipline allows a pitcher to feel his individuality, his inner strength, his talent. He is master of, rather than a slave to, his thoughts and emotions.

— H. A. Dorfman

SPIRITUAL CONTEMPLATION: Do you feel financially free or burdened by debt? What causes you to go into debt?

AFFIRMATION: I live a free and abundant life! I am open to all the ways abundance flows into my life! I am a good steward over what I have. I am debt free!

Programming for Abundance

It's valuable to stop mistaking your stories for the truth. The physical realm is the printout of your awareness. It's no different from writing a letter on your laptop, hitting print, and having the printer reproduce what's on your screen. If you notice a mistake, correcting the printout isn't enough—you've got to change what's on the computer. Similarly, if there's something you don't like being printed out in your world, it's not about rearranging the players in your life but rather you must reprogram yourself. Your experience of abundance with ease and flow is defined by your programming more than by outer circumstances.

The key to abundance is meeting limited circumstances with unlimited thoughts.

— Marianne Williamson

Constricting circumstances that aren't deleted from your programming will strangle your intuition and inspiration for re-creation. Live by intent rather than default. You are more than a creature of conditions—you are a creator of conditions. Life is biased toward life. Whatever is life-affirming gets Life's flow. It's right to have your needs easily fulfilled and live in the affluent flow of abundance where your soul's yearnings are joyously and spontaneously met. The nice thing about your physical printout is that it's a direct demonstration of whether or not you've got your programming correct.

SPIRITUAL CONTEMPLATION: Take a look at your life's printout. Is there anything appearing in your life that feels wrong? Take your focus off attempting to shift things around in your outer world and correct the programming that is producing them in the first place.

AFFIRMATION: I am the conscious creator of all in my life and I program for abundant good!

Paying Attention

We know that whatever we pay attention to in our consciousness grows in our world of experience. This is how the Creative Process works. On the one hand, It takes the primary focus off our thoughts and feelings and uses this as the filter through which we see our life. So if our filter is one of debt, lack, and never enough, then no matter how much we have, it won't be enough. On the other hand, the Universal Law actually takes this sum total of our thoughts and feelings, and uses it as the mold from which it manifests our reality. So if our mold is one of "not enough," that is what will we continually experience.

> *Be thankful for what you have; you'll end up having more. If you concentrate on what you don't have, you will never, ever have enough.*
>
> — Oprah Winfrey

This Creative process can just as easily be used for our benefit and abundance, however. If we consistently focus our thinking and feeling on having enough, then this is not only the filter through which we see life, it actually becomes the mold from which our life is manifested.

SPIRITUAL CONTEMPLATION: What are you paying attention to today—enough or not enough? How is that manifesting in your life?

AFFIRMATION: I have enough because the Universe is an abundant place. I know this is true for myself and for each and every person.

October 18
The Monster Wasn't So Big

Not too long ago, my electric garage door stopped working. The repair company found more parts broken than I even knew a garage door had. Springs, pulleys, and pole needed replacement and rails needed adjustment, all for a significant amount of financial exchange. It worked perfectly for a few months—then it didn't. I'd press the remote only to have the door go up about a foot and come to a dead halt. I'd have to get out of the car, go inside, and press the opener on the wall to make it work. I did this for about a year because I'd lost the repair receipt and couldn't call the company and complain. Finally I called another company.

One resolution I have made, and try always to keep, is this: To rise above little things.
— John Burroughs

This repairman took a look and said the springs from the first company were technically correct, but because my door was heavier than most it needed larger ones. I was beginning to feel like it was a bait and switch and went into the house to take a breather from my rising frustration. But then the technician discovered that actually his company had done the original work almost twelve months prior and he would replace the springs for free.

For almost a year I had put up with inconvenience and hassle because of small thinking on my part. This is the kind of thinking that creates issues in life. You avoid what's before you as it becomes ever bigger in consciousness. Then when finally you deal with it, you find the monster wasn't so big after all. It was only your petty thinking that blew it out of proportion.

SPIRITUAL CONTEMPLATION: Where in your life do you have a petty annoyance you keep putting off? Wouldn't you get a good laugh at yourself if you found out it wasn't that big of a deal? Why don't you go find out and make that call to the repair person today?

AFFIRMATION: I now put my annoyances behind me!

Sourceful Surge

A brisk fall walk in the woods can leave your cheeks tingling from the cool air and everything brighter from all the fresh clean oxygen in your body and head—this is a great way to start a day with renewed energy. And although an invigorating jaunt through the pines is not always possible when you're in the midst of the city with honking cars instead of Canadian geese honking in the sky, you can still find respite. When you feel the pressure of the demands of the day, you can face them by taking a few moments to go within.

No matter where you are, you can start your day with an inner jaunt through your inner kingdom. Take the time to close your eyes to connect with

When you see a new trail, or footprint that you do not know, follow it to the point of knowing.

— Grandmother of Charles Eastman, Santee Sioux

the abundant blessings within. When you touch that something which is greater than your own interests, there is a sourceful surge that refreshes, revitalizes, and uplifts. Holding sacred the space within, it gracefully imparts that which is needed to those who are responsive to its flow. The Divine Presence has the power to provide you with all you need if you can just remember to take that stroll.

SPIRITUAL CONTEMPLATION: Notice how you feel, then take a walk outside today and check the difference after your stroll. Why don't you do this every day? Notice how you feel, take some time to meditate, and then check the difference after your stroll through your inner kingdom. Why don't you do this every day?

AFFIRMATION: I do what it takes to honor my time to walk with God today!

October 20
Go Big

Do you spend your time fishing for anchovies while at the same time the hundred-pound tuna are running? What do you miss out on because you're too busy thinking small? Isn't it time for you to proclaim that you're worth more than you're getting compensated for? Aside from the wasted energy on small rewards, in the end small goals are harder to land than the bigger ones anyway. Small clients bring their small-mindedness to the table and attempt to impose their limitations on you. Abundance doesn't show up by your being exhausted and overworked. No sir, it arrives when you're in your power and expanding.

Instead of lamenting your fate, create your world.
— Vilayat Inayat Khan

Take a look at where you are losing interest but are plugging on anyhow. Progression is a way your soul emerges in this world. If you keep tolerating what has become old and bothersome, your soul will catch your attention with a dynamic that may or may not be fun— but it will definitely get your attention. You might as well remain in the captain's seat and go big with your creativity rather than have wild, unpredictable currents toss you around and strand you who knows where. What excites you about the potential for your world? What small fish do you need to throw back in order to land some of the big expressions of God!

SPIRITUAL CONTEMPLATION: What are you doing just for money that is no longer soul-satisfying? Where are you being called to go big in life, but instead you're listening to all the limiting thoughts as to why you shouldn't? What activities keep you too occupied and tired to be available for the greater abundance of your life?

AFFIRMATION: I am courageously aligning the progression of my soul's emergence.

Masterful Manifester

Some people head off to Las Vegas or Atlantic City to have some fun, and hope that they don't lose their shirts at the craps table. Now isn't that an interesting consciousness around money—just hoping to either not lose too much or minimally break even? Masterful Manifesters approach creation with the intention of creating abundance. Strugglers hope to have enough to pay the bills. The next step up from this is to be comfortable, but there's a world of difference between being comfortable and being wealthy.

You must be clear about what you want to create in your life and stop sending mixed messages to the Universe. People don't get what they want because they aren't clear about what they want. They often think themselves in and out of possibilities, and their lack of clarity bewilders the Universe as a result. Those grappling through life make their choices based on fear of what could go wrong rather than what they want to go right. They stall by saying they're still preparing as they watch potential move past them day after day. Alternatively, Masterful Manifesters move forward confident in their creative abilities to make what they touch turn to gold and engage the necessary support. Masterful Manifesters take whatever action is needed to put the opportunity into play.

> *We live in a world of constant juxtaposition between joy that's possible and pain that's all too common. We hope for love and success and abundance, but we never quite forget that there is always lurking the possibility of disaster.*
>
> — Marianne Williamson

SPIRITUAL CONTEMPLATION: What limiting conversations in your head keep you from being a Masterful Manifester? Are you stalling because of your ambiguity? In order to leave that fear behind, what opening must you step through to make your dreams come true?

AFFIRMATION: I am a Masterful Manifester!

October 22
Success Is What You Make of It

My favorite definition of success comes from Ralph Waldo Emerson: "To laugh often and much; To win the respect of intelligent people and affection of children; To earn the appreciation of honest critics and endure the betrayal of false friends; To appreciate beauty, to find the best in others; To leave the world a bit better, whether by a healthy child, a garden patch or a redeemed social condition; To know even one life has breathed easier because you have lived. This is to have succeeded."

This is the attitude we should assume, that life holds nothing against us. It desires only our good; it wants us to be well, happy, and successful, but it wants us to play the game of life the way it is supposed to be played—in unity and cooperation with others.

— Ernest Holmes

While success definitely includes having material things, they alone will never be enough. Success also includes having healthy relationships, making a meaningful contribution, enjoying life, and becoming more of yourself every day. The quality of your life experience is as important as the way your life looks on the outside. Live up to your own definition of success, not anyone else's, and discover that you are living Joy!

SPIRITUAL CONTEMPLATION: How do you define "success"?

AFFIRMATION: I choose my own definition of success. I know that Spirit supports my success in every way.

Defining My Abundance

When I first began exploring a spiritual path, everyone I knew wanted to manifest a Mercedes sports car. I knew a couple of people who actually did so. But I couldn't really understand what the big deal was. If I had that much money I wouldn't spend it on a car—I'd spend it on a cabin in the woods. I wondered if this meant I had some kind of limited idea about what I deserved or could have. Gradually I discovered that I just had different aspirations and things that I wanted to do and experience. Not too much later I purchased, and lived in, my cabin in the woods.

The highest consciousness is not one of possession, but of being. The greater your consciousness of being, the more automatically will the Law flow from this consciousness into the acquisition of the things you desire.

— Ernest Holmes

What do abundance, success, and prosperity mean to you—money, fulfillment, happiness? Living a healthy, joyous, meaningful life? Family, Love, Beauty? Everyone's idea or definition of Abundance ought to be their own. Don't be swayed by others' ideas of what you should have or do. Follow your own guidance to greater abundance!

SPIRITUAL CONTEMPLATION: Spend some time writing about what an abundant life means and looks like to you.

AFFIRMATION: I know Spirit supports my joyous, happy, fulfilled, and abundant life in whatever way I choose to experience and express it!

Comparison Robs Our Joy!

It's amazing to me how many of us think that everyone but us has his or her life together. We point to saints, celebrities, spiritual leaders, and successful people and envy them. We look to TV characters and movie sets and think they show us how most people live. Then we look around our own house and feel inadequate.

I generally find that comparison is the fast track to unhappiness. No one ever compares themselves to someone else and comes out even.

— Jack Canfield

On the other side of the coin, if we look at the truly amazing lives we live—with opportunities and indoor plumbing, a floor and a roof, car and cell phone, and all the things of a First World lifestyle, we have more than most of the people on the planet today.

So the reality is that you can always find someone better off, and worse off, than you. Comparing just doesn't help you find your place and experience your abundance. Express your life! Be happy with who you are! Be proud of your own growth and learning. Be aware of the good in your life and what you have available to share with others. That is enough to move you into joy!

SPIRITUAL CONTEMPLATION: Who are you always comparing yourself to in a way that focuses on your lack or sense of inadequacy? Is there another way you could look at this?

AFFIRMATION: I am grateful for my life and all the good in it. I share it joyfully with others.

The Missing Piece

Transcending the ordinary comes from a deeply held desire to move from limitation into a more abundant and free state of expression. Exhaustion from the mundane and a sense of hopelessness have the potential to create even more negative experiences in your life. Because there's something stirring in your soul that hasn't been satisfied, a temporary fix won't last. This emptiness is a deep suffering that is waiting for a Divine touch.

It can't be fixed by thinking your way out. Now is when the brush of grace is most needed to propel you to the next rung on the spiral of your journey.

People do not decide to become extraordinary. They decide to accomplish extraordinary things.
— Edmund Hillary

The missing pieces, like your talents and gifts, have always been there despite the fact that you can't see them in your present state. They haven't been withheld—they're just awaiting your discovery. Only by going deeper than the ordinary, mundane, la-di-da daily grind can you unearth them. But you can't go deep if you've turned yourself off so as not to feel the pain of a seemingly meaningless life. Fear will thrive when the light goes out within, and you'll never survive the darkness if you believe that what you fear has more power than what is within you. Whatever it takes, be it crisis or creation, what turns on the light within will awaken and realign you with your higher purpose and passion. Dispelling the doubt in your life will transform the ordinary into the extraordinary.

SPIRITUAL CONTEMPLATION: What creative project breathed life through you and made that time in your life extraordinary? What heartbreaking event bumped you into a deeper realization of the preciousness of life? Sit in those passionate energies for a while. Remember what they felt like moving through you and know that vibrational match is still waiting for you.

AFFIRMATION: My life moves from ordinary to extraordinary!

Letting Your Buried Brilliance Out

Spiritual living is based on your ability to experience the Divine presence—not on your knowledge about it. You might be able to recite what John said about God being love, or what Moses taught about law, or even what the New Thought philosophy says about God being principle. You can quote these perspectives until you are blue in the face, but there's a big difference between talking about God and experiencing God. All that God is, you are! You have got to let that out. To demonstrate abundance, you must allow it to move through you into the world.

You are the only real obstacle in your path to a fulfilling life.

— Les Brown

Some people look to get their good from the outside, but don't limit yourself by trying to do the same. That's just an exercise in futility. Spirit is all the abundance you will ever need, and it's already within. Open up and allow your gifts to come out from your buried brilliance within. You are not here in this world to get—you are here to contribute. When you realize the infinite abundance of your nature, you will move out of your limited perception of humanhood and into the awareness of your true spiritual identity. Your concerns will no longer be "Where is my good coming from" but rather "Where can I share my good next."

SPIRITUAL CONTEMPLATION: Do you feel that your abundant good lies outside you and is dependent on someone else opening the door for it to flow? How can you refocus your perception to recognize the Divine qualities of your own being?

AFFIRMATION: I let pour forth from me my gifts for the world!

What Are You Waiting For?

After a mom calls her child to come to the dinner table for the umpteenth time, she finally resorts to the age-old ultimatum: "What are you awaiting for, an engraved invitation?" No answer is needed here—just swift and appropriate action if the kid doesn't want fury to rain! An incredible banquet of delectable delights is likewise awaiting you. What's up with needing a formal invitation to partake of what has already been offered? Do you need all hell to break loose before you realize how precious life is?

> *Life is a banquet and most poor fools are starving to death.*
>
> — Mame in *Auntie Mame* by Patrick Dennis

God's voice is eternally calling you to the banquet of abundance. Nothing created by the Divine was ever intended for your distress. You don't care about the call to the banquet if you're full on fast food and fixated on the kids' table set boldly with judgment and the appearance of lack. You are being called to use your discernment. Feast or famine has always been your choice. Get up from where you are and realize you can't appreciate the greater gourmet offerings while entertaining childish tastes.

SPIRITUAL CONTEMPLATION: Where are you waiting for a clearer invitation before joining the greater options in life?

AFFIRMATION: I say yes to the banquet of Life!

It's a Lot Like Breathing

Try this experiment, right now, while you read this. First take a deep breath and notice how much air you inhaled. Now breathe normally for a moment. Next, push out all the air in your lungs, as much as you can. Then take in a deep breath and notice how much more air you inhaled this time. But you can't take in any more air until you actually exhale again.

The attitude of getting is the law of life in a congested state or a repressed action. As long as getting dominates our mind, that mind is in a paralyzed condition being limited in its action in accordance with the fundamental law of creation.

— Bob Proctor

Claiming our Abundance is a lot like that. If we continue to pour into a full glass it simply spills over, which shows that something needs to be given out before more can be taken in. In spirituality this is called the Law of Circulation. Giving and receiving are actually two sides of the same process. One is defined by the other: to receive more, you have to give more; to be able to give more, you have to receive more.

SPIRITUAL CONTEMPLATION: In terms of your abundance, which do you try to do more—inhale or exhale? How could you even things out so you feel the rhythm of the Law of Circulation?

AFFIRMATION: I joyously receive. I joyously give. I joyously use the Law of Circulation for greater abundance for everyone!

The Spiritual Practice of Sacred Giving

Giving is the way to prime the pump for your good! Giving opens the channels and releases the flow, allowing more good to come to you. Become a generous giver because Spirit mirrors back to you whatever you think and do. So be generous, and Spirit will be generous to you!

Regular and committed giving, which is tithing, is a profound spiritual practice. Tithing comes from the desire to say thank you for the abundance you have already received. It's an act of faith in that you can give away 10 percent, save 10 percent, and still have more than enough left over. Make your claim on Spirit and expect your abundance. Then say thank you by giving back!

> *When the law of circulation is retarded, stagnation results. It is only when we allow the Divine current to flow through us, in and out, we really express life. The law of giving and receiving is definite.*
>
> — Ernest Holmes

SPIRITUAL CONTEMPLATION: Where is the Law of Circulation stagnant in your life? What do you need to start giving? Are you a committed giver, tithing of your good?

AFFIRMATION: I joyously give of my abundance. I know it blesses and prospers our world!

October 30
I Came to Give

Too often people think abundance is about what you can get and save, when in truth you didn't come to the earth plane to get and store, but to share what's inside of you. You came with a gift to give that is uniquely yours. You feel best when you are in that flow of sharing your talents and distinctive expression. There is an "I" behind your mind. This I-that-is-you thinks through and reasons with the mind and is greater than the mind that tries to accumulate. This I-that-is-you has come here to bring forth from within its contribution to the emerging whole.

You live in a realm of Infinite opportunities that are forever seeking to express through you.
— Ernest Holmes

Abundance means being a conduit from the Infinite into form. You live, move, and have your being in the Infinite Reservoir of good. Unlimited possibilities are forever seeking to express through you. Your concern for supply dissolves when you live in a generous giving mode because you see the unending resource. Life presents you with an unshakable sense of peace and security because you're not seeking to be sourced from this world. Rather you are here to give to this world from the Inexhaustible Abundant I Am of your being.

SPIRITUAL CONTEMPLATION: Remember how good it feels to share yourself.

AFFIRMATION: I live in the abundant joy of giving!

Happy Halloween

As ghosts and goblins become more visible this time of year, the veil grows thinner between the world of the ancestors and those who now walk this realm. The earth-based traditions that predate Christianity believed that the end of the harvest was a time of gratitude and thanksgiving when the spirits of the beloved departed would return home to share in the bountiful feast. Death didn't sever their connection with loved ones, and people left offerings for the departed and candles so they could find their way home.

> *Only those who have dared to let go can dare to re-enter.*
> — Meister Eckhart

Now we set out lit pumpkins and give the offerings to our children—who just might be our ancestors returning home in their newest expressions. Whether literal or metaphorical, this is a time to appreciate and bring alive once again those who have passed from this world by sharing their stories with the newest generations.

SPIRITUAL CONTEMPLATION: In addition to dressing up and having fun, remember the spiritual practice to raise a loved one or two from the dead by sharing your memories of them with the next generation. Then this night will be filled with the living departed, and their memory will remain alive.

AFFIRMATION: I honor my loved ones who have gone before me!

November

An Abundance of Gratitude

RAOK

This would be a good day for some random acts of kindness. It's human nature to be empathic to others, whether they are in need or just to make them feel good. You never know how bad a day someone might be having and how much just a cup of coffee or a surprise at the register that their lunch has been paid for will mean. A smile, being present for a conversation, stopping to assist a child in need, being patient with a dumb question, or giving away your last chocolate chip cookie are all selfless acts of kindness. Whatever generous expression of love moves through you, so does the butterfly effect, as one small gesture becomes a tsunami of inspiration to others. In addition to the waves of blessings you cast, imagine the upsurge within you when you contemplate how you can be a bringer of blessings.

Carry out a random act of kindness, with no expectation of reward, safe in the knowledge that one day someone might do the same for you.

— Princess Diana

The more places you leave your little acts of nicety, the fuller your heart becomes as you look through the screen of giving out kindness. As abundance flows through you, the giver can't help but be a recipient of exponentially expanding blessings. Yet that isn't why you give. Giving is an extension of your consciousness, and when you give, you are being the activity of God in your life. When you choose to participate in RAOK, you not only set forth a tidal surge of abundant good for the world, but for yourself as well.

SPIRITUAL CONTEMPLATION: How and where can you leave some anonymous random acts of kindness in your wake?

AFFIRMATION: My actions create a tsunami of blessing!

November 2
What Are You Radiating?

Remember the old comic strip with the little guy who was always followed by a rain cloud? This sort of summed up how he walked through life. We might call this our mental atmosphere and the energetic that we radiate into the world around us. We can tell, can't we, whether we are with someone who transmits negativity or someone who radiates a positive, joyous atmosphere.

There wells up from within us a trust, a consciousness that we are surrounded by an infinite Goodness . . . First at home, in the silence of our own thought, let us heal ourselves of fear, of doubt, of uncertainty. Let our lives be peaceful; let our lives be whole. Then shall that Peace which is God abiding within us radiate from us.

— Ernest Holmes

Our thoughts, feelings, attitudes, and beliefs become the mold through which Love and Life take the form of our life and everything in it. It often takes a crisis to shake things up in our life. This is an opportunity for us to reevaluate what we send out into the world. When we're confronted with something that isn't working in our life and we look inside, we want to pay attention to when we broadcast lack instead of Life, or criticism instead of Love. We want to notice how much negative energy we give out in the situation, or just in general.

SPIRITUAL CONTEMPLATION: Is there an area where you automatically transmit negativity from an old pattern? Examine the values and directives you are living by. Is it still how you want to be?

AFFIRMATION: I radiate peace in stressful situations and love whenever it is needed. I radiate a positive attitude and a joyful mental state wherever I go!

Share in Another's Joy

Everyone equally deserves as his or her birthright all the abundance that you deserve. Realize that the rich, meaningful life that you want to create for yourself is what each person seeks to experience. One of the quickest ways to open channels for your own good is to celebrate the good that someone else is enjoying. This generosity of Spirit is a powerful demonstration of your ONENESS!

Every time we look at what someone else has and feel envious or left out, we are focusing on what we don't have. This is the very lens, or filter, that colors the way we see and interact with others. Seeing and revealing another's Good to them or simply celebrating their Good is a joyful way of expressing our oneness. Lifting up another is a powerful way to affirm Good for everyone.

The greatest good you can do for another is not just share your riches, but to reveal to him his own.

— Benjamin Disraeli

SPIRITUAL CONTEMPLATION: When or with whom do you have the most trouble sharing in their joy and success? What is the root of this in you?

AFFIRMATION: I joyously celebrate others success!
I joyously share in another's good!

Defuse and Deactivate

Masterful Manifesters appreciate the successful creations of others, whereas some people who struggle tend to be sarcastic, and put down or demean other people's accomplishments. They also tend to be fans of trashy talk shows, gossip, and buyers of sensationalist headlines at checkout stands. But resenting another's success will only keep your good from showing up for you. If you find negativity creeping into your mind, immediately defuse and deactivate it. Resentment is a powerful way to keep your abundance at arm's length. Why would good want to show up to an unappreciative, unwelcoming place? Let yourself cheer the accomplishments you see happening in the world.

Rejoicing in the good fortune of others is a practice that can help us when we feel emotionally shut down and unable to connect with others. Rejoicing generates good will.

— Pema Chödrön

Appreciation is a prayer of acknowledgment and has nothing to do with getting Life to do something for you. It's an awareness of the abundant Universe you live in. Someone else's good doesn't diminish yours—it's not like a pie where less is available when one piece is gone. It's more like lighting a candle with an existing flame and having greater light without depleting the originating source. Recognition of good expressing has nothing to do with influencing God to do something. Being grateful that life is blessing others brings you into alignment with being a channel and recipient of graceful abundance.

SPIRITUAL CONTEMPLATION: Notice when a tinge of resentment creeps into your awareness in judging someone else's success. Immediately observe yourself with that feeling and consciously neutralize it by acknowledging to yourself for them, "Nice job, way to go, thank you for doing that in my presence."

AFFIRMATION: I am happy when I see other people's good fortune!

Appreciating Others

Appreciation increases the value of things in our own eyes and in the eyes of others. Through appreciation we are reminded that others make valuable contributions, and more importantly, that they are intrinsically valuable just in themselves. These realizations enhance our relatedness and connection so that interactions move more smoothly as we seek to do our best for each other.

Giving thanks centers us in the Divine Reality of Love. The simple act of grace at a meal is a deep realization that we are completely interdependent with all of life. Each bite is a surrendering of life so that life may continue. This life is the ONE LIFE that emanates through all creation with a pure and unstinting Love. It gives itself freely and completely into all of Life, and to us, holding nothing back. Thanksgiving opens our heart to the humble realization that we have done nothing to earn this Divine grace, for it is freely and forever being given.

> *No one who achieves success does so without acknowledging the help of others. The wise and confident acknowledge this help with gratitude.*
>
> — Alfred North Whitehead

SPIRITUAL CONTEMPLATION: Who graces your life with their presence? How have you appreciated them?

AFFIRMATION: I easily and joyously appreciate those around me. I am aware of everyone's contribution to my life. I am grateful to contribute to the lives of others!

November 6
The Single Thing That Guarantees Success

I read this headline, "The Single Thing That Guarantees Success," the other day and thought that someone was making an outrageous claim so they could sell me something. I was still intrigued, so I looked into their claims. To my astonishment, I discovered sound spiritual advice for everyday living and for creating success in business, relationships, and one's own life experience.

What is this secret? It is the attitude of gratitude, the expression of appreciation, the ability to give thanks throughout one's day and interactions. What a novel concept . . . neither a program nor elixir designed to make me a better manager or cure my ills, but rather a simple and elegant spiritual truth.

As we express our gratitude, we must never forget that the highest appreciation is not to utter words, but to live by them.
— John F. Kennedy

Gratitude focuses us on what is good in what is present. We know that what one focuses on continues to grow in consciousness and in reality. Growing dreams into reality and valuing others and ourselves while experiencing Love as the very wind beneath our wings—this seems like a perfect recipe for success and a powerful platform from which to make a meaningful contribution to life.

SPIRITUAL CONTEMPLATION: Are you grateful to, and for, the people in your life—at home and at work?

AFFIRMATION: I easily express and share my gratitude for those in my life. I appreciate everyone who shares the journey with me!

Blessing or a Downer

When you have a great thought about someone and you don't share it with them, what good does it do them? If you think someone is beautiful, kind, generous, or helpful, and you don't acknowledge how you've been touched, you withhold a reciprocating gift. Why hold on to a blessing when giving it makes everyone feel better? You can feel good thoughts until the cows come home but they won't have a positive impact or bring any blessings if they stay in your head. You must voice your thoughts.

Do your little bit of good where you are; it's those little bits of good put together that overwhelm the world.

— Desmond Tutu

It's as if some people feel it's their birthright to be a critic and point out what's not working. Ask yourself whether you want to build people up—or tear them down. Do you want to walk in the garden and see the gifts that abound, or do you want to walk in a barren desert devoid of the richness that nurtures life? It's your choice as to how you perceive and talk about your world. How do you want your friends to feel after you leave? Do you think your presence makes them feel better or worse? Do you want to be known and remembered as a blessing, or a downer? Do you make positive deposits to your relationships, or do you withdraw the good? Are you a giver or a taker? By sharing a kind thought that costs you nothing you leave the world blessed.

SPIRITUAL CONTEMPLATION: Find at least ten places where you can share a kind thought today. Notice how that feels.

AFFIRMATION: I am aware of blessings filling my life!

A Powerful Wildness

I have spent years wilderness hiking and camping. For me, it counts as wilderness only if I can walk for a day and not see any people or man-made structures. Out there in the wilds, I encounter a different side of the Divine Reality—unfettered by boundaries, unconfined and uncomplicated. The wilds offer a moment of deep peace because everything is simply what it is. The river doesn't need me to ride it, enjoy it, or even see it. The water simply flows how it will. In this unpredictable jumble of leaves, twigs, and stones, shines a glorious beauty. The trees don't need me to love them; they simply are there, being themselves in all their beauty. They stand tall and short, straight and leaning, intertwined and interwoven, creating soaring cathedrals and intimate quiet groves. I have a sense of curiosity and possibility—will there be a shy doe in the meadow or a bear crossing the trail? The sheer unknown quickens my heart and invites me to open to every possibility.

In Wildness is the preservation of the world.

— Henry David Thoreau

In the same way, there is a powerful wildness in your Soul that is the infinite, awesome mystery of Life itself. Do not seek to be too outwardly perfect. Rather, seek to perfectly allow your soul to break through the confines of worldly acceptability. Let the unpredictable beauty of you run through everything you do. Allow yourself to simply be who you are.

SPIRITUAL CONTEMPLATION: When and how do you experience the wildness of your soul? What has tamed you beyond endurance?

AFFIRMATION: I revel in the wildness of my Soul and allow the mystery of being to shine forth in me.

The Secret Whispers of the Wind

The enchanting sound of chimes dancing in the wind reveals the secrets they have to tell from faraway places. Tantalized and lured by the mysterious resonances echoing in harmony with the swaying trees and rustling bushes, the soul is enticed into a secret dimension beyond the realm of typical thinking. Traveling on the sound waves of the imagination, enthralling possibilities seem possible. The mystical comes alive—the soul exposes herself, inviting a delight to come alive within your being.

Come Fairies, take me out of this dull world, for I would ride with you upon the wind and dance upon the mountains like a flame!

— William Butler Yeats

In this bewitching respite from the analytical, nature calls you into remembrance of her Omnipresence. Evoked from within is the reminder that you live, move, and have your being in this Invisible Power that carries with it all that it has seen, knows, and will be. The tales it tells are for those who can decipher its mystery from its swing between the realms of here and now, and what was and what will be. Close your eyes for a second and the moment is gone. You can no longer see it, but like the wind, you can feel it.

SPIRITUAL CONTEMPLATION: Sit outside in the wind, close your eyes, feel nature's breath upon your body, and let her take you away.

AFFIRMATION: I hear the secret whispers the wind has to tell!

It's Just an Owl

Your higher self is constantly communicating with you, but do you notice what it has to say? Often it may look like a sign from "beyond," when what you are really witnessing is a reflection from your intuitive self. A cat crossing your path is just a cat crossing your path, but if something in you takes it with a significant impress then it's yours to interpret however you wish. Often the interpretation is what your deeper yearning is for, but you haven't yet consciously embraced. When you take a stroll with a friend who finds a feather on the path, which has great significance to her, you see it as just a feather. Neither is right or wrong. A sign is a sign only to the one who gets it.

The owls are gathering; find out why soon.

— J. K. Rowling

As I sit writing in the predawn hours, my wakeup call is a screeching owl perched unapologetically outside my window. I find its presence quite unusual for my urban neighborhood. Although it's just a bird in the fall hoping to attract a mate, an awakened imagination stirs inside of me saying that this is a messenger from one who flies between two realms, enticing me to get to the keyboard to catch what's stirring in the universal subjective. Whether this is a bunch of hogwash or just good fodder for creation, it's fun to think about the interplay of Spirit looking for an outlet.

SPIRITUAL CONTEMPLATION: What signs have you received in your life that were so clear, you had no question as to the significance of what they meant in your world?

AFFIRMATION: I am now hearing the communication from my higher self!

November 11
Veterans Day

From Valley Forge to the Middle East, brave men and women have stepped forth with a promise to sacrifice everything they have to make this world a safer place for the rest of us. Today we honor all veterans who have served this country whether in peace or war. We show our gratitude to those young ones who left their families and homes to accept not only the risks to life and limb but also the soul-transforming burden of taking up arms. No amount of medical care or GI benefits can compensate for the innocence they lost. It has been said that veterans are those who wrote a blank check made payable to the United States of America for service up to and including their life. Whether you agree or disagree with what the leadership is doing, today is a day to remember those who signed that check so you could be safe in your freedom.

Veterans Day gives all Americans a special opportunity to pay tribute to all those men and women who throughout our history, have left their homes and loved ones to serve their country. Their willingness to give freely and unselfishly of themselves, even their lives, in defense of our democratic principles has given our great country the security we enjoy today.

— Former president
Ronald Reagan

SPIRITUAL CONTEMPLATION: Pause today at 11:00 a.m. and open your heart in appreciation of all those who were willing to risk everything for their belief that they were making a better world for you.

AFFIRMATION: I am grateful for my freedom!

November 12
Grateful to Be Alive

You are an incarnation of Divine Reality, a place where Consciousness reveals itself. You are a radiant being of Light and Love. This is the absolute truth—and the only unchanging truth—about you. The Universe is infinite with an infinite number of ways that Love and Light can incarnate. You are one of those ways. You are absolutely necessary for the Universe to fully come into being and express itself. If you didn't exist, the Universe would have "infinity minus one" ways of expressing and becoming more of Itself. That's how much you matter!

We are each that incarnation of a divinity, and against each presses the insistent urge that will not let anyone alone because it is there: life and more life.

— Ernest Holmes

This is the inner urge that presses on each of us to live our life fully. Whenever we feel depressed, anxious, and unable to go on— or when we want to hurt others or ourselves—this urge cannot be fully expressed. So it turns in on itself within us. We must begin to see and realize how important we are to Life itself. The way we show up, no matter what anyone else thinks, matters to the Whole of the Radiant One Life.

SPIRITUAL CONTEMPLATION: Are you grateful to be alive? How do you express your life urge?

AFFIRMATION: I matter! I am a part of the Whole Universe! I am grateful to be alive and to express my unique self!

Grateful for the Mountain Peaks!

Every so often we have peak experiences along our path. Enjoy the moment and savor it for all the good it has to bring. Don't try to hold on to it, however. Seeking to hold on only causes it to pass more quickly. There is a natural rhythm to our life from peak to ebb and back again. Not holding on to the peak reminds us that the ebb, too, will pass. Only the Presence of Spirit/Love is the changeless constant.

> *Peak experiences are experiences of wonder, awe, ecstasy, altered consciousness, universal oneness, revelation, or transcendental states of being.*
>
> — Abraham Maslow

SPIRITUAL CONTEMPLATION: What peak experiences have you had this past year? What insight have you gained from them?

AFFIRMATION: I am present in the peak moments of my life. I know they bring me closer to my full potential as Spirit incarnate!

November 14
The Morning Stats

Starting your day by checking the morning stats, whether sports, stocks, or social media, is a curious and entertaining way to fire up your brain for the day. Your first activity sets the tone for what's to come, so be careful not to allow words or numbers on a page to provoke your emotions before you even get out of the house. Facts are fine but don't let them control you. Who you are is more important than what's being reported. Let your brain process the physical specifics but remember it's your heart that enables you to face what this world throws at you.

Statistics are used much like a drunk uses a lamppost: for support, not illumination.

— Vin Scully

You are not bound by statistics. Insurance companies know the percentage of those who will survive a particular challenge and those who won't. What they don't know is which side of the equation you fall into. It's your spirit that determines how you'll process information and how much it will impact your life. So don't give your power away to the morning news—it's only information and has only as much impact on your world as you allow it. Be grateful that you always have the ability to enhance the stats of your life.

SPIRITUAL CONTEMPLATION: How do you allow reported information to stir you? Is that response all right or would you prefer to process it differently? Knowing that you are more than physical specifics, can you look at information from a greater distance with a more detached perspective? Or is it fun to be stirred by the news of the day's sports, stocks, or social media for a brief while?

AFFIRMATION: Who I am is greater than the law of averages!

You Are Welcome to the Banquet

There is so much wonder, love, and joy in life. The banquet of life is lavishly prepared, and it's there for you every moment! Don't stand at the table thinking you are not worthy and don't deserve to partake of life's richness. Take a plate and take what you want, but not more than you can enjoy. Come back as often as you like—the table is continually replenished. Savor each bite. It's all there for you, catered from Spirit's boundless Love.

SPIRITUAL CONTEMPLATION: Are you enjoying the banquet of life? What keeps you from savoring every bite and going back for more?

Peace Be Unto Thee, Stranger

Peace be unto thee, stranger, enter and be not afraid. I have left the gate open and thou art welcome to my home. There is room in my house for all. I have swept the hearth and lighted the fire. The room is warm and cheerful and you will find comfort and rest within. The table is laid and the fruits of Life are spread before thee. The wine is here also, it sparkles in the light. I have set a chair for you where the sunbeams dance through the shade. Sit and rest and refresh your soul. Eat of the fruit and drink of the wine. All, all is yours, and you are welcome.

— Ernest Holmes

AFFIRMATION: Spirit has set a lavish table and I enjoy the feast of life!

November 16
Self-Righteous Tizzy

The next time you're in the grocery store and someone beats you to the empty checkout lane, or the clerk is incredibly slow and you find the energy inside you rising because they should have more clerks (and you're probably right)—breathe. Yes, breathe and look at your full shopping basket and those of the people in front of and behind you, and appreciate the abundance around you. Embrace the fact that you have all you need—plus you didn't have to hunt and kill something for dinner. Nor are you filthy and exhausted from tilling the soil. So why work yourself up into a self-righteous tizzy just because you're going to be home five minutes late?

I want to know if you can be alone with yourself, and if you truly like the company you keep in the empty moments.

— Oriah Mountain Dreamer

Not only are you in the grocery store with so many choices for your table, you're also at the banquet and free to choose how you will behave. Your graceful behavior is not dependent on anyone or anything outside of you. You might make the excuse that someone prompted you to be less than kind, but that in fact is merely an excuse for a poor choice you made. You wouldn't fill your basket with food that you didn't like or would make you sick, so what in the world are you thinking by choosing behavior and ingesting thoughts that make you cringe?

SPIRITUAL CONTEMPLATION: When you notice energy beginning to escalate in your body, breathe and become conscious that you are at choice for your response. What kind of experience are you going to put in your cart to take home with you?

AFFIRMATION: I am always at choice in my life!

Outburst, Was It Worth It?

A story is told of a young boy who continually lost his temper. So to help him gain control of his emotions, his dad gave him a bag of nails and a hammer and told him to go out to the back fence and pound a nail into it every time he got angry. At first the boy made a couple of dozen trips a day to that fence. But then over the next few weeks his trips diminished as he discovered it was easier to hold his temper than drive nails through a fence.

Whatever is begun in anger ends in shame.

— Benjamin Franklin

After the outbursts decreased, his dad told him that for each day he held his temper, he could pull a nail out of the fence. Finally all the nails were gone, and the young boy took his dad by the hand to show him. His dad responded with great pride, but then he also pointed out that the fence, scarred with the wounds of nail holes, would never be the same.

Be careful with your outbursts of temper because even though the recipient of your energetic display says things are fine afterward, a scar is left on the psyche. You can kick someone and say you're sorry, but the wound has been inflicted and you can't control how it is interpreted or internalized. When you feel your emotions rising, it's always best to still the body, quiet the mind, and remember Spirit first.

SPIRITUAL CONTEMPLATION: When have you allowed your emotions to damage a relationship? Even though the other person said everything was fine, you knew it wasn't. Was this worth your outburst?

AFFIRMATION: I quiet my mind in all emotional moments.

November 18
Making Friends with the Ego

Jill Taylor Bolton, a brain scientist, had a stroke. As she was having it, and afterward, she analyzed what was going on to learn more about the brain. During her stroke her cognitive faculties, what she calls her left-brain, stopped functioning. All she had was her intuitive, right brain experience of reality, which

The Ego is an exquisite instrument. Enjoy it, use it— just don't get lost in it.

— Ram Dass

enabled her to feel and see her oneness with everything. It was a powerful mystical experience. The only problem was that she couldn't distinguish between her own body and the wall against which she was leaning. Then when she finally got to the telephone she couldn't recognize the numbers, nor remember that she had to dial them in sequence. Her TED talk about her experience is truly amazing and worth watching.

Through her description, we are reminded of two things. First, that we are actually wired to sense and experience Oneness. Second, we are also wired to be able to function in the space-time continuum. She says it's the left brain that does this. Others ascribe this functionality to the ego, which helps us understand why the ego is necessary. It helps us function in linear time, prioritize tasks, classify things, and choose what's next. These are all useful and necessary functions, and we should be grateful for our ability to do them. The ego is only a problem when we forget and think that its view is the only way to see and engage in life.

SPIRITUAL CONTEMPLATION: Explore the difference between the ego/left brain functions and having a "big ego," or being so caught up in the ego that you don't experience your connection and oneness.

AFFIRMATION: I am not afraid of my ego, nor do I let it rule me. It has a place in helping me operate in the world but I do not forget and think it's the master of my life.

You've Always Had Enough

Gratitude has the knack of transforming everything, be it good, bad, or ugly, into a gift. Life is often made into a battleground when it was intended to be a playground. Appreciation has a way of brightening all the aspects of life, and Thanksgiving is a way of saying yes to life. If all you want is a break from stress and a little calm in your crazy world, you've forgotten there's so much more than getting away from it all.

I don't have to chase extraordinary moments to find happiness—it's right in front of me if I'm paying attention and practicing gratitude.

— Brené Brown

Waking up with grace and gratitude for the newness of a day is a blessing. Don't get caught in the cruel memories of the past but instead, face each day with a joyous soul. Expect all to be blessed, and if not, grateful to be the one who gets to bring blessings to the playground. Just to be able to do the next right thing is a blessing, and to be thankful for the chance to do that alone is a gift. You may not feel as if you have all the tools to be the blessing, but you've always had enough. Be grateful that your path has prepared you for your life's work and whatever's next. Your appreciation could very well be the game changer for someone who's watching you without you knowing it.

SPIRITUAL CONTEMPLATION: Go to sleep, and upon waking, take time to contemplate all the things you have to be grateful for. During the day, doodle out a gratitude list and keep it handy on your desk so you can keep expanding it.

AFFIRMATION: I am grateful!

A Thanksgiving Season

Celebrate a day of thanks and gratitude for your family and friends, your prosperity, your caring for one another, and the Presence of Love in your Life. A bountiful Divine Reality showers you with blessings.

"Thank you" is the best prayer that anyone could say. I say that one a lot. Thank you expresses extreme gratitude, humility, understanding.

— Alice Walker

Developing an attitude of gratitude is a deliberate spiritual discipline that we can begin or increase, starting today. Take time in the morning, before a meal, over a cup of coffee, or in a conversation to be grateful for three things that seem important in the moment. Do this as regularly and often as you can. Let every day be a day of thanksgiving.

SPIRITUAL CONTEMPLATION: How much of your life are you living in the attitude of gratitude?

AFFIRMATION: I am so grateful for my life and everything about it. I am grateful for . . .

Gratitude Knows No Barriers

In Dallas, we have a beautiful institution called "Thanksgiving Square." Both a place and a reminder, Thanksgiving Square is based on the notion that there is one thing EVERY faith and spiritual tradition agree upon—the power and importance of thanksgiving.

Cultivating gratitude is a life-long process that aids in a person's centeredness and depth.
— Elizabeth Goudy

SPIRITUAL CONTEMPLATION: How have you learned about the importance of gratitude?

AFFIRMATION: Thank you in any language is a beautiful prayer!

November 22
Thank-You Notes

Writing thank-you notes is a wonderful way to warm the heart with thoughts of how you've been loved. When you're busy it's easy to forget to tell others how they have blessed your life. But when you pause to write a thank-you letter you are doubly blessed because you enter into the remembrance of that field of love. Taking time to appreciate people is an important part of a healthy daily routine that will prolong your life in an enjoyable way.

Take time to be kind and to say "thank you."

— Zig Ziglar

A grateful heart greatly revitalizes the body. It lifts the soul out of bondage to your needs and wants and instead places the awareness on blessings. As you turn your attention to the grateful side of life through appreciation, you bring yourself into harmony with a multiplying frequency of what you are looking at. All increase is from the seed. You will have stepped into the magnetic force of duplication of expanding your good. Your subjective goes into overdrive attacking only the experiences that support your present state of mind. Looking through the filters of thanksgiving draws forth more to be grateful for.

SPIRITUAL CONTEMPLATION: Make some time, grab some stationery, and enter into your heart. Then handwrite some thank-you notes to those individuals in your life that you've been wanting to extend your love and appreciation to.

AFFIRMATION: My heart is filled with gratitude for those who grace my world!

Prayer of Gratitude

God is always and forever giving of Itself into Creation. Spirit is always providing everything that is needed for life—It is the fountain of Love and Joy and Abundance. We don't thank the mountain for being a mountain—we feel overwhelming awe and gratitude that it exists and we get to see it in all its grandeur and beauty. In that same way our prayer of gratitude is because we so are grateful for all the beauty and mystery and blessings in our life and that we get to experience and share them. We don't say thank you to God because God needs our thanks. We say thank you because we need to be grateful for our blessings.

In everything give thanks. An attitude of gratitude is most salutary, and bespeaks the realization that we are now in heaven. How we love to do for those who cooperate with, and are grateful for, our small endeavors! Gratitude is one of the chief graces of human existence and is crowned in heaven with a consciousness of unity.

— Ernest Holmes

SPIRITUAL CONTEMPLATION: What is your prayer of Gratitude?

AFFIRMATION: I am so grateful that Spirit is my life and that I am experiencing and expressing it in every way I possibly can! I am grateful for all the ways Spirit shows up and blesses me.

November 24
Happy Thanksgiving

One of the great things about life is that at every point, Spirit gives you a reason to be grateful if you have the heart to see. Gratitude is an attitude of the heart emphasizing your relationship with the abundant giver of all of life. Thanksgiving is a pure vibration. In the God-given gift of 86,400 seconds today, will you use any of them to say thank you? If you forget to be appreciative for the small gifts in your life, you won't be given much to be thankful for. Aldous Huxley made an interesting observation: "Most human beings have an almost infinite capacity for taking things for granted." What comes to mind is a Chinese proverb that states, "When eating bamboo sprouts, remember the man who planted them."

He is a wise man who does not grieve for the things which he has not, but rejoices for those which he has.

— Epictetus

When you're really thankful, you can't help but want to share the abundant blessings. It's important to remember in all things to give thanks. Thanksgiving is that pure, vibrational, bountiful seed that when planted will grow into abundant joy as your life. Allow gratitude to sweep through your life and attract blessings like bees to honey.

SPIRITUAL CONTEMPLATION: Take some time today to fill your heart with the pure vibrational energy of gratitude. Look upon the many abundant blessings you presently have gracing your world. Write those thank-you notes today. Make some calls and let people know how much you appreciate them.

AFFIRMATION: I have so much to be grateful for in my life now!

Potluck Time

The community potluck is one of the mystery miracles of life. No one is really in charge but somehow there always seems to be enough, and even more miraculous there's always a perfect blend of salads and an abundance of chips, protein, vegetables, and sweets. Thank goodness for the subtle competition for the best dishes, which ensures there will be some good eats! What could be more satisfying than praise for your broccoli concoction when you know your friend bought her version of the same dish from the deli section of the local market? Yes, there's also the mystery dish that no one is quite sure of and doesn't touch until you find yourself standing next to its chef who tells you, "You've got to try what I made—you'll love it." You are polite in covering some valuable real estate on your plate with this unknown creation only to discover that everyone was correct in passing it by.

If you can't feed a hundred people, then feed just one.
— Mother Teresa

You better cut the pizza in four pieces because I'm not hungry enough to eat six.
— Yogi Berra

He was a bold man that first ate an oyster.
— Jonathan Swift

In life, we all bring our gifts to share. There are some rivalries that will help raise the bar of what is being offered. There will be moments of mystery. Others will just cruise by and take without contributing to the party, and some will care with all their heart to make sure it all looks beautiful. Then there are those you can always depend on to stick around and help make sure the place is cleaned up before going home. It's the soul that is added to the friendships, conversation, and listening that keeps you coming back. There is acceptance, understanding, appreciation, marvel and, of course, a lot of love. Bon appétit!

SPIRITUAL CONTEMPLATION: What do you bring as your offering to the potluck of life?

AFFIRMATION: I am grateful to be a contributor to life!

November 26
Sacred Pearls

Share gentle truths with those around you, but be careful not to go too deep with those who aren't ready or don't want to hear them. Many have their eyes on the demonstration part, but don't want the principle behind it. This is not the right time to blurt out the sacred pearls of spiritual truth. Ridicule is sure to follow, leaving you with an empty feeling inside. It will be as if you offered a pearl of great value and it was taken and lost, leaving you with less than what you had when you began.

Do not give what is holy to the dogs; nor cast your pearls before swine, lest they trample them under their feet.

— Matthew 7:6

Share some easy pieces, not a whole boatload. When you experience the depth of the Divine merging with the Whole and have your awareness expanded and filled with truth, there's no need to flaunt it or convince anyone else of your experience. You can't save people who aren't ready by telling them about your mystical moments because they'll put you under a sarcastic light and challenge you to prove what you say. Whether they want you to manifest cash for them on the spot or perform a healing of their choice on demand, skeptics will expect miracles without concern for the principle behind it. You never have to convince others because when their mystical moments appear, it will be in their own right time. In the meantime those who do their work in secret will be blessed. Share your gifts where they are appreciated.

SPIRITUAL CONTEMPLATION: Are you offering pearls that are just not being embraced? What is it that makes you think you know what's best for others at this time in their life? Let it go and just be the expression of Truth.

AFFIRMATION: I give up being spiritually pushy!

Practice with the One You've Got

Be careful not to fall into the complacency of taking your partner for granted. Express your gratitude often and share why your partner blesses your life. Tell them regularly whatever it is you love about them. No matter how long you've been together, don't forget those special dates and getaways—they are the lifeblood of your future.

Romance will always liven things up, so remember to flirt with your sweetheart, and whisper those playful teases into one another's ears. Don't get stuck in a rut. Spice things up with a little variation to your normal routine. Keep it fresh by experimenting with some new experiences together.

If you age with somebody, you go through so many roles —you're lovers, friends, enemies, colleagues, strangers; you're brother and sister. That's what intimacy is, if you're with your soul mate.

— Cate Blanchett

Life is stressful enough, so it's up to you to make sure you share plenty of laughter so that togetherness becomes a place of healing. Just because you can say anything to your partner doesn't mean you should. Some remarks can create a lot of pain, so be wise in what you say. But it's important to communicate what you want because no one can read minds. If responsibilities have taken charge of your world, be careful not to lose sight of what's most important to you—the love between you two. Continue to inspire good health with each other and always express gratitude for the love you've come to share.

SPIRITUAL CONTEMPLATION: What can you do to infuse a fresh moment of love into your relationship today?

AFFIRMATION: I am grateful for my trust in intimacy!

November 28
The Power of Gratitude

Gratitude is the most powerful way to increase your blessings. Be grateful for all you have, and it increases. Be grateful for situations in which you are learning, and you deepen. Be grateful for what you are becoming, and you grow. Gratitude blesses your whole life.

Gratitude is where freedom and destiny meet, because gratitude is a divine doorway to the fulillment of destiny. When you consciously choose to express thanksgiving, this sets causation into motion to manifest your destiny of Wholeness in every expression of life.

— Dr. Michael Beckwith

SPIRITUAL CONTEMPLATION: What people, things, and experiences are you easily grateful for? Which ones are difficult to be grateful for?

AFFIRMATION: I am grateful for every person and experience in my life for they grow and prosper me in ways I can't even begin to know!

The Eye of the Beholder

Beauty is in the eye of the beholder, and so are joy, truth, love, peace, and every good thing you desire. It's not what you're looking for that counts. It is where you are looking from. The consciousness with which you look is what you will see. The best way to see the truth of this phenomenon is to start looking at new cars. Once you narrow the field and choose a car you like, doesn't it seem like you see those cars all over the place? You are looking at life "from" the eyes of seeing that particular car.

A negative way we experience this is when we collect evidence in support of our limiting beliefs. Because we easily feel left out or overlooked, we notice all the times, no matter how small, that we are left out or overlooked. We have a tendency to completely miss all the times we are actually included.

> *He who sees Beauty,*
>   *sees the Whole within*
> *Apparent parts;*
>   *the beauty of the dawn*
> *Is not the sun, nor mist*
>   *nor spuming sea,*
> *Nor oak-tree challenging*
>   *the raging wind.*
> *For Beauty lies in him*
>   *who sees and what*
> *He sees and how he sees*
>   *and what he feels.*
>
> — Ernest Holmes

SPIRITUAL CONTEMPLATION: Where are you looking from? What kind of eye are you beholding your life from?

AFFIRMATION: I behold my life from the eye of Beauty, Joy, Peace, Love, Abundance, and Wholeness.

November 30

Trust in Your Dreaming

You are a multidimensional being with many potentialities and possibilities. Allow mystical flashes of the Infinite that illuminate your mind and activate your heart to take you to a deeper awareness of yourself. Trust in your dreaming!

The biggest adventure you can take is to live the life of your dreams. What God intended for you goes far beyond anything you can imagine.
— Oprah Winfrey

SPIRITUAL CONTEMPLATION: What are your potentials and possibilities? What are you dreaming?

AFFIRMATION: I live the life of my dreams. This is the Life that Spirit wants to live in, through, and as me!

December

Abundant Light and Grace

December 1—7
Stoked

December 8—15
The Illusion of Separation

December 16—22
Winter Solstice
Rare and Precious Light

December 23—31
Christmas
No Room

December 1
It's a Balancing Act

Too often we polarize things because we are so much more comfortable with black and white than we are with shades of gray. We want to know the right answer, the best way, and what we are supposed to do. This attitude tends to create pendulum swings in our culture, teachings, and within our own selves. Yet the truth is usually that it's "both/and." Sometimes one side is "right" or needed, and sometimes the other. Most often what's needed is a dynamic blending of both sides. In spiritual teachings the pendulum often swings between the head and the heart. Yet scientists now tell us that there are brain cells in the brain, heart, and stomach, and that they are all equally important in different ways.

Keep your head and heart going in the right direction, and you won't have to worry about your feet.

— Unknown

Balancing the head and heart, Law and Love, invites us to step into the fullest expression and experience of Life. Do not be afraid to be all that you came here to be! Your mind is brilliant and your heart is deep. Allow all of Life to play through you like your breath plays through a flute, making beautiful music throughout your whole being.

SPIRITUAL CONTEMPLATION: Do you have a tendency, between the head and the heart, to make one primary and the other wrong? What would it be like if they actually formed a single heart/mind unity?

AFFIRMATION: I treasure my heart and my mind, for both operate from a consciousness of wholeness and the presence of the One.

Living the Grace of Love

Divine Grace, which is Spirit's givingness, is always percolating just under the surface. It invites you to give and forgive, even when part of you wants to withhold or hang on to hurt and resentment. Your rational mind doesn't always know what to do with this. There's no question that it's important from a psychological point of view to develop healthy boundaries and not enable others, and to speak up when something isn't okay. However, there is also a place of spiritual living that sees through the foibles of others to the truth of their essence. This is especially important during the holidays as we manage all our family obligations. Rather than falling into the same old arguments or relationship dynamics, we might simply allow Grace to bubble up and take over. A more compassionate, kinder way of engaging in the world emerges without effort or force. Allow Love to spring forth throughout this holiday season.

> *In its broadest sense love is the impartation of the self, the givingness of everything we are or hope to be or have, and giving it in joy and without reservation, in complete abandonment.*
>
> — Ernest Holmes

SPIRITUAL CONTEMPLATION: With whom might you allow Divine grace to soften your relationship? How can you bring more love into it?

AFFIRMATION: I see with the eyes of Love and open my heart to my family. Divine Grace flows through me in all our holiday gatherings.

Giving Back

How wonderful that no one need wait a single moment to improve the world.
— Anne Frank

Nobody made a greater mistake than he who did nothing because he could do only a little.
— Edmund Burke

Now is the time to share your final tithes and gifts for the year. You have been well supported and nourished by Life this whole year, in many different ways. Make your "Declaration of Abundance" by willingly giving of that abundance. Think of those places and people who have spiritually nourished you. These are the perfect places to contribute a little extra to. It's like planting seeds in the fall, knowing they are busy preparing to burst forth into new growth at the first hint of spring.

SPIRITUAL CONTEMPLATION: Where have you been spiritually or personally nourished? How much support are you willing to give back?

AFFIRMATION: I cheerfully and joyfully give back. I lovingly support others as the Universe has supported me.

Stoked

One day a member of a spiritual community who participated regularly just stopped attending. After a month the minister decided to visit her. Guessing the reason for his call, she welcomed him in and offered him a chair by the fire. He made himself comfortable, and together they watched the fire dancing around the logs. After a time of reflection and silence, he arose, picked up one of the burning logs with the tongs, and placed it away from the fire. Returning to his chair they watched as the log slowly lost its radiance and glow and eventually died. Not a word had yet been spoken when the minister looked at the clock and indicated he

> *The best index to a person's character is how he treats people who can't do him any good, and how he treats people who can't fight back.*
> — Abigail Van Buren

had to go. He stood, returned the cold log to the fire, and they watched as the other embers immediately brought the life and glow back to it. As the minister went to the door, his hostess got up, gave him a big hug, and thanked him for his message—she said she'd heard him loud and clear, and she'd see him next week at services.

Sometimes when the routine of life knocks you off course, you might think you'll find some extra time if you give up your spiritual practices. But when you feel depleted and tired, a community has a central flame that blesses you, and a love that can rekindle and awaken your spirit when it goes into slumber. The more you isolate yourself when you're feeling down, the wider the chasm becomes. The gift of community is the energy and love it offers you in the downtimes. Don't remove yourself—reach out and know the fire burns with more light when you are there to receive your blessings.

SPIRITUAL CONTEMPLATION: Do you have a spiritual family from whom you've withdrawn? Drop back in and see if there is still fire there for you.

AFFIRMATION: My life is brighter with a community!

December 5
Iconic Memories

Every now and then, a scent or a thought of a taste triggers childhood memories, and one of those is Bazooka Bubble Gum, the classic bubble gum with the Bazooka Joe comic inside the wrapper. One of my earliest candy-buying memories was being knee-high to the counter as I selected those little individually wrapped pieces of bubble gum from the bottom shelf at Mr. Chinn's candy shop. It's what a whole generation of kids learned to blow bubbles with, and I couldn't even play a Little League game without some in my mouth. So it's sad to report that Bazooka Bubble Gum as you knew it from your childhood is no longer. In an effort to appeal to a new generation, the taste, shape, and packaging have all been changed and Bazooka Joe rests among the fallen.

The Topps Company developed its Bazooka Bubble Gum product in Brooklyn, New York after the end of World War II. It was named after the humorous musical instrument which entertainer Bob Burns had fashioned from two gas pipes and a funnel in the 1930s. (This contraption also gave its name to the armor-piercing weapon developed during the War.) Bazooka Joe comic Bazooka, with its distinctive name, taste, and red, white and blue logo and packaging, soon became a familiar part of Americana.

— OldTimeCandy.com

Nostalgic moments live in your heart and soul forever, occasionally transporting you to a more innocent and simple time in your life. Today's kids are creating memories of their own that in a few decades will trigger the same kind of smile from those warm remembrances. This heart experience allows all to meet in the subjective space that transcends linear time.

SPIRITUAL CONTEMPLATION: Find a quiet space and allow a pleasant memory, scent, or taste to transport you to an innocent time that warms your heart and puts a smile on your face. Then notice how real it is now and how you just transcended time and space.

AFFIRMATION: Innocent and simpler times that make me smile are alive within my heart!

The Power of Grief

The Holidays may bring you face to face with the loss of someone you love. Grief is a powerful experience and requires expression. Speak the name of your loved one, and remember his or her gift to you and your life. Remember how much more you have to bring to life because of the time you shared.

Death leaves a heartache no one can heal, love leaves a memory no one can steal.
— From a headstone in Ireland

SPIRITUAL CONTEMPLATION: Write a love letter to the one you've lost and whom you miss.

AFFIRMATION: My grief is an outward sign of my love. I allow my grief to be a gentle and tender expression of my heart. I know the Love of Spirit supports me always.

December 7
Closer Than a Phone Call

Losing a dear friend after many years of sharing and loving is painful. Of course you can't help missing them, but indeed your life is richer for all the memories of caring and love you received and gave. You have so much more to bring to the world and your relationships with others because they were such an important part of your life. Their tender touch lives in your heart, and all that you do will move through a piece of them in you for the rest of your life. They truly are part of your every act and thought. They are closer than a phone call, but you must now learn a new communication system.

I hope it is true a man can die and yet not only live in others but give them life, and not only life, but that great consciousness of life.

— Jack Kerouac

Your loved one would not want you to remain overly sad for too long, but rather be a place where aliveness and joy are part of your daily experience. Isn't that what you'd want for the ones you love? Love transcends time and space, and the link of love that brought you together has not been severed because of death. It is Omnidimensional, and just as true of the spirit that animates your physical body. This plane of human form is only one stopping place on its evolving journey. When the soul is complete here, it leaves behind the physical body, which is the ideal vehicle for this plane of expression, and continues on its forward journey otherwise unchanged, but enriched by the love experienced here. One doesn't die to become immortal—you are immortal now, and a living person can never die.

SPIRITUAL CONTEMPLATION: Allot some space in this day to find a quiet spot and bring a loved one who is no longer in this world into the memory of your loving heart. Spend some time connecting with them.

AFFIRMATION: I believe in the continuity of the individual soul that is forever expanding!

Nothing to Overcome

If it weren't for some challenging situation in people's lives they probably would never have wandered into the teachings of the New Thought movement with its universal metaphysical principles of truth from the ancient wisdom. It's easy to get caught in the idea that this power can be used to overcome the challenges of your life.

The difficulty is not an error of a real nature that must be overcome, but a belief in the physical expression as the truth of who you are. New Thought isn't about using a bigger power to overcome a lesser one, but a knowing that

Seek first the kingdom of God and his rightness and all other things shall be added to you.

— Matthew 6:33

the so-called error doesn't exist as the spiritual truth of who you are. Healing has moved beyond looking for a mental cause to knowing the dis-ease cannot exist in the realm of the Infinite because there can be no otherness, no other power, hence nothing to overcome.

When you move into the realization that God is your very awareness and live in a spiritual alertness, you'll find your needs being forever fulfilled. As you shift into being a beholder of spirit, then that which is unlike it falls away. Spirit isn't sending your good to you; rather, it is emerging as your healing. So don't turn to God to improve the situation, but for the consciousness of God appearing as the perfect expression that is already available. The Infinite takes on all forms. So let your demonstration be in the consciousness of the omnipresence even in the midst of the challenge at hand.

SPIRITUAL CONTEMPLATION: Where do you believe the physical fact is the truth of who you are and is greater than the spirit of your being?

AFFIRMATION: My life is spirit appearing!

December 9
Slow Down, Be Still

Take time to be aware that in the very midst of our busy preparations for the celebration of Christ's birth in ancient Bethlehem, Christ is reborn in the Bethlehems of our homes and daily lives. Take time, slow down, be still, be awake to the Divine Mystery that looks so common and so ordinary, yet is wondrously present.

— Edward Hayes

I love Christmas carols, and one of my favorites of the traditional carols I grew up with is "O Little Town of Bethlehem." I love how it talks about the stillness of the town and how quiet everything feels as the Christ is born. Other lovely songs in both English and German talk about the stillness of the forest in a snowfall at this time of year. How wonderful to be reminded to seek out stillness and quiet in the midst of the hustle and bustle of our preparation for the holidays.

SPIRITUAL CONTEMPLATION: How will you find stillness and take time to slow down during this season?

AFFIRMATION: I invite in the stillness and the quiet as I slow down and take time to nourish my soul with the Presence of the Christ Child.

What a Ride

When an imposing issue looms large it seems natural to look at it. But what you focus on grows more real and often increases the discomfort around it. It's similar to what happens when your car goes into a skid. The natural tendency is to look at what you're skidding toward. Wrong. Because you steer toward what you're looking at, you end up driving right into the very collision you want to avoid. Race car drivers know to look away from the skid and with that comes the ability to steer away from the impending disaster, such as a wall.

> *Life should not be a journey to the grave with the intention of arriving safely in a pretty and well preserved body, but rather to skid in broadside in a cloud of smoke, thoroughly used up, totally worn out, and loudly proclaiming, "Wow, What a Ride!"*
>
> — Hunter S. Thompson

Remember though, the car's response time isn't immediate—there's a natural delay between the turn and the response of the vehicle. The same is true about life—when you change your focus there may be some gap time between your new cause and its effect showing up in your world. Be patient with the responsiveness to the new form taking shape in your body, mind, or world of affairs. Form does follow consciousness; it always has and always will. It's your job to turn away from where you don't want to go, and life's momentum will fulfill its part.

SPIRITUAL CONTEMPLATION: Are there any walls you seem to be racing toward? It doesn't matter if this wall is a doctor, a bank, or relationship—call it to your attention and look in the other direction to avoid a crash.

AFFIRMATION: My path is clear!

The Illusion of Separation

Getting caught in your human struggle can cause you to question your Oneness with Spirit. You might imagine yourself like a windowpane. No matter how dirty the pane is, it doesn't affect the sunlight itself. The sun always shines brightly. It's every false idea of who you are, every smallness, littleness, resentment, and unforgiveness, that clouds the windowpane. Every time you feel unable, unworthy, or unnecessary, you are fogging the window with the illusion of separation.

The God that is in us is the same God that is universal. There is no wall of separation, no barrier, no place where one begins and the other leaves off. All is one and one is all.

— Ernest Holmes

Clean your dirty window with deep spiritual truths and a new way of seeing yourself and the world. The birthing of the Light that we celebrate in so many ways this season is all about this eternal light that is always shining. When we see with the eyes of the ONE, look how bright the light becomes! This brightness is your eternal Oneness with Spirit. You only sometimes seem separate from it. Remember, you never really are.

SPIRITUAL CONTEMPLATION: What beliefs or stories do you carry that separate you from your ONENESS?

AFFIRMATION: The eternal Light is revealed within me and within all people. In this light our Oneness is revealed.

Maya

One of the secrets of an illusionist is to guide you to look in a certain direction while the trick takes place outside your view. A live elephant can be made to appear and disappear as you watch from your seat. The illusionist distorts reality, knowing that your brain makes general assumptions during its perception. You are lost in the trance of believing your perceptions, or what the Hindus call Maya, the illusion.

When you look in the mirror, what do you see? Do you see the real you, or what you have been conditioned to believe is you? The two are so, so different. One is an infinite consciousness capable of being and creating whatever it chooses, the other is an illusion imprisoned by its own perceived and programmed limitations.

— David Icke

You operate in your thoughts as well as the collective consciousness of the world, which guides you to look in certain directions. But it's important to note that who you are is the witness to this activity. As the Knower you understand it's all Maya—the body, the mind, and the world of form that lures you into a trance by directing what you are led to perceive as the truth. Your body grabs your attention and speaks of discomfort, and you believe you are the body; your finances are a bit short for a desired purchase, and you think you don't have enough. But as you evolve a new spirituality, you leave behind the limiting beliefs that no longer define you and embrace the unlimited truth of who you are. You are infinite consciousness capable of creating and being whatever it chooses. Are you going to believe what you see in the mirror of life or are you going to create a new reflection?

SPIRITUAL CONTEMPLATION: What illusion in your life has you trapped into believing it's the truth of who you are? Now observe yourself thinking those thoughts, feeling those feelings. Ask yourself who is observing you having those thoughts and feelings? Then listen to this witness guide you to a higher place beyond the trance of that illusion.

AFFIRMATION: I am the clear observer of my life!

December 13
It's Time to WAKE UP!

My mom used to tell my sister and me, "It doesn't matter that you are girls; you can grow up to do or be anything you want to do or be!" This was a great positive message and I believed it. Not everyone, however, treated me this way. There were many things I learned, subtly and overtly, that I couldn't do or have because I was a girl. The reverse happened to my guy friends. A box was laid out that we were each supposed to fit into—a box that defined what our life was supposed to look like, what success meant, and how we would know if we were happy.

We are born with the capacity to learn how to dream, and the humans who live before us teach us how to dream the way society dreams. The outside dream has so many rules that when a new human is born, we hook the child's attention and introduce these rules into his or her mind. The outside dream uses Mom and Dad, the schools, and religion to teach us how to dream.

— Don Miguel Ruiz

But now it's time to wake up from the societal trance. Your good, your joy, happiness, love, or peace isn't out there. It's not in your bank account, the gifts under the tree, the job, or the house. Stop being run by what you think should make you or others happy! Listen to your own inner being; follow your inner guidance; find out where your joy lives. Bliss is an inside job, and it requires you to be awake.

SPIRITUAL CONTEMPLATION: Are you still living inside the box and asleep to your true desires?

AFFIRMATION: I am awake. I desire only that which supports my bliss and the bliss of others!

The Gift of Grace

Ernest Holmes writes, "Every sacred book is a Divine document insofar as it is true. Any note of pure harmony ever struck on any instrument or by the human voice is a harmony of God, a revelation of God, an action of God, and an impersonation of God. Every step in a dance that is pure symmetry and grace is that which is the essence of loveliness. Every essay ever written that speaks the truth is God proclaiming it. There is only God; and we must not deny the slightest fact to affirm the omnipresence of God—over all, in all and through all."

> *The grace of God means something like: "Here is your life. You might never have been, but you are, because the party wouldn't have been complete without you."*
>
> — Frederick Buechner

Grace is Spirit's gift of life to us, unearned and joyfully given. What we do with it is our gift back to the Whole, or as some people say, "Grace without works is dead." Every time we live, act, and move from the center of our being, we give the Divine Presence reality in human expression. This is what is meant by the incarnation, and this is what we celebrate throughout the season of light.

SPIRITUAL CONTEMPLATION: How are you manifesting and sharing the gift of Grace, your very life, with the world?

AFFIRMATION: I accept the gift of Grace as the Presence of the Divine. I return that gift with the work of my hands, my heart, and my life.

December 15
Cultivate Childlike Wonder

"Star of Wonder, Star of Light" reminds us to see life with wonder and awe. There is so much more going on than just the outer forms of our ordinary lives. Through the eyes of a child, an ordinary toy car becomes an extraordinary monster drag-racing winner. This holiday give yourself the gift of stopping and seeing the extraordinary in your life. It's there! You just have to open your God-eyes with childlike wonder, anticipation, and joy. These eyes will enliven what seems to have lost its sparkle and renew you. Let the Season work its magic on YOU!

Never lose the childlike wonder. Show gratitude . . . Don't complain; just work harder . . . Never give up.
— Randy Pausch

SPIRITUAL CONTEMPLATION: How much childlike wonder do you have these days? Where do you find it?

AFFIRMATION: I see the world with the eyes of wonder. I am in awe of its beauty and love!

Notice You Observing You

Have you ever watched the clouds taking on their unique shapes and then transform into something else before they just float out of existence? Have you ever watched a forceful storm blow in from the horizon in all its fury? Maybe you've even seen a tornado twisting through the sky or sucking the water out of the ocean. Or watched the whole sky disappear in a white-out from falling snow or dense fog. Where did the sky go in all of these scenarios? Nowhere, of course! It remained the constant, unchanged space as all the activity blew through with a convincing performance that it was the sky, but the truth is, all of it was just passing through the unbothered space we call "sky."

Feelings come and go like clouds in a windy sky. Conscious breathing is my anchor.

— Thich Nhat Hanh

Your observing consciousness witnesses your thoughts, dramas, and soul-searching defining moments without being impacted in the least. The higher aspect is not impacted by your stories. A part of you that has never been hurt or violated, lovingly beholds your unfoldment without any judgment. It's like the sky with all the weather passing through it—the weather is not the sky, and your experiences are not you. Weather takes place within the sky, and the dynamics of your life take place within your field of awareness. You are not your stories any more than the weather is the sky. Watch your happenings and narratives pass through who you really are like clouds passing through the sky.

SPIRITUAL CONTEMPLATION: Sit and watch your thoughts form and dissipate through your mind without attachment. Then notice you observing you as you watch those thoughts.

AFFIRMATION: I gracefully observe myself moving through life!

Rare and Precious, Who Me?

Growing into your future with health and grace and beauty doesn't have to take all your time. It rather requires a dedication to caring for yourself as if you were rare and precious, which you are, and regarding all life around you as equally so, which it is.

— Victoria Moran

Spirit sees you as infinitely precious and worthy. You are, after all, an incarnation of Itself, expressing and experiencing life as you. There is only one of you. Spirit always wants the highest and best for you, and sees you having it through the eyes of Love. Start seeing yourself as Spirit sees you, as Love sees you. Take time today to explore how you could. Now, open to what will allow you to express more Spirit, live more Joy, and be more Love.

SPIRITUAL CONTEMPLATION: Do you know that you are rare and precious? Do you treat yourself with the tender care you deserve?

AFFIRMATION: I treat myself and everyone else as the rare and precious beings we are!

Got Vibration?

When you feel trapped, whether in a relationship with another person or in a situation with your employer, you feel dependent on all the outside energies for your well-being. If you're stuck in a cubicle farm at work, it can be a struggle to maintain optimism when you hear others cursing at their computer screens all day. Being reliant on your income will put you in a stuck position if you can't communicate from your place of self-worth. Chances are, you tolerate behavior that you would otherwise reject

> *It is better to light a candle than curse the darkness.*
> — Eleanor Roosevelt

because the mortgage and car payment don't care how stuck you feel. The way you bring the light to darkness that is seemingly out of your control is through choice. Choosing to move outside of your own personal power and surrender your self-pity to become a conduit for the power that is greater than your own is the means by which you will be freed.

When you choose to be a generator of radiating light, luminescence washes over the dissonance. The emanation of all power is then held until your body vibrates in perfect harmony and accord. No possible harm can come to you while you are in harmony with that God vibration. This isn't a special privilege for just a few—it's for all. Anyone who is intentionally being nasty is eliminated from your world by the wave of light. When the infinite in you comes forth, there is nothing that's contrary to it. No inharmonious vibration can enter this sphere. Dissonant energy merely falls away.

SPIRITUAL CONTEMPLATION: When are you unable to turn off negative energy around you? Practice turning on the Divine generator, that which channels an infinite source of vibrational abundance, and is greater than your own personal source of light. Vaporize the nastiness and move into your vibration of harmony.

AFFIRMATION: I am a generator of harmony in every situation!

December 19
A New Picture

Forgiveness is a mystical alchemy that frees your awareness from the entire human desire for retribution for the injuries you have received. To enter the realm of forgiveness it takes more than what is humanly possible to transcend the pull of justice. It takes a Divine grace to enter the equation because it makes no sense to the rational mind. You must move out of the realm of the thought of law and order into your soul and expression of unconditional love. Being hostile and destructive is not a normal behavior of your spirit. It has to be fed motives by the human mind to remain engaged in resentment. To have a clearer understanding of what would free you, you've got to drop the tapes you've been running.

Forgiveness is the scent that the rose leaves on the heel that crushes it.

— Source Unknown

Your mind will choreograph, rehearse, and cling to sometimes truly horrific scenarios of the past, embellished by others to keep you clinging. You must be willing to go deep in your yielding of what's going on for you so a better way may emerge. Remember that your intellect cannot understand the spiritual side of forgiveness. It wants to play in this realm, but it's not its natural domain, nor does it have the capacity, and it doesn't do well letting go of the lead. You must surrender to grace's repatterning of your whole matrix where forgiveness neutralizes the pain from the past. Pictures and memories that you are holding on to from across your life's spectrum of occurrences will lose their hold on your psyche, and that release will open the heart to a Divine guidance. When you turn your attention to God instead of revenge, the human mind must surrender its smallness, and a new picture emerges from the heart.

SPIRITUAL CONTEMPLATION: Where could you use some Divine intervention on your thoughts of justice and retribution?

AFFIRMATION: Grace now guides my thoughts and experiences!

Leaving Selfhood Behind

A goal on the spiritual path is to move from being an individual who is under the law of the world of form to one who lives by spiritual principles—to leave behind the earthly selfhood that is caught in good and bad, ease and struggle, the law of opposites, and walk this world as an expression of the Divine emanation of all that Spirit is. Either you are a branch on the tree of life that has been cut off and will eventually wither and die, or you are connected with the trunk and draw nutrients from the depths of the roots that feed the whole tree. Every problem you face comes from a sense of separation from the whole. The tree already knows how to heal. It knows the proper disbursements of the abundant resources.

In creating this world below, the world above lost nothing. It is the same for each Sepfirah (progressively unfolding emanations as God becomes manifested): if one is illuminated, the next loses none of its brilliance.

— Kabbalah

As you meditate and reconnect with your life source, you come to remember what principles govern your life. In this conscious realignment you are lifted above the laws of this world to that which animates your very life as a branch of the tree. The branch is unaware of the many sources feeding it—sunlight and rain and nutrients from the soil—yet it benefits from them all. You may not be cognizant of the invisible flow backing the totality of your happiness and well-being, or even the people playing an unseen influence. Your meditation establishes your oneness in the flow of the spiritual sustenance that is ever available to you as a branch on the tree of life.

SPIRITUAL CONTEMPLATION: Where in your life do you feel disconnected from your source?

AFFIRMATION: I feel my connection to the Tree of Life!

December 21
The Divine Spark

The winter solstice is one of the oldest seasonal festivals of humankind. It seems right to place the birth of the light at the time of the greatest darkness. Today we know the sun will come back but our ancestors weren't quite so sure and didn't take that return for granted, particularly since they were impacted a lot more by the winter elements than we are today. As an agricultural society that depended on crops, the sun's return was definitely worth celebrating.

And God said, "Let there be light," and there was light. And God saw the light, that it was good: and God divided the light from the darkness. And God called the light Day, and the darkness He called Night.

— Genesis 1:3-5

What a powerful metaphor was embraced by the Egyptians with the birth of Horus, the Persians with the birth of Mithra, and the Christians with Jesus, to mention just a few of the Divine child saviors. How interesting that they all share the same story of a miraculous virgin birth and of the winter solstice celebrating the return of the light to a world of darkness. Amazing how people separated by time and space tapped into a universal story of truth that is as relevant today as when it was originally told and celebrated. Unaware of your slumbering spiritual magnificence, you walk this world oblivious to your greater potential. Winter is the germination and preparation for the flowering of spring as all things that come into existence must first be born. There is a Divine spark in you that is ready to make its return and birth itself into expression. As cold as the dark times may get for you, remember that from the beginning of recorded history the return of the light has been celebrated, and the return of that light is your story.

SPIRITUAL CONTEMPLATION: Where in your life has it become so dark that you've begun to question whether the light will return for you? Remember, the birth of the light comes at the time of the greatest darkness. Take some time to contemplate this ageless celebration and its relevance to your world today.

AFFIRMATION: Today the light returns to my world!

Multiplying Joy

My son has the ability to disrupt the orderliness of a room almost instantly. He has a creative energy that leaves a wake of colorful toys—Hot Wheels and their accompanying tracks, books, and marbles—in esthetic disarray in the blink of an eye. I can hardly fathom there's that much potential waiting for placement even possible. Seemingly, out of nowhere, an abundance of stuff is strewn on the floor like a minefield that awaits my bare feet as he calls me in to join him in his play.

My happiness grows in direct proportion to my acceptance, and in inverse proportion to my expectations.

— Michael J. Fox

You might put a limitation on everything in your world while others bask in an understanding of the God Consciousness with no limits in any field of their endeavor. You can create from what might appear to be nothing by enjoying what you have to play with. Somehow from somewhere, another piece materializes from almost nowhere and then another and before long you are sitting in the midst of God's colorful abundance that brings you multiplying joy. It's only natural you'd look for a playmate to enjoy your expanding good fortune.

SPIRITUAL CONTEMPLATION: Where are you multiplying your joy and where are you multiplying your fears? Do you realize you are using the same neutral energy for both actions?

AFFIRMATION: My abundant good seems to appear out of nowhere!

December 23

The Christ Consciousness Revealed

To practice the Presence of God is to awaken within us the Christ Consciousness. Christ is God in the soul of each one of us.

— Ernest Holmes

There is no way to force yourself into the mystical realm of the Christ Consciousness. As you dance between the dimensions of self-awareness and unity, you simply get seduced into surrendering your sense of self into the radiance of the Whole. You merge your self with the Self, and Oneness is all that is left.

SPIRITUAL CONTEMPLATION: Take these words by Ernest Holmes into your spiritual contemplation: "As the human gives way to the Divine, in all people, they become the Christ."

AFFIRMATION: I awaken to the Christ Consciousness within and I see it in everyone.

Contemplating the Christ Consciousness

Christ means the Universal Idea of Sonship, of which each is a member. That is why we are spoken of as members of that One Body; and why we are told to have that Mind in us "which was also in Christ Jesus." Each partakes of the Christ nature, to the degree that the Christ is revealed through him, and to that degree he becomes the Christ.

— Ernest Holmes

Christ is the embodiment of divine Sonship which has come, with varying degrees of power, to all people in all ages and to every person in some degree. Christ is a Universal Presence.

— Ernest Holmes

There is no one particular man predestined to become the Christ. We must understand the Christ is not a person, but a Principle. It was impossible for Jesus not to have become the Christ, as the human gave way to the Divine, as the man gave way to God, as the flesh gave way to Spirit, as the will of division gave way to the will of unity—Jesus the man became a living embodiment of the Christ.

— Ernest Holmes

SPIRITUAL CONTEMPLATION: What do Jesus and the Christ Consciousness mean to you?

AFFIRMATION: I awaken to the Christ Consciousness.

December 25
No Room

It's almost unimaginable to think of a very pregnant young woman about ready to give birth showing up at your door in the middle of winter and being told, "Sorry, no room for you here." Can you even fathom telling someone to go deliver her baby in the barn with the animals? That's not quite the romantic version of the story, but

Joseph went up from Galilee, out of the city of Nazareth, into Judea, to the City of David which is called Bethlehem to be taxed with Mary his wife who was great with child. And so it was, that, while they were there, she brought forth her firstborn son, and wrapped him in swaddling clothes, and laid him in a manger, because there was no room for them in the inn.

— Luke 2:4-7

a powerful precursor to an unfolding saga of no room. Herod learned of Jesus's birth from the gossip of the day and sent soldiers to Bethlehem to eliminate all children. There was no room for his teaching, no room for his miracles, and the leading religious leaders wanted him gone. Even in death he didn't get his own tomb—it was borrowed from Herod.

This story comes from two millennia ago, but the question is still valid today. Do you have room for the birth of Christ Consciousness in your world? Having no room at the inn is not nearly as significant as having room in your

life for a higher awareness to birth itself into your experience. Is there room in your expression or are you full? Is there room for peace, or is war taking up too much space? Are your pursuits leaving too little time for your spiritual revelations? If you are too busy to create space for God in your life, you are too busy.

SPIRITUAL CONTEMPLATION: Are you so full that you don't have the energy or inclination to create space for something greater to enter into your life?

AFFIRMATION: I always have room for God!

The Garden of Grace

The garden of the Divine has fragrances you can't describe. Surrender your need for explanation, and wander in the mystical realm beyond reason. You will be uplifted by Grace, empowered by Vision, and revitalized by Life Itself. When you return, you may not have any words, but your healing and transformation will impact everything.

Connect with your Center, and you connect with the Source of All. You are a portal of the Divine where the Infinite and the finite merge, one into the other. Your being is the fulcrum where Spirit becomes matter and human becomes Divine. Breathe into the still point at your Center, and you breathe in the Heart of the One.

Grace because the Universe is Itself an infinite givingness— It can't help it; that is Its nature.

— Ernest Holmes

SPIRITUAL CONTEMPLATION: When do you experience the presence and gift of Grace?

AFFIRMATION: I am open to the gift of Grace as the Presence of the Divine. I open myself to the mystery and mystical experience of the One.

Wisdom of the Samurai

A story is told of a Zen master who was a great and legendary samurai warrior. He eventually settled down in a small mountain village where students still came to him to receive his teachings and insights. One day, a young arrogant warrior, wanting to prove himself superior to the old ways, journeyed a great distance looking for this master teacher. Along the way he boasted of his skills and conquests upon unassuming bystanders, and eventually found his way to the monastery to challenge the former samurai so he too could be added to his list of conquests. He tried everything to provoke the old guy into a fight. He hurled insults, rocks, and even spit on him, but being true to the way of spirit, the Zen master didn't respond to this childish behavior. The arrogant youth, humiliated by the lack of response, left the town by the end of the day.

If we accept being talked to any kind of a way, then we are telling ourselves we are not quite worth the best.

— Maya Angelou

Many of the old samurai's students questioned their master as to why he didn't engage with the youngster and show him that people shouldn't be treated that way. To this he responded simply, "If someone offers you a gift and you don't accept it, who does the gift belong to?" "To the giver, of course," the students replied. "The same is true when people throw their emotions at you, whether they are in the form of anger, hate, or insults," said the master. "When you do not accept them, they remain with the one who's holding them."

SPIRITUAL CONTEMPLATION: Have you taken on emotional trash that isn't yours when it was thrown your way? When have you let other people's emotional garbage remain with them, and how did it feel to walk away clean? Where in your life are you being challenged to embrace other people's toxic emotions? What are you going to do about that?

AFFIRMATION: I accept only the gifts that bless my life!

Celebrating Kwanzaa

We all should know that diversity makes for a rich tapestry, and we must understand that all the threads of the tapestry are equal in value no matter what their color. – Maya Angelou

We have religious holidays and we have secular holidays. I see Kwanzaa as an opportunity for African-Americans to reaffirm ourselves if we choose to, a chance to rebuild and renew our focus. I see Kwanzaa as a holiday of the spirit. – Jessica Harris

Kwanzaa is a pan-African celebration of heritage and culture and family and community. The principles and the manner of observing the holiday lift up traditional values that are key to our lives. – Janine Bell

The seven principles of Kwanzaa—unity, self-determination, collective work and responsibility, cooperative economics, purpose, creativity and faith— teach us that when we come together to strengthen our families and com- munities and honor the lesson of the past, we can face the future with joy and optimism. – Former president Bill Clinton

Our children need the sense of specialness that comes from participating in a known and loved ritual. They need the mastery of self-discipline that comes from order. They need the self-awareness that comes from a knowledge of their past. They need Kwanzaa as a tool for building their future and our own. – Jessica Harris

Kwanzaa is a holiday that should be celebrated by everyone, not just the black community. – Jacqui Lewis

Kwanzaa isn't a replacement for Christmas or even Hanukkah. Kwanzaa has nothing to do with religion and while some may twist it to be political, in its nature it is not. Kwanzaa is not the tool of its creator. Kwanzaa has a life of its own. Kwanzaa is about the spirit of people—all people regardless of color or race. Kwanzaa is a holiday of the human spirit—not the divine. The two were meant to co-exist peacefully. – Author Unknown

---

SPIRITUAL CONTEMPLATION: Be with these quotes in your medi- tation today.

AFFIRMATION: I affirm the unity and interdependence of all humanity as we are One with each other and One with God!

December 29
Freed from Karmic Debt

The God of many people punishes evil and rewards good, but just because many people believe in this concept of God, it doesn't make it so. You don't need to attempt to influence God or sacrifice for God in order to win favor. If you believe that the creative Life Force is the truth of you, then this Presence, this eternal good, is forever seeking to express through you. God is love and all-knowing, today and tomorrow and forever more. If you make a mistake, let it go and become something other than that mistake. The law of cause and effect, often labeled karmic law—as you sow, so shall you reap—does not need to imprison you.

All's love, yet All's law.
— Robert Browning

You can't convince God to give you your good, nor can you earn it—because it's already been given and only awaits your recognition. You are a child of the Divine and because of that you have been given nations as your inheritance. As Jesus said, "Today you shall be with me in paradise; your mistakes are forgiven, go and sin no more." Those are statements of grace transcending punishment. When you stop doing what is bringing hurtful consequences to you, you are able to break free of the karmic wheel because you've chosen to embrace love and forgiveness. When you no longer entertain thoughts and deeds of human realm, you free yourself from human law. What a gift you give yourself! The way to stop sowing in the physical dimension is to recognize your spiritual identity. There is law, but there is also grace. But behold, there is only one power in the Divine, not two. When under grace in the spiritual realm there is no room for clashing. In this state of harmony there is only your abundant good to express.

SPIRITUAL CONTEMPLATION: Where are you waiting for your karma to play out? How about accepting being in paradise today? Embrace the concept that all blunders are already forgiven, and go and create from a new level of awareness.

AFFIRMATION: I am now free of my karmic debts!

Dimensions of Consciousness

You have been graced with two dimensions of consciousness—the mental and the spiritual. The mental dimension allows you to overcome obstacles, create material form, and move toward your dreams. This is the realm of affirmations, visualizations, and knowing that you are captain of your ship and master of your fate. It is a powerful state to co-create life from, according to your choices and desires. You have complete freedom to co-create anything you want.

The key to growth is the introduction of higher dimensions of consciousness into our awareness.

— Lao Tzu

The spiritual dimension invites you to commune with the Divine, sip from nectar of Presence, and know the Truth of who you are. This is the realm of meditation, the mystical experience and the consciousness of Oneness. It is a powerful state of oneness and connection with everything and everyone, with Beingness Itself. By living from the spiritual dimension of consciousness you invite and allow the impress and impulse of the Divine to move through and as you, sensing and feeling that the Presence is as near as your breath and as close as your heartbeat.

Both dimensions are yours to play in, and you can move freely between them. One is not "better" than the other. You are a being that operates in both realms simultaneously.

SPIRITUAL CONTEMPLATION: Are you aware of when and how you move between these two dimensions of consciousness?

AFFIRMATION: I live from my higher dimensions of consciousness as I move through my life and the world.

Closing the Chapter

New Year's Eve is a defining moment that can close a chapter and cast a new one in your life. History shows us that the date for the celebration of a new year has been all over the calendar reflecting different religions, moons, and seasons. December 31 is pretty much an arbitrary demarcation of the cycle around the sun that says this day is where we agree we start the new cycle. So rather than starting in a winter month we could go back to agreeing that the new year begins in the spring. What is more significant than the starting date is what you choose to do with the celebration itself. Symbolically, resolutions of today are similar to the secular version of spiritual vows of the past. What's impactful for you today is your crucial soul reflection of what you are doing with your endless infinite trek through time. On this day nostalgia will rise, remembrance of people, places, joys, sorrows, and yearning for finding the comfort of home again will fill your field of awareness.

> *For last year's words belong to last year's language and next year's words await another voice.*
> — T. S. Eliot

Leave behind anything that doesn't belong in your new year. Write down those things that are no longer welcome in your new chapter for this coming year and burn them in the fireplace tonight. Or get together with some friends and create a dissolution ceremony for this list of particulars that aren't going to hitch a ride any further through time with you. Proclaim your completion with the past and join your friends in throwing your lists in a bowl of fire and watch them turn to ashes. Letting go of what doesn't belong in your life expands your abundance potential as you start a new chapter of your life!

SPIRITUAL CONTEMPLATION: Write that list of what you are committed to leaving behind in the old year. Then, burn it ceremoniously tonight. Don't wait.

AFFIRMATION: I let go of that which no longer serves me.

Acknowledgments

Deep gratitude to my prayer partners and Rev. Karen Fry and the staff at CSLDallas for all the loving support while I worked to finish my half of this year's journal. I could not have completed it without you! So much appreciation for my co-author, Christian, for keeping his unwavering focus and commitment to this project! What a blessing and a joy it is to work together, and how effortlessly things flow!

— *Petra*

Heartfelt appreciation goes out to Lori Gertz whose soulful editing and immense patience made sure every one of my words was perfectly placed. Great gratitude to my spiritual community, Seaside Center for Spiritual Living, who encourages and supports all my spiritual undertakings, and special love to the team of co-ministers I partner with there every day. Lots of thanksgiving I send to all my students over the last thirty-five years who kept me stretching to articulate the ineffable. What a joy it's been to create with Petra more than a thousand days of joy to leave our world through our three books together. Lots of gratitude to Judy Morley for believing in this project before the first book was ever edited. Finally to my beloved wife, Kalli, who put up with me leaving our bed every morning at 4 a.m. to rendezvous with my keyboard and create this next year's journey for us all.

— *Christian*

Also by Petra Weldes & Christian Sørensen

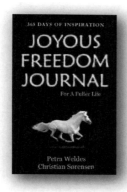

JOYOUS FREEDOM JOURNAL

Do you want to survive . . . or thrive? Each day gives you the opportunity to consciously make this decision and Spiritual Living Press has the workbook that will help you joyously thrive and freely flourish! The soul craves freedom and joy the freedom of self expression and the joy of being. This is your inheritance and your birthright. Sometimes, though, it takes practice to recapture the joyous freedom of your true self. Explore and discover a unique path to joy and freedom through 365 days of thoughts designed to engage you and help you practice, respond, and explore new ways of moving forward in life. Run through this world with joy. Discover that you are truly free to create heaven on earth. Your joy and freedom bless you, those around you, and the entire world.

Paperback: 392 pages
ISBN-10: 0972718494
ISBN-13: 978-0972718493

JOYOUS LIVING JOURNAL

We all know that it is more pleasurable and ful-filling to go through life happy rather than miser-able. In fact, we are designed and intended to live rich, full, blessed and prosperous lives. Taking joy from our inner being, sharing joy through our relationships, and bringing joy into the world through our meaningful contribution is what Spirit is trying to live and express through us, as us, in our everyday, ordinary experiences. Every moment we are invited to choose joy, love, peace, or simply the Presence of Spirit as our ground of being. When we do so, Joyous Living becomes our reality.

Paperback: 392 pages
ISBN-10: 091784906X
ISBN-13: 978-0917849060

About the Authors

Christian Sørensen

A gifted and eloquent speaker and author with a unique and engaging style, Christian lights up audiences all over the world with his expansive vision, passion, and heartfelt enthusiasm. He has authored nine books, numerous articles and pamphlets, and hosted two television programs on spirituality, New Thought, and growing one's consciousness. Christian leads spiritual tours and works with orphanages and schools around the world to raise global consciousness. His intention is that his life be his message.

Rev. Christian Sorensen, D.D., is the spiritual leader of the Seaside Center for Spiritual Living in Encinitas, California. His weekly talks can be viewed at www.seasidecenter.org.

Petra Weldes

A highly-regarded, deeply-admired teacher and speaker, Petra engages others with her deep wisdom and wealth of knowledge—as well as humor—awakening others to their unique expression and creative, joyful potential. She has authored two books, numerous articles, and led countless retreats on Spiritual Living. Petra has a passion for youth, interfaith service, global transformation, and expanding consciousness. She speaks at conferences and leads sacred site journeys around the world. Her intention is to grow people and things into their greatest purpose and self-expression.

Rev. Petra Weldes, D.D., serves as spiritual director of the Center for Spiritual Living in Dallas, Texas. Her messages can be heard at www.csldallas.org.

For More Information

For more information on Spiritual Living, Science of Mind, and a practical, positive spirituality that teaches tools for personal transformation and making at the world a better place, go to either of the websites listed above. To find a community in your area, go to www.unitedcentersforspiritualliving.org.

Notes

Notes

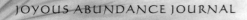